Take Back *the* Sky

Take Back the Sky

Protecting Communities in
the Path of Aviation Expansion

Rae André

SIERRA CLUB BOOKS
San Francisco

The Sierra Club, founded in 1892 by John Muir, has devoted itself to the study and protection of the earth's scenic and ecological resources—mountains, wetlands, woodlands, wild shores and rivers, deserts and plains. The publishing program of the Sierra Club offers books to the public as a nonprofit educational service in the hope that they may enlarge the public's understanding of the Club's basic concerns. The point of view expressed in each book, however, does not necessarily represent that of the Club. The Sierra Club has some sixty chapters throughout the United States and in Canada. For information about how you may participate in its programs to preserve wilderness and the quality of life, please address inquiries to Sierra Club, 85 Second Street, San Francisco, California 94105, or visit our website at www.sierraclub.org.

Published by Sierra Club Books
85 Second Street, San Francisco, CA 94105
www.sierraclub.org/books

Produced and distributed by
University of California Press
Berkeley and Los Angeles, California
University of California Press, Ltd.
London, England
www.ucpress.edu

SIERRA CLUB, SIERRA CLUB BOOKS, and the Sierra Club design logos are registered trademarks of the Sierra Club.

Library of Congress Cataloging-in-Publication Data
André, Rae.
        Take back the sky : protecting communities in the path of aviation expansion / Rae André.
             p. cm.
        Includes bibliographical references and index.
        ISBN 1-57805-116-9 (alk. paper)
             1. Aeronautics. 2. Sustainable development. 3. Aeronautics-Environmental aspects.
        I. Title.

TL507.A53 2004
363.73'1-dc22   2004042822

Book and jacket design by Elizabeth Watson

Printed in the United States of America on New Leaf Ecobook 50 acid-free paper, which contains a minimum of 50 percent post-consumer waste, processed chlorine free. Of the balance, 25 percent is Forest Stewardship Council certified to contain no old-growth trees and to be pulped totally chlorine free.

08 07 06 05 04

10 9 8 7 6 5 4 3 2 1

In memory of Ed Lieberman,

gentleman and activist

Contents

Preface 9

1
The Quest for Environmentally Sustainable Aviation 11

2
The Airport in My Garden 16

3
Aviation Pollution Today 24

4
Facing Up to Airport Expansion 43

5
Massport: The Aviation Industry's Model Organization 68

6
How the Air Transportation Industry Pursues Growth 84

7
How Noise Laws Fail Communities 96

8
How Will Citizen Involvement Solve These Problems? 121

9
The People Play Defense 133

10
Aviation with Representation 152

11
How to Work for Sustainable Aviation 167

Epilogue 174

Appendix A:
The Targeted 100 Smaller Airports
the Aviation Industry Wants to Expand 179

Appendix B:
Resources on Aviation and the Environment 183

Appendix C:
Federally Designated High-Speed Rail Corridors 187

Epigraph Sources 189

Notes 191

Bibliography 215

Index 227

Preface

SEVERAL PEOPLE urged me to write a short preface that sets the ideas and experiences of this book about communities standing up to the aviation industry within a larger context. Today many communities face crises created by powers beyond their borders, typically government and business interests. Many will feel frustrations similar to those of the communities represented here and will seek similar remedies—petitioning government for redress of grievances, hoping for broad solutions that also solve immediate problems, and urging the wider world to pay attention, adopt responsible behaviors, and join their struggle. Some communities will have had some measure of success; others will have tried all of these approaches and given up.

Developing a collective understanding of what works to protect communities is an important goal. Perhaps if you, the reader, find commonalities between the situations described in these pages and your own, you will be kind enough to let me know your thoughts.

Many people have generously supported the research for this book with their valuable time and expertise. They include Marty Pepper Aisenberg, Michael Barrett, Les Blomberg, Julian Bussgang, Margaret Coppe, Tony Galaitsis, Gigi Estabrook, David Knapp, Neil Rasmussen, Jack Saporito, Peter Schilling, Kay Tiffany, Dede Vittori, and Anna Winter. The list also includes many helpful others who have preferred to remain anonymous.

My daughter deserves special recognition because she has attended patiently many dull adult meetings, licked her portion of stamps, and comforted me when, because of nighttime flyovers, I was a grumpy mom.

My sincere thanks to all these, and to the many people who are supporting the quest for sustainable aviation—indeed, for sustainable transportation—with their own research and active involvement.

1

The Quest for Environmentally
Sustainable Aviation

We cannot be free without being secure in our property.
   —Abigail Adams

*Remember how long it took the tobacco industry to
acknowledge that their products are hazardous to your
health? Or how hard they fought the warning labels? They
didn't want us to know we were being poisoned either.*

   —Lynne Pine, president,
   Witham Airport Action Majority

TODAY AMERICANS face a momentous conflict between commercial
aviation and community interests. Companies in the highly competitive aviation industry seek to survive and maximize profits,
while citizens want aviation that is community-friendly and
environmentally sustainable. Currently more than 500 of the
13,000 airports in the United States have commercial service, and
their expansion, along with the commercialization of many other
airports, is on the drawing boards. These expansions will affect the
communities near the airports immediately, and because flight
paths can be changed, they threaten any community within a
thirty-mile radius. Already an estimated 2 to 4 million people are
affected by noise pollution alone. Even now, hundreds of citizens'
groups representing 1.5 million people are challenging the industry by fighting the expansion plans at 3,300 airports.[1]

The millions of people who live near airports can testify to the noise pollution, ground pollution, and air pollution generated by the air transportation industry. Many experience increased anxiety. Many are sleep deprived. Many find that their health has been jeopardized. Yet their complaints are dismissed by an industry that brands them as radicals, and their requests for relief go unanswered by state and federal governments that have crafted laws to protect the industry. Little by little, in one of the most serious cases of incremental environmental degradation in our day, homes, livelihoods, and health are being damaged.

The issue of aviation expansion is so complex that it is seldom fully grasped by anyone other than industry professionals and a handful of transportation activists. This book hopes to redress that imbalance. It is a layperson's introduction to the laws, community impacts, and political realities surrounding the conflict. Here you will learn why it is that pollution from airports affects so many people yet is largely uncontrolled by state and federal governments. You will come to understand how, over recent decades, the national noise laws in the United States have been revised to protect the industry while abrogating a person's right to a quiet home. You will learn from the experiences of several communities exactly how incremental growth is being used every day to defeat their opposition to airport expansions. You will understand more fully why the United States urgently needs a multimodal transportation policy based on values that meld private profit and customer service with environmental sustainability.

This book invites you to ponder how democratic values and processes are being threatened by the modern emergence of a remarkably powerful industry. For in no small part, this book is about the effect of special-interest influence on government. The salient fact is that, today, communities in the United States have no local control over their skies. Their airspace is controlled by the Federal Aviation Administration, which is itself highly influenced by the air transportation industry. The industry is subsidized heavily by the federal government. Even since September 11, 2001, when the public turned to trains and the strategic importance of rail transportation was clearly established, funding for rail has languished. Meanwhile the aviation industry has received a multibillion-dollar subsidy and even more funding for airport expansion, as well as significant financial relief as part of the funding for the Iraq war.

When a special interest grows as powerful as the aviation industry has, the community and state rights on which our democracy was founded are at risk. The cases described here illustrate at the local level how that has happened. They show how the civil society that we trust to be a foundation of local power has ceded that power to a set of unresponsive corporations and government bodies. The stories of the ill-fated communities in the path of aviation expansion suggest what citizens facing the consolidation of power at the federal level must do to protect themselves and to reclaim critical rights that in recent decades have been eroded.

This book examines American aviation expansion as an urban and a suburban phenomenon, as an issue that affects every city and hundreds of towns. Communities near large American airports have suffered for decades under significant airport expansions, and now the aviation industry is expanding the thousands of general aviation airports that exist in residential suburbs and near smaller cities. The National Air Transportation Association has compiled a list of the 100 smaller airports the aviation industry has targeted for expansion (see appendix A).[2] In towns where large-scale aviation simply does not belong, the industry is working to turn its small airports into busy commercial jetports. How large will these airports become? If the industry has its way, they will become as large as possible, destroying the quality of life in nearby communities.

One of the aviation industry's prime strategies is to divide and conquer urban and suburban communities, to play one set of sufferers against another. In Boston, for example, Massport, the state agency that owns key airports, is attempting to pit suburban communities fighting expansion of their local airport against the urban communities fighting growth at the city's major airport. The agency asserts that if those communities near Hanscom Field, in the suburbs west of Boston, accept more air traffic, those near Boston's Logan Airport can have less. At the same time, over continued local opposition, Massport has sought to build a new runway at Logan. The agency is also part of an aviation industry coalition to promote the construction of more runways nationwide.

It makes sense, for a variety of reasons—including transportation efficiency and national security—that there should be a national policy supporting rail over air for travel distances up to 350 miles. Yet there is no national plan that combines all modes of transportation into a workable solution that meets the nation's transportation challenges. There should be a national policy that humanely regulates aviation noise pollution, but the noise pollution office of the Environmental Protection Agency is defunct, and airplane noise is regulated by the FAA itself. There should be a national policy that removes dangerous and polluting flight paths from all residential areas, yet today planes routinely fly low over homes and schools, and not only has this threatening situation come to be seen as normal, the industry wants to do a lot more of it.

In greater Boston we have learned from experience exactly how powerless communities have become to influence aviation expansion. Citizens have come to understand that they must stand together if they want "environmental justice" to mean something more than equal insensitivity and equal stupidity in urban and suburban communities. The reality is that even as Logan gets its new runway and Hanscom Field is turned into Boston's LaGuardia Airport; even as citizens are being driven out of their homes in established communities near Logan; and even as, after years of increasing degradation, the enviable quality of life in both downtown Boston and suburban communities such as Bedford, Concord, Lexington, and Lincoln is ruined, the government's failure to impose reasonable limitations on the growth of air transportation leaves all citizens, in all of these communities, and *in every community nationwide,* powerless to protect their homes and manage their communities' future.

At the deepest level, preserving local autonomy and quality of life is what the national appeal for sustainable transportation must be about. It is crucial to develop pollution regulations that contain real protections and that remain in effect consistently over time. If our country is to preserve essential values of justice and local empowerment, the quality of life in our communities has to matter just as much as customer convenience and inexpensive seats, and our laws must reflect this sentiment. In *Who Will Tell the People,* author and journalist William Greider describes the national political context for such initiatives. I urge you to read it.

The United States today needs to emphasize multimodal transportation. Voters must demand significant investment in responsible transportation planning that promotes safe and environmentally sound transportation systems. This will undoubtedly mean more emphasis on rail travel. Our country needs the kind of high-speed trains that take the French from Paris to Marseille—the distance from Boston to Washington, DC—in three hours. On the principle that the polluter pays, new transportation policy will require the aviation industry to take responsibility for the pollution it generates.[3] On the precautionary principle that the prevention of environmental damage is better than the remedy, communities must no longer be burdened to prove they have been harmed before action is taken.

Concerned citizens must send the message to Congress, their state legislatures, and their local governments that they will vote against anyone who allows the irresponsible expansion of air traffic, and for those who promote sustainable alternatives.

We must challenge our government to initiate responsible transportation policies that balance the interests of all stakeholders, and we must do this now, before the creation of more aviation infrastructure makes significant increases in pollution and suffering in our communities inevitable.

2

The Airport in My Garden

Some men don't care for nature and would sell their share in all her beauty. . . . Thank God they cannot fly and lay waste the sky as well as the earth.

—Henry David Thoreau

The airlines are coming, the airlines are coming.

—Jay Kaufman, state representative,
Lexington, Massachusetts

THE STORY OF how my town and three neighboring towns are fighting the commercialization of the local airport is typical of struggles against airport expansion nationwide. Like so many others, from rural communities to urban centers, our communities are stacking up their relatively meager local resources against one of the most powerful special interests in the world, and they are losing.

On a Saturday morning in August of 1997 I stood on the deck of a small yellow house and looked out over its charming garden to the neighborhood beyond. My daughter was four, and soon she would need a good public school. I had been searching for a home for five months, but for buyers in popular Lexington, Massachusetts, during a real estate boom, half a year of looking was not unusual. This particular house was offered for sale on a Friday, with all offers for purchase to be delivered at 4 P.M. on Sunday. Numerous bids were expected. I was standing on the deck, peering at the conspicuous green colonial out back and pondering whether I could camouflage it or learn to live with it, when a small plane flew over the crest of the hill just beyond it.

I turned to the realtor and said, casually, "Oh yes, Hanscom's flight path. But it's over there." I gestured away from the house. "Yes," she agreed readily, gesturing herself. "Way over there."

I had lived directly in the flight path for Hanscom Field for two years, and it had been no big deal—little planes cruising overhead, the occasional military transport lumbering beyond the trees. It reminded me pleasantly of my childhood, as I'd grown up near a small airport. So the next day, in an auction among five bidders, I bought the house.

We took possession in November, and during the following year I put my own stamp on the place. I had not owned a house for many years, and installing bird feeders was a pleasure. One morning in the summer of that first year we were awakened by planes practicing for the biannual air show hosted at Hanscom Field. For a couple of days we were treated to the sight of unusual aircraft gliding down the flight path. We were buzzed by fabulous fighter jets. It was fun. Afterward we went back to business as usual, tending the garden and watching the frequent flying hobbyists and the occasional corporate jet overhead.

In June of 1999 I read in the local paper that a start-up commercial airline was applying to fly out of the airport. I thought, That is just ridiculous. You can't have airlines flying this low over people's homes and schools. You can't diminish the historic sites of Lexington and Concord—places like the Old North Bridge, the Battle Road, the Louisa May Alcott House, and Walden Pond. You can't have even more planes flying over the Great Meadows National Wildlife Refuge. Massport, the state agency that manages air transportation, will take care of it, I thought. They have promised to keep the airport as it is—for small planes. They will turn down the airline's application.

I, like many of my neighbors, went away on a summer holiday.

When we returned, the local newspaper informed us that
Massport had not, in fact, turned the airline down. On June 7,
Massport notified the community that the airline was proposing
to start up service at Hanscom Field and gave the Hanscom Field
Advisory Committee only two weeks to respond. HFAC is the
advisory group of airport users, neighbors, local town officials, and
other interested groups officially designated by Massport to provide input to its decisions. The June HFAC meeting was attended
by seven hundred citizens, but their arguments against the airline
proposal did nothing to move the agency, for on July 15 Massport
announced its formal approval of the airline's start-up.

Down at the school bus stop the parents all agreed that this
was just politics. Massport had to give the appearance of supporting commercial efforts, we believed, but it is a state agency ultimately responsible to the community, and the community clearly
did not want commercial traffic overhead. Nobody in his or her
right mind would want commercial traffic over Lexington. Over
established residential areas and schools? Historic landmarks?
Wildlife areas? Suddenly, without warning? You'd have to be kid-
ding. Put more traffic on our already crowded roads? We thought,
something will prevent this.

Our community leaders, who obviously knew more than we
did, sought a temporary restraining order against Massport.

Uppermost in our minds was the worry that this airline represented the toe in the door. We suspected that where there were a
few flights, there would be more; where there was one airline,
there could be many.

Local activists warned us about the development of Westchester
County Airport, north of New York City. Like Hanscom Field it
had been created for the military in the 1940s on about five
hundred acres. After World War II both facilities had become
general aviation airports. In the late 1980s Westchester had allowed
commercial passenger service to start. Community activists there
told us that because they had failed to do enough at the outset,
their airport was, in 1999, handling almost a hundred passenger

flights a day and a million passengers a year on such carriers as US Airways, Northwest Airlines, American Airlines, and Continental Airlines.

Like many of the thousands of small airports established in the 1940s and 1950s, Laurence G. Hanscom Field exists on property taken by eminent domain. In 1941, the land was appropriated by the federal government from the town of Bedford for use in World War II. Immediately after the war, the airport was converted to a military base, and in 1959 it was turned over to the state.[1] Today Hanscom Field is owned and operated by Massport, formally titled the Massachusetts Port Authority; Hanscom Air Force Base is an adjacent, separate facility that sometimes uses the airstrips.

Over the years the Massport property, which is ringed by four residential communities, has grown to an estimated 1,300 acres. Of these, about 500 constitute the current airfield.[2] The airfield has two runways, one 7,000 feet long by 150 feet wide, and one 5,000 feet long by 150 feet wide. By comparison, LaGuardia Airport, near Manhattan, consists of 680 acres, with two main runways, each 7,000 feet long by 150 feet wide, and has seventy-two aircraft gates.

Hanscom Field is the second-busiest airport in New England, with about 580 incoming and outgoing flights daily (year 2000 figures), more than either T. F. Green Airport in Rhode Island or Manchester Airport in southern New Hampshire. It supports private planes, corporate aviation, flight schools, charter operations, light cargo flights, military planes, and of course, since September 1999, commercial aircraft. The Boston Bruins and the Celtics lease jets there.[3] Companies that have planes based there include Raytheon, Liberty Mutual Insurance, EMC Corporation, Avidyne Corporation, and CTC Communications.

During recent decades, the airport has been developed strategically as a general aviation reliever airport for Logan Airport, which is about fifteen miles away. The myriad small planes and corporate jets that use Hanscom Field would have pushed Logan beyond its capacity years ago.

In 1999, the new airline at Hanscom Field started up slowly, with a mere four flights, as announced in its publicity release. Actually, as we experienced it, there were four flights in and four flights out of the airport for a total of eight "operations" per day. Beginning on September 28, they served Buffalo, New York, and Trenton, New Jersey, with morning, midday, afternoon, and early evening departures.

At 7 A.M. on Tuesday of the inaugural flight, a crowd of 250 to 650 people converged on the airport to protest. Counts differed, but it was still a lot of citizens. People came and went as their schedules dictated. Many of the protesters were at least middle-age—those citizens not constrained by jobs or school.

The rally was organized by a grassroots citizens' group. It was high energy and positive, despite the news that the community's appeal for an injunction against the start-up had been dismissed on the grounds that it would damage the investment that the airline and Massport had already made and injure the reputation of the airline.[4] The judge ruled that the towns had failed to prove their case on any of three counts: failure to allow the Hanscom Field Advisory Committee ample time to review the airline's proposal, violation of Massachusetts Environmental Protection Agency regulations, and irreparable harm to the public interest.

The protesters heard speeches from their representatives and admired one another's slogans. I particularly liked a sign that read "No Aviation Without Representation," which the holder credited to Lexington's state representative, Jay Kaufman. After hearing speeches from Kaufman and others, people marched in front of the terminal chanting and waving their signs. A photographer wanted a picture with a protester holding a sign in the foreground and the first flight taking off in the background. "Quickly. You," he said. Me? I gulped. Well, OK. For the cause. I held up the sign—"No Commercial Airlines at Hanscom"—and he snapped. Who are you taking the photograph for? I asked. The Associated Press. I hoped the sign had hidden my face.

Back home I erected the sign in the front yard and slapped a bumper sticker on my van. I got on the Web and boned up on statistics like the correlation between airplane noise and children's stress, crashes around small airports, and the pollution caused by de-icing agents.

One evening I could hear that planes were landing at an enormous rate, and I called the airport to find out what was happening. The polite woman who answered the phone informed me that Hanscom Field is a twenty-four-hour facility operated by Massport and that planes may land any time they wish. Planes landing at night must pay a penalty, she said. The current fine for operating at Hanscom Field between the hours of 11 P.M. and 7 A.M. is $40 for aircraft 12,500 pounds or under, and $290 for aircraft over 12,500 pounds. If an airplane operates at night more than five times during a calendar year, these fines are doubled, she said. She attributed the recent surge in traffic to private planes arriving for the Ryder Cup golf tournament being held in a nearby suburb. Complaints, she said, should be directed to the Hanscom Field noise report line.

Complaining about the noise of one airplane after another didn't seem like an effective use of my time, but I decided to try it just to see what would happen. I filed my first aircraft disturbance report the last week in September. After being awakened in the night, I dialed the number, listened to the recording and left my complaint as directed, stating date, time, general location, and the nature of the noise incident. I was invited to leave my name and address for Massport's records and in order to receive a written response. I wondered what Massport would do with the records.

The first time I complained I said the heck with filing. But the next time, October 4, I was still curious about the process, so I left my name and address and asked for a response. I received a written reply from Massport on November 5. Their form letter told me only the type of aircraft that had flown over (it did not name its owner—this information is not given to the public), and the amount of its fine, if any, for operating during the night.

Between my two calls to the noise complaint line, the airline had more than doubled its operations, from eight to twenty.[5]

The story of how American communities are failing to stop aviation expansion in their backyards illustrates how weak they have become in the face of special-interest influence on government. While we Americans are less cynical and apathetic than some analysts suggest, when it comes to managing the system of government-by-special-interests affecting our lives, we are much less powerful than we imagine ourselves to be.

One reason is that those lucky enough to live in privileged communities like Lexington have rarely encountered intractable civil problems. Crime levels are low, our schools and transportation systems are excellent, and we can afford to maintain them. If they choose to, individuals can usually avoid the difficult issues that do arise. Whether this means ignoring a problem for the sake of personal peace, treating it at academic arm's length, selfishly disregarding it, literally moving away from it, or delegating a solution to others, the privileged often stay above the fray. As to issues of the wider world, from geopolitics to global warming, we may choose to ignore these, too, or at least to deal with them from a distance.

For many Americans, the fact is that if an issue does not touch us personally, there is little incentive to get involved, and there are so many reasons not to. We are busy with jobs and families. The airport is in another part of town. When it comes to holding government accountable, our intention to be good citizens may fall into the same category as the wish to change a bad habit—fervent but ineffectual.

Yet today the fact is that in our town—which is, ironically, the birthplace of American democracy—the ability to sleep through the night is not protected by the law. Our children's well-being—from their learning environment to their very safety—is threatened by low-flying jets. The pollution from airport chemicals is seeping into local streams and soil. Increasing numbers of large planes are flying low over our homes and schools, and at least in the short term, we are powerless to stop them.

As a privileged American, I have up to now had no particular need to think deeply about how the power of special interests is growing in our country, except to wish, like many others, that special interest money could be driven out of the election process. Yet, as I have come to understand the extent of aviation industry power, I have realized just how urgently we need to do this. When I experienced the reality of pollution in our communities, I was motivated for the first time to grapple with the sea change in the balance of community, business, and government power that is taking place—indeed, has taken place—in the United States.

As I joined the effort to stop the expansion of Hanscom Field, I wanted to understand the extent to which unbridled commercial interests have come to dominate our government and our lives. How can our beloved communities be held hostage to self-serving corporations? What can we do to make the aviation industry more environmentally responsible? These are questions all American citizens should ask themselves, because if powerful commercial interests have not yet come to your community, they are on their way.

3

Aviation Pollution Today

*On a round-trip from New York to London, a Boeing
747 spews out about 440 tons of carbon dioxide, the main
greenhouse gas. That is about the same amount that
80 SUVs emit in a full year of hard driving.*

—Harry Rijnen, *New York Times,*
citing data from Edinburgh Center
for Carbon Management

*Any person living within 30 miles of an airport is just one
flight path change away from a noise disaster.*

—Les Blomberg, executive director,
Noise Pollution Clearinghouse

NATIONALLY, AIRPORTS rank with chemical factories, oil refiner-
ies, and power stations among the top four emitters of noxious
nitrogen oxides and volatile organic compounds.[1] Chicago
O'Hare International Airport, with approximately 900,000 operations per year (an operation is either a takeoff or a landing), is
believed by local citizens to be the largest stationary source of pollution on earth.[2] While it is difficult for citizens to get the data
needed to assess what this pollution costs in terms of clean-up and
health effects, in Great Britain alone, government estimates for the
environmental cost of the CO_2, nitrogen and sulfur oxides, hydrocarbons, water vapor, "and other gunk spewed out by aeroplanes"
ranges from £1 billion to £6 billion a year.[3]

Seventy percent of the United States population resides within twenty miles of a major airport.[4] Moreover, many major airports in the United States are located in large metropolitan areas where air pollution levels exceed national health-based standards, and twenty-two of the largest thirty-one airports in the United States are located in areas of the country where ozone levels persistently exceed national standards.[5] Yet the federal government has ignored or downplayed most aspects of aviation pollution.

Noxious emissions? The EPA monitors only the emissions that come from large commercial aircraft engines—those with at least 26.7 kilonewtons, or about 6,000 pounds, of thrust. These are the engines used on midsize to large passenger planes—generally those planes with more than fifty passengers—and the occasional luxury jet. The EPA does not monitor any emissions at all from general aviation, corporate jet engines, military jet engines, or piston-powered engines—which constitute the primary types of planes that populate most smaller airports. Furthermore, the EPA monitors only engines, not planes. In practical terms this means that it measures emissions only at the factory when the engines are first built, not later after the planes have actually been flown.[6]

Noise pollution? The standard for noise pollution by aviation is far higher than the threshold recommended by the EPA and used by most governmental agencies, including the Federal Transit Administration, the Federal Energy Regulatory Commission, and the National Research Council of the National Academy of Science. The EPA ceased most noise abatement activities after the Office of Noise Abatement and Control was defunded in 1981 under the Reagan administration.[7]

Toxic chemicals? The government does not monitor one of the worst ones used by aviation. In 1997 a coalition of organizations, including the Natural Resources Defense Council, Defenders of Wildlife, the National Audubon Society, and the Humane Society of the United States—together representing over 5 million members and constituents—petitioned the Environmental

Protection Agency to include transportation by air on the list of industries that must report the use of the major toxic ethylene glycol, but the petition failed.[8]

Few government studies have been done on the health effects of airplanes and airports. Nobody really knows how badly airports are polluting their nearby communities. An emerging body of research is, however, suggestive.

In addition to being noisy, airports and airplanes spew out a great deal of toxic material. A 1993 EPA-sponsored study of a sixteen-mile area around Chicago's Midway Airport, which at the time was about one-tenth the size of Chicago's O'Hare, found that landings and takeoffs were a local source of pollutants—including particulate matter, benzene, 1,3-butadiene, and formaldehyde—that far exceeded the industrial pollution sources in the area.[9] Ten years later an EPA study in the Northeast found that toxic emissions (in this instance, fourteen air toxics known or suspected to be human carcinogens or to have noncarcinogenic, adverse health effects) from aircraft greatly exceeded those of the largest stationary sources in Connecticut, Massachusetts, and New Hampshire.[10]

It is also clear that local populations are experiencing health effects from aviation pollution. In Sweden researchers have found significant increases in blood pressure among those exposed to moderate airplane noise levels, with an 80 percent increase in high blood pressure in people in the noisiest areas.[11] In Great Britain a study of deaths from childhood leukemias and cancers has found relative excesses of these diseases near airfields.[12] In the state of Washington a report by the Seattle-King County Department of Public Health contrasted hospitalization rates for a community near the King County International Airport (Boeing Field) with other Seattle communities, and it found that near the airport there was a 57 percent higher asthma rate, a 28 percent higher pneumonia/influenza rate, a 26 percent higher respiratory disease rate, an 83 percent higher pregnancy complication rate, and many other higher illness rates.[13]

Increasingly, citizens and communities themselves have stepped in to do the research that is needed. Exasperated by the lack of state and federal government action to evaluate pollutants or assess the health risks to communities near O'Hare Airport, the City of Park Ridge, Illinois, with financial assistance by several other communities, in 2000 hired an environmental firm with expertise in air pollution sampling and toxic health assessment to study the impact on nearby residential communities of airborne toxic emissions from the airport.[14] The study was based intentionally on toxic emission data from a 1999 consultant's report commissioned by the airport's owner and operator, the City of Chicago, because these data were believed to actually understate both the quantity and types of toxic pollutants generated by O'Hare.

The Park Ridge study found 219 different volatile compounds in the air. Of these, 92 were identified, and 78 were found to be at increased levels downwind of the airport. The study found that near O'Hare particulates were also contributing to the dust in the air downwind from the airport. (As we shall see, the presence of particulates alone poses major health risks.) The consultants reported that in ninety-eight Chicago-area communities (including the City of Chicago), covering an area of approximately one thousand square miles, these toxic air emissions caused the cancer risk to exceed federal health goals. The risk was greatest at the airport fence line, where the hypothetical lifetime cancer risk was approximately 100 cases of cancer out of 1,000,000 people—which is five times higher than the risk in a typical town of the region, and 100 times higher than the federal standard of 1 cancer in 1,000,000 people. The study concluded that, "While public health assessment and potential control measures need to be carefully evaluated and debated, one thing is clear. Given the massive and widespread impact of O'Hare's toxic emissions on the health risk of hundreds of thousands of residents . . . O'Hare should not be expanded."[15]

The citizens of Winthrop, Massachusetts, a residential community on a peninsula east of Boston's Logan Airport, have been exposed consistently to such pollutants as noise, odors from burned and unburned Jet Fuel A, and burning rubber from airplane tires. Like the citizens of Park Ridge, the citizens of Winthrop have tired of being ignored by federal and state regulatory authorities. Facing further airport expansion, the town decided to organize its own study of respiratory disease incidence. The expansion of Logan Airport will "markedly increase operational capacity and the generation of pollutants," the town asserted in its 1999 report. "While potent arguments in favor of this expansion are being presented from an economic standpoint, once again no consideration is being given to the possible public health impact." [16]

From a scientific standpoint, Winthrop is ideal for a controlled study because some of its neighborhoods are located within a few hundred feet of major airport runways, while others are located as much as a mile and a half away. Also, unlike other urban communities near Logan Airport, the town is little affected by such pollution sources as power plants, industries, and heavy road traffic.

The 1999 Winthrop study was well crafted. It was based on sound questions delivered in closed-ended interviews and carried out by volunteers trained in objective interviewing techniques. Questions were posed to residents regarding the presence in their homes of each of five respiratory diseases that have been connected with exposure to fossil-fuel exhaust. The study required that a physician make the diagnosis of the diseases, and the results of the study were controlled for confounding variables like gender, age, and smoking history. The results showed that the most common of all respiratory diseases, asthma and allergies, were twice as frequent in the part of town most heavily exposed to the airport, and that chronic sinusitis was also strongly correlated with the most highly exposed area.

Faced with such growing evidence, we clearly should be monitoring aviation pollutants. What are the major pollutants that concern our communities? Here is a compendium.

Air Pollution

Our friends who have lived at the end of runways near large airports tell us that departing jets drop so much fuel combustion residue on their homes that the smell seeps in through their closed windows. I experienced a similar effect at our local park when, after a dozen small jets had flown over, there remained an intense smell of jet exhaust. At our small airport, nearby residents have already noticed that clothing put out on a line is blackened by the air traffic exhaust. Exactly what is being dropped on the communities near airports?

According to an EPA study by the Northeast States for Coordinated Air Use Management (NESCAUM) and the Center for Clean Air Policy (CCAP), the list of aviation pollutants that adversely affect public health and the environment includes nitrogen oxides, hydrocarbons, particulate matter, carbon monoxide, and numerous toxics.[17] In the United States, aviation fuel for piston planes is the only commonly used fuel that contains lead additive.[18]

Nitrogen oxides and hydrocarbons are precursors to ozone formation. Ozone is a powerful oxidizer that at ground level causes lung irritation and aggravates diseases such as asthma, chronic bronchitis, and emphysema. Ozone produces many acute effects including coughing, shortness of breath, and impaired lung function.[19]

Particulates have adverse cardiopulmonary effects and also contribute to haze and acid rain. Like all engines that burn fossil fuel, airplane engines emit particulates—simply, soot. Recent research has discovered that this component of air pollution is responsible for more serious health consequences than many more commonly studied components. A 1995 Canadian governmental review of many scientific health studies concluded that increases in particle concentrations in the air are associated with increases in death rates.[20] In 2000, a comprehensive study of ninety large American cities by the Health Effects Institute of Cambridge, Massachusetts, separated out the effects of particulates from other air pollutants such as ozone, sulfur monoxide, and carbon monoxide, and confirmed the relationship between the particulates themselves and higher death rates.[21] A study using data collected by the American Cancer Society concluded that the adjusted risk of mortality in cities with the highest level of particulate pollution was approximately 15 to 25 percent higher than in cities with the lowest particulate levels.[22]

In the "toxics" category emitted by airplanes are such known or probable human carcinogens such as benzene and formaldehyde.

How much of these and other noxious substances do airplanes emit? In 1995, Chicago's O'Hare Airport had 383,363 operations, and these were putting into the air of its local communities 1,428 tons of volatile organic compounds and 4,650 tons of nitrogen oxides annually.[23] In 2003, with 900,000 operations, O'Hare is the world's busiest airport, and under plans approved the same year by the Illinois state legislature it will expand to 1.6 million operations. Assuming airplane engines continue to pollute at about the same rate, the expansion will spread more than four times the amount of these pollutants, amounting to almost 6,000 tons of volatile organic compounds and more than 19,000 tons of nitrogen oxides per year, or 16 tons and 52 tons respectively *per day* over the local communities. In the context of the entire state of Illinois, which has 8,000 active (nonaviation) sources, it would represent about 4.4 percent of the volatile organic compounds and 3.7 percent of the nitrogen oxides. One concern is that airplane pollutants are not dropped over the entire state, they are concentrated in the communities over which the planes land and take off.[24]

To cite another suggestive example, the NESCAUM-CCAP study of three major airports in New England examined ozone-creating nitrogen oxide emissions and found that the annual amount of tons of nitrogen oxide emissions in 1999 was 2,664 tons at Logan, 676 tons at Bradley, and 187 tons at Manchester. Most of these emissions are attributed to air carriers (commercial planes rather than small planes or ground vehicles), the study pointed out, for three reasons: on an engine-per-engine basis, air carriers produce more pollutants per minute and burn more fuel per minute than general aviation aircraft; at these airports they account for more landings and takeoffs; and they have more engines per plane.

Comparing the airport emissions to other stationary sources, the researchers wrote, "In Massachusetts . . . aircraft from Logan International Airport currently emit approximately 20 percent as much nitrogen oxide as the largest power plant in the state. By 2010, aircraft nitrogen oxide emissions at Logan are expected to exceed those of any single power plant in the state, without further regulation." [25]

In a separate category the researchers studied 14 aircraft toxics emissions, including benzene, formaldehyde, toluene, and xylene. While apologizing that their calculations were based on only a few data points, the research team found that the airports' emissions already "greatly exceed" those of the largest stationary sources in the three states. Among these emissions is lead. The researchers noted that when the lead-containing aviation gasoline (used only for general aviation aircraft, as differentiated from the jet fuel used by air carriers) is burned, about 75 percent of the lead is released into the air. [26]

The study concluded that, in 1999, "the total emissions contribution from three airports in the Northeast was already significant, relative to other major emissions sources in the area. Moreover, given the predicted increase in aircraft [landings and takeoffs] over the next ten years at the three airports studied, and the relatively lax emissions standards for aircraft and [ground service equipment], emissions are expected to increase at all three airports. . . . Given current growth rates and planned controls on existing stationary sources, airport-related nitrogen oxide emissions will be greater than nitrogen oxide emissions from the largest stationary sources (power plants) in the vicinity of the airports studied by 2010." [27]

Of course, in addition to planes flying overhead, the increased ground traffic in and around airports contributes significantly to the local air pollution. Even with modest growth at a small airport, ground traffic escalates dramatically. If even one commercial airline flies 50-seat planes for 20 flights a day at 50 percent capacity, 500 passengers a day will have to get to or from that airport. If the flights are at 100 percent capacity, this number will climb to 1,000 passengers a day and nearly that many car trips to the airport. If Hanscom Field, for example, develops as Westchester County Airport has, at 100 flights a day it will process a million passengers a year, which will add an average of over 2,000 passenger trips per day to the local roads. Much of this traffic would be bunched at peak commuter flying times in the early morning and late afternoon, which are also peak commuter driving times.

A line of 150 cars, traveling thirty miles an hour, stretches over two miles long.[28] Thus, in addition to the pollution, the congestion locally can be extreme. In the case of Lexington, the sole access road to Hanscom Field is the two-lane Battle Road through Minute Man National Historical Park, and access to that road is through residential areas of Lexington to the east, Lincoln to the south, and Concord to the west—where residential routes are already crowded—and via Route 128 to the east, which is clogged with stop-and-go traffic every workday morning and evening. In addition to severely increasing congestion, it is inevitable that cars and taxis will cut through residential neighborhoods.

Of course, air pollution is caused not only by the planes themselves but by the many vehicles that service them, and by the local motor vehicle traffic of the passengers who ride them. It is the combined effects of ground and air traffic that make O'Hare Airport, for example, the major polluter that it is.

Climate Change

Emissions from jet aircraft contribute to the destruction of the earth's protective ozone layer. A 1999 intergovernmental European report on climate change estimated that, conservatively, aircraft are responsible for 3.5 percent of the warming caused by greenhouse gases.[29] This estimate is based on a compromise among scientists and includes some influential assumptions about how waste emission will be improved. The actual percentage could easily be as high as 7 percent, and some of the study's authors thought it could be as much as 10 percent. Of these emissions worldwide, about half are accounted for by international aviation and half by domestic aviation.

Emissions from aircraft are predicted to double every ten years. This makes aviation emissions the fastest-growing source of greenhouse gases.[30]

Although emissions from domestic aviation are included in the Kyoto Protocol targets for reduced emissions internationally, because the Kyoto negotiators could not agree on how to allocate responsibility for emissions made during international flights (the same problem occurs with international shipping), emissions from international aviation are excluded.[31]

A recent American report indicates several other important effects of aviation emissions. A primary concern is that because these emissions are deposited directly into the upper atmosphere, some of them have a greater warming effect than gases like automobile exhaust that are emitted closer to the earth's surface. Second, the primary relevant gas emitted by jet aircraft engines is carbon dioxide, which has an atmospheric lifetime of up to one hundred years. Third, when combined with other gases from jet engines, carbon dioxide can have two to four times as great an impact on the atmosphere as carbon dioxide emissions alone.[32]

A related concern is the projected introduction of a fleet of supersonic jets that would cruise at altitudes much higher than the current subsonic craft and would consume more than twice as much fuel per passenger mile as subsonic aircraft. Were this fleet to be built, the projected rate of increase of total aircraft emissions would be even larger.

Contrails, or condensation trails from jet aircraft, are an increasingly recognized factor in climate change. Contrails are the ice crystal streams that form around particles extruded from airplanes at high altitude, and of course, they are most often observed near major commercial air corridors. Contrails seed cirrus cloud systems that can trap heat, according to research by the National Aeronautics and Space Administration.[33] Even one individual contrail can create a cloud system up to sixty miles long.

Probably as a result of the contrails from increased air traffic, the number of clear days over the United States has decreased in the last thirty years. Researchers at the University of Wisconsin–Whitewater conducted an experiment during the three-day quiet skies period from September 11 to September 14, 2001, and it showed that without contrails the average temperature range in regions of high plane travel was significantly wider than normal. This is further proof that the contrails act like artificial clouds, preventing temperatures from climbing by day and dropping by night.[34] In other words, they change local climates. The effects of contrails are conservatively expected to increase by a factor of six by 2050.[35]

Ground Pollution

The water runoff from smaller airports typically goes into the water table under neighboring communities. It contains, among other toxic substances, all of the chemicals that are routinely used in airplane maintenance. For instance, since de-icing of commercial planes is required, and there are no holding tanks, the chemicals from de-icing simply run off into local watersheds. Many of these chemicals are documented health hazards.

It is known, for example, that the main ingredients in aircraft de-icing/anti-icing fluids (ADAFs) are glycols. Some de-icing formulations use ethylene glycol. According to the Occupational Safety and Health Administration, ethylene glycol "causes eye irritation, central nervous system depression, and kidney and liver damage" in lab tests.[36] In humans, exposure to ethylene glycol by either ingestion or inhalation causes eye and upper respiratory tract irritation and headaches, thus threatening airport workers. Other de-icing formulations use propylene glycol, which is believed to be less toxic to humans but which, when introduced in large amounts, does not degrade before reaching groundwater. If glycols enter streams at even fairly low concentrations, they may have negative effects.[37] Glycols use high amounts of oxygen, reducing the amount of dissolved oxygen available for fish and other aquatic organisms. In Canada, the Environmental Protection Act has regulated glycols because of the high biochemical oxygen demand measured in waters receiving airport storm-water discharge. This is in part because fish kills have been associated with discharges of de-icing chemicals.[38]

Additives, usually 10 to 20 percent of the ADAF formulations, include such substances as wetting agents, corrosion inhibitors, surfactants, dyes, and thickeners. According to a 1998 study in *Environmental Science & Technology*, a number of researchers have found that ADAFs have significant toxicological effects and that additives contribute to these. One research report based on analyses of groundwater samples in the water table beneath "an international airport" in Milwaukee, Wisconsin, found the samples to be "potentially extremely toxic." In this instance, the key contaminant was tolyltriazoles, a common class of corrosion inhibitor used not only in de-icing agents but also in automobile engine coolants and other products.[39] Subsequently, Steve Corsi of the United States Geological Survey in Madison, Wisconsin, verified that, especially when heavy de-icing has been carried out, water taken from the stream that drains that airport destroys aquatic life. He has pointed out that while current environmental regulations monitor glycols, they ignore additives. He also makes clear that at larger airports, which typically collect the excess fluid when planes are sprayed, there is still runoff as aircraft taxi down a runway and take off.[40]

In an industry profile, the EPA found that toxic chemicals used by airports, airline terminals, and aircraft maintenance facilities, some of which must now be reported, also include trichloroethylene, methylene chloride, acetone, chloroform, methyl ethyl ketone, isopropyl alcohol, glycol ethers, toluene, xylene, and other petroleum distillates.[41]

In Lexington, Massachusetts, when the state initiated commercial air service at our local airport, no prospective environmental impact studies were done regarding water pollution, air pollution, noise pollution, or traffic. The state argued that none was needed. Yet uncontained spills of jet fuel and hydraulic fluid, along with the de-icing compounds, enter the storm drainage system and the water table. Already, because of its aviation usage over decades, Hanscom Field sports a SuperFund pollution site, and town wells have been closed. Groundwater and subsurface soil are contaminated with chlorinated solvents, jet fuel, and other petroleum compounds, and people who come into direct contact with or ingest these are at risk. At Hanscom Field the EPA has ranked the possibility for groundwater migration of these pollutants as high.[42]

Noise Pollution

From a community's perspective, the most urgent and obvious environmental problem is usually noise pollution. Research has linked noise pollution to harmful effects ranging from reduced learning in children to increased blood pressure in children and adults.[43] To begin with, there is a strong and growing body of research on the effect of airport noise on children. A 1997 study examined the effects of airplane noise on children attending school in the flight path of a New York international airport.[44] The children experienced phases of peak activity when single planes created noise in their classroom of up to 90 decibels every 6.6 minutes, and they suffered significant reading deficits. A study of children living near London's Heathrow airport found that chronic aircraft noise exposure (defined as having an average continuous equivalent sound level of aircraft noise approximating 66 dBA for 92 days) is associated with impaired reading comprehension and high levels of noise annoyance.[45] A third study discovered long-term physiological effects on children after a large new airport was opened near Munich, Germany.[46]

Despite the alarming findings, I had trouble imagining events of this magnitude occurring in our community. I thought, Hanscom Field isn't a major airport! It's only a general aviation facility! Air traffic in Lexington is low compared to the traffic in these research studies. I guessed the noise, at least, would not affect my child, our children.

I was forced to think again. In Lexington, planes using the longer flight path descend directly over a middle school at about 1,000 feet, and several elementary schools are also affected. In a letter to the editor of the local newspaper, a seventh grader in the middle school wrote, "During school, the teachers always have to stop when a plane flies over, they are just too loud. Once a plane flew so low that it looked like it might crash into the building—that's ridiculous!"[47] I might add, as a parent, that scenario is also frightening.

Because the range of sound intensity that a human ear can detect is so large, the scale most frequently used to measure it is a decibel scale, which is logarithmic rather than linear. Thus, a small increase in the number of decibels actually represents a very large increase in sound intensity: each time the decibel level increases by ten points, it means that the noise intensity is *multiplied* by ten.

In the decibel scale, the threshold of human hearing is assigned a sound level of 0 decibels (0 dB), while a sound that is ten times more intense is 10 decibels, and a sound that is one hundred times more intense is 20 decibels.

A source of frequent confusion to the layperson is that decibels (dB) may be measured in more than one way. In assessing human impact the measurement or metric most conventionally used is the decibel measure called dBA (also referred to as the A-weighted decibel), and in this book, when I refer simply to "decibels," this is the metric I mean.

Although dBA is the measurement most widely used by government policy makers and others, *it has been heavily criticized* by acoustic experts because it accurately captures only what humans experience when they hear low-pressure sounds. For sounds that exceed 60 dB the reliability of A-weighting decreases,[48] and high-pressure sounds are what typically emanate from an airplane. There exists a different decibel metric (dBC) that more accurately captures airplane noise, but it is seldom used.

In any case, currently most policymakers deal in dBA. Using this metric, how loud is loud?

A sound of 90 decibels (dBA) is as loud as a vacuum cleaner or a large orchestra. A sound measured at 100 decibels is the equivalent of listening to a Walkman at maximum level. A decibel level of 110 is like sitting in the front row of a rock concert.[49]

How do such figures translate into aviation noise for communities? A propeller-driven plane flying at 1,000 feet creates a sound of about 88 decibels for persons on the ground, which is equivalent to the noise experienced when standing next to a food blender or a lawn mower. It is louder than standing next to a garbage disposal. A jet plane flying over at 1,000 feet yields 103 decibels, which the average person perceives as louder than an unmuffled diesel truck or a motorcycle passing by 50 feet away.[50] In Lexington we already have a mix of jet and propeller aircraft flying at low altitudes over our schools and homes. My experience is that aircraft routinely fly over many homes at altitudes of about 500 feet.

According to World Health Organization guidelines for community noise, individual sound events over 45 decibels impair sleep if a window is open. Outdoor sound levels above 50 decibels create moderate annoyance. What does it take to get a good night's sleep with the windows closed? The WHO guidelines are that background noise in the room should not exceed 30 decibels.

Outdoor sound levels above 55 decibels create "serious" annoyance, and repeated exposure to events above 100 decibels causes hearing impairment.

The probability of being awakened increases with the number of noise events per night, so multiple noise disturbances create increasingly disturbed sleep. Typically, research has shown, any 8 to 10 decibel spike, meaning any such change over existing background sound levels, will cause a person to wake up.[51]

Lack of sleep causes many problems, among them general irritability and reduced capacity to work. There is even consistent evidence that noise above 80 dB causes reduced "helping" behavior, such as reduced kindness, and that loud noise increases aggressive behavior in individuals predisposed to aggressiveness. In children, high levels of chronic noise may also contribute to feelings of helplessness.[52]

When I applied these findings to a town like ours, I realized that in the future, assuming again that Hanscom Field develops as the Westchester County Airport has, there could easily be 100 commercial flights, or a total of 200 commercial operations, in the air over our residential communities every day. Hanscom Field has two runways. The longer one at 1.3 miles in length can handle the world's largest aircraft.[53] If we assume that these flights would use only the longer one, and if the airport is open from 7 A.M. to 11 P.M., or sixteen hours, planes, if evenly spaced, would be taking off or landing every 4.8 minutes. Because they take off and land in different directions, this translates into a commercial aircraft going over one of the Lexington middle schools every 9.6 minutes.

These calculations account for only commercial traffic, which at this time is a small percentage of the total Hanscom Field flight operations. Many private companies also have planes based at the airport, and in the wake of the 9/11 tragedies, corporate jet traffic is rapidly increasing.[54] Massport talks of turning Hanscom into a major small-jet port. Small corporate jets are also quite noisy, and there is no limit on the size of jet a private company may use. These calculations also do not include small private planes or military planes. Nor do they account for the increase in private jets that are shared by several owners, a practice that is also expected to expand significantly as a direct result of the concerns for security and convenience at major airports since September 11, 2001.

Taken together, even 200 commercial and 70 jet operations per day on a runway translate into one disruptive flight over our middle school every seven minutes.

Another way to look at our situation is to consider the total number of operations now and in the future. Up until the September 11 attacks, our airport had run roughly 200,000 operations a year, while 320,000 operations a year is the point at which the Hanscom Field Master Plan suggests the community would begin to be significantly impacted by various types of pollution. There is no prescribed mix of aircraft types for the additional 120,000 operations. Theoretically, were new ground infrastructure to be built, the additional planes could all be large jets, commercial or private. Assuming they were, and based on our other assumptions about runway and takeoff direction, 120,000 new operations would translate into 164 more planes per day, or one commercial airliner every 2.2 minutes flying over our middle school.

The FAA itself has recognized the need for community relief and protection from the noise of such low-flying aircraft. It advises pilots operating over noise-sensitive areas to voluntarily "make every effort to fly not less than 2,000 feet above the surface, weather permitting," even when flight at a lower level may be consistent with the minimum safe altitudes set by the FAA.[55] Of course, flying at such high altitudes is simply not possible when landing at suburban airports embedded in residential communities.

The EPA also recognized the general noise problem as early as 1976, when its chief administrator, Russell E. Train, stated, "We need a national air transportation system which is healthy as well as safe. The evidence is overwhelming that, unless we make that system quieter, both human health and the financial health of the industry will continue to suffer.[56]

But measuring the noise is only the first part of the equation. What do we really know about its effects on children and learning?

A 1997 study by Gary Evans and Lorraine Maxwell, environmental psychologists in the College of Human Ecology at Cornell, with funding by the National Heart, Lung, and Blood Institute and the U.S. Department of Agriculture, matched first and second graders from two elementary schools in one urban area and discovered that the children bombarded by frequent aircraft noise do not learn to read as well as the children in quieter schools.[57] The major reason children in noisy schools don't learn as well is that they tune out speech. Although they hear perfectly well, they learn to avoid listening. The authors speculated that other factors may also be at work, such as the irritability of teachers and parents—who may be reluctant to talk as much, use as many complete sentences, and read aloud as often as teachers and parents in quieter schools.

A 1981 review of several studies concluded that, after controlling for socioeconomic factors, academic performance of children is better in quiet schools than in noisy schools.[58] Reading achievement is affected, particularly when the children's homes are also in noisy areas. One 1993 study showed that reading impairment in twelve- to fourteen-year-olds was about 23 percent if exposed to aircraft or train noise.[59] A 1992 study indicated that children, especially girls, exposed to the noise of low-flying aircraft developed more anxiety disorders.[60] There is a history of studies showing similar results, so many that noise-disrupting communication in the classroom has led to the nickname "jet-pause teaching."[61]

In 1998, a second study by Evans and some German and Swiss colleagues, funded by the Society for the Psychological Study of Social Issues, the National Institutes of Health, and the Swedish Environmental Protection Agency, among others, examined the physiological effects of noise on children.[62] The researchers found detrimental effects on third and fourth grade children near Munich eighteen months after a new airport opened. The children who experienced chronic noise experienced increases in blood pressure and in the stress hormones epinephrine, norepinephrine, and cortisol, while the children in quiet areas experienced no significant changes. The exposed children also reported a significant decline in their quality of life.

The Evans study suggests, "Although the increases in blood pressure were modest in the children living under the flight path, they may predict a greater likelihood of having higher blood pressure throughout adulthood," since elevated blood pressure in childhood predicts higher blood pressure later in life.[63] Increases in stress hormones in adults are linked to such adult illnesses as high blood pressure, elevated lipids and cholesterol, heart disease, and a reduction in the body's supply of disease-fighting immune cells.

In sum, noise pollution has important physiological and psychological effects on both children and adults. Responding in 1990 to Continental Airlines' proposal to begin commercial service at Hanscom Field, Dr. Donald Goldman, a professor of pediatrics at the Harvard Medical School, observed that public health authorities in other countries take the cardiovascular effects of noise "very seriously," and that it is well known that "the startling, repetitive intrusion of noisy aircraft overhead raises our blood pressure." Dr. Goldman declared, "What we are really talking about here is nothing more nor less than the traditional conflict between commercial business interests and profits on the one hand and public health and welfare on the other. This battle is as old as history itself. . . . [The airlines] want to win our hearts and minds, and we simply want to protect them."[64]

Regretfully, today the friendly skies have become the polluting skies. In the next chapter we will look at how small airports are growing.

4

Facing Up to Airport Expansion

*No person shall own or keep in this town any dog or pet
which, by barking, biting, or howling, or in any manner,
disturbs the peace and quiet of any person. No person shall
own, or keep in this town any bird or fowl which, by
screeching or crowing or in any other manner, disturbs the
peace and quiet of any person.*

—Bylaws, Town of Lexington, Massachusetts

*Would we as a nation, if there were 598 flights a day over
Yosemite National Park, say, "That ought to stop?" Yes, I
think we would.*

—David McCullough, historian

IN CITIES LIKE Minneapolis and New York, residents near large
airports have fought aviation pollution for decades. Yet of the
more than 2,000 airports in the United States that are currently
targeted for expansion,[1] most are in smaller cities, cities where
citizens have less experience tackling government agencies.
Suburban citizens are unfamiliar, in particular, with the incrementalist tactics by which an airport is expanded into a major facility.
First, there may be a runway extension, then a new terminal
building, then a new control tower, and before the citizenry is
aroused, suddenly there is a major airport in their backyard and,
given the cumulative investment in infrastructure, there is no

turning back. The cumulative effects of such growth should be monitored under existing environmental laws, and in some cases are, but such laws as exist are typically ineffective.

This chapter relates the stories of three smaller communities, each confronting a different stage in the expansion of its airport. The first, our airport in Lexington, is well into the process of commercial development. In Westchester County, New York, the local airport has already matured into a full-fledged commercial facility. In Stuart, Florida, the airport is described during an early stage of commercial development. These cases illustrate how sub-urban communities react when their airports begin to expand. They show how, in the face of incrementalist and often-deceptive business and government tactics, communities struggle, and usually fail, to prevent airport expansion.

Lexington, Massachusetts

Lexington is a suburban town with more than thirty thousand residents located in the high-technology corridor west of Boston. It is a bedroom community to many area professionals, including administrators and professors at Boston's many institutions of higher learning, and engineers and managers for nearby high technology companies. Lexington's schools are among the best in the nation. Ninety-six percent of its high school students take the SAT examinations, and their average combined score for verbal and math is 1207. The town has 20,532 registered voters, mostly independents and Democrats. Approximately one mile of the town's western border abuts Hanscom Field.

People move to the town because of its excellent school system, its proximity to the city, its parks and recreation facilities, its wonderful library, and its small-town atmosphere. Walking on the high school track in the early morning, one fairly inhales the citizens' sense of well-being. Strolling across the historic Battle Green on a fine fall afternoon, one's mind scrolls readily through two centuries of democratic destiny.

Over the years the town has made choices that have kept it connected with other communities—participating in the metropolitan cooperative program that buses children from less-privileged schools, voting to turn a railway right of way into a popular bike path that joins several towns, redesigning streets to facilitate tour bus access to the Lexington Green. It has also made choices that have separated it from other communities, such as voting down a Boston area subway extension through the town.

Lexington is the epitome of a modern suburb that captures the image of the small towns of yesteryear while living squarely in the current times. The nature of the town is so increasingly rare that over the last decades housing has gone to the upper middle class and the rich. It is hard to buy your way into Lexington, where the median home price in 1999 was $410,000, and mansionization is rampant. Certainly most new, young families must have two breadwinners. The economic isolation of a town like Lexington is accentuated by the strong Boston economy—housing costs in the area are among the highest in the country—and by the national trend of the rich getting richer while the poor and middle classes stagnate.

Economically it is not the diversified town of the American dream, but rather it is today an upper middle class enclave. In recent decades Lexington's problems, like those of similar communities, have become increasingly complicated. Not only does the town deal with utilities, roads, and schools, these days it faces significant problems that originate beyond its borders—pollution, traffic, and cellular towers, to name just a few—issues that tie citizens inextricably to powerful commercial and global interests. Indeed, the social, governmental, and commercial environment in which all towns operate today is more complex and hostile than it has ever been. Even staying informed on these concerns, let alone involved with addressing them, requires a major commitment. Small towns, even affluent ones, are stretched to the limit.

Fortunately, many of Lexington's citizens are eager to participate in local organizations and politics. The town is rife with active civic groups, churches, and synagogues. Volunteering in schools is a particular focus.

The other three towns contiguous to Hanscom Field are similar in character to Lexington. Bedford, Concord, and Lincoln all have the pretty look of the traditional New England village, all share the pains of suburban growth along the Route 128/Route 2 high-technology corridor, all are populated by the middle and upper class. Together the four towns have about 74,000 residents.

While Lexington and Bedford have more commercial development, Concord and Lincoln are more affluent. Lincoln is nationally renowned for its foresight in planning extensive town-owned conservation land. This land and the state-owned Walden Pond in Lincoln and Concord are important natural and recreational resources for the greater Boston area. Concord is home to the Great Meadows National Wildlife Sanctuary, a 3,000-acre link in the north-south flyway for annual bird migrations along the East Coast; the sanctuary receives 600,000 visitors a year. Walden Pond, the Minute Man National Historical Park, Lexington Green, the Historic Homesteads of the Alcotts, Emerson, Thoreau, and Hawthorne, and hundreds of sites on the National Landmark and Historic Register are in these towns, all within about three miles of Hanscom Field.

The Minute Man National Historical Park borders Hanscom Field on the south. The 950-acre park was created by Congress in 1959 to preserve for the American people historic structures and properties of outstanding national significance associated with the opening of the War of the American Revolution. The park, one of the top tourist attractions in Massachusetts, hosts about a million visitors a year. It includes dozens of historic landmarks and the 5.5-mile Battle Road Trail, site of the running battle that began April 19, 1775, when colonial militia pursued British troops from Concord to Boston following the fight at the Old North Bridge. At considerable federal effort and expense, the Battle Road Trail has been kept rural in nature, with stone walls, wooden guardrails, and a rustic walking path adjoining it. Unfortunately, the only access road to Hanscom Field is the Battle Road itself. Development of the airport threatens to further clog this already busy two-lane road, where more lanes and traffic lights will be needed. To handle the increased traffic, the state already has on the drawing board the reconfiguration of the historic intersection Meriam's Corner.

The inevitable increase in noise and pollution from a large airport has already diminished visitors' experience of the historical sites, which are best contemplated under conditions of reasonable quiet. Park rangers giving talks at the North Bridge in Concord are often interrupted by planes passing over and must stop speaking until the planes are gone. The six hundred thousand people who visit Walden Pond each year are also increasingly subject to airplane noise.[2] When planes roar over the nearby Thoreau Institute every few minutes, speakers have to pause until they pass.

Because the four towns are relatively small and intimate—hardly anonymous urban environments—they are probably better organized than many communities. Organizing is convenient here, and citizens are also resource rich—in contacts, money, and professional expertise. Citizens bone up on town budget overrides. They vote. They volunteer in places they value—making lunches for food pantries, running a Girl Scout troop, or helping the town's initiative on racial diversity. On Patriots Day at 6 A.M. many congregate at the Lexington town green to see the enactment of the first shot fired in the American Revolution. The town is proud of its history and its present.

At the same time, many of our citizens work long hours. Today's Americans work longer hours than any workers in the industrialized world,[3] and the average American is working one month longer per year than twenty years ago. Level of income does not predict how much free time workers have: all income classes are working equally hard.[4] People move into Lexington and raise their kids in a mad flurry of work and carpools. Although a significant proportion of the population is retirees, it is also common practice in these communities to take your profits and buy a home in a cheaper place after the kids have finished school.

Given the nature of these communities, and of dozens of middle and upper class suburbs across the country, it should come as no surprise that until the fall of 1999 many, probably most, residents believed that they were well protected by their active citizenry and their local government. Certainly, it was unimaginable to most of us that we should be seriously threatened by air traffic and all its attendant problems. After all, there was an airline here in—when was that—the late 1980s?—and we got rid of it. That issue was settled over a decade ago, and our continued opposition to development is voiced by the state-authorized advisory group of Hanscom Field stakeholders—the Hanscom Field Advisory Committee. Isn't it?

When in 1999 the Commonwealth of Massachusetts, through its state agency Massport, promised the communities that Hanscom Field would continue to serve the region as a general aviation airport, which is an airport for private, corporate, charter, and light cargo planes *only,* many of us, the average citizens of our towns, naturally believed them.

Officially, the four-town area has developed several groups that look out for its interests vis-à-vis the airport. First, the towns themselves have formed the Hanscom Area Towns Committee (HATS) to coordinate their efforts on the airport and other issues of common concern. At one point they also instituted a regional advisory review board, an extra planning step that would require developers in areas contiguous to the airport to present any plans for property located in one town to all four towns, but this effort seems to have died.[5]

Second, the aforementioned Hanscom Field Advisory Committee established in 1978 by the state also represents the citizens of the towns in a monthly forum that includes general aviation pilots and commercial interests at the airport.

Third, there are also two volunteer organizations devoted to the airport issue. Safeguarding the Historic Hanscom Area's

Irreplaceable Resources (ShhAir) is a 2,000-member citizens' group whose concern for the last ten years has been the threat of increased noise, ground traffic, and environmental pollution from expanded air traffic or changes in the character and use of the airport. ShhAir's broader and longer-term goals are to preserve open space, areas of historic importance, and environmentally sensitive land and water resources. For years ShhAir (and its former incarnation, People Against Hanscom Expansion) has served as the community watchdog, opposing several commercial developments at the airport and pushing environmental reviews. It has done extensive legal research, solicited expert opinion, collected 17,000 petition signatures against commercial development at Hanscom, maintained a Web site, lobbied, organized pickets, and kept members informed of important meetings and events. Its volunteer board consists of about fourteen citizens from the four towns.

The second volunteer organization is Save Our Heritage, a group of local citizens who want to achieve permanent protection for the national historical, cultural, and environmental resources in the community. This organization's operating objectives are to educate the public about the special nature of the resources surrounding Hanscom Field, the impacts of airports on health and environment, and the practices of the FAA and the aviation industry; to ensure that limits are placed on the increased noise, ground traffic, and environmental pollution resulting from the expansion of air traffic; to prod state authorities to honor "their 25 year commitment not to develop Hanscom Field into a commercial airport"; to ensure that future development at Hanscom bears the costs of damage to the historical and environmental resources of the area; and finally, to encourage the development of federal programs that will reduce the impact of aircraft on people and the environment.[6] Save Our Heritage has created a national board of directors that includes historians David McCullough and Shelby Foote; actors and humanitarians Joanne Woodward, Paul Newman, Gregory Peck, and Christopher Reeve; director Ken Burns; and the heads of such organizations as the National Trust for Historic Preservation and the Walden Woods Project.

In 1999 the four towns appropriated $200,000 to hire the prominent Boston law firm Hale and Dorr to represent them in suing Massport for illegally initiating commercial traffic at Hanscom. While this suit has been criticized by a few townspeople, most agree it is a small investment to protect, among other things, the towns' tax base. Studies by the FAA and the state of Washington have shown that when a suburban area is significantly impacted by aviation, property values drop by about 15 percent.[7] Other research has suggested that a buyer's willingness to pay for a particular house drops 2 to 4 percent of the house value per decibel of environmental noise pollution.[8]

One citizen calculated that even a 15 percent loss of value on only 20 percent of the homes in Lexington would result in an approximately 3 percent reduction in tax revenues.[9] This would translate into a loss of one million dollars per year to the school systems in each town. These calculations do not account for additional public services needed in the towns as a result of increased traffic. Nor do they consider the potential for increased tax revenues from airline-related local businesses; however, because of the towns' primarily residential character, projections have suggested these would be modest. In this sense, suburban towns differ from towns near major airports, where businesses often depend on the airport and the airport creates many jobs.

There is more to Lexington's concern about the local airport expansion than even health and property issues. It took us a while to articulate what it was about the commercialization of the airport that was really getting to us. While sleepless nights, the subsequent reduction in our efficiency at work, and the stress on our families constituted one set of problems, it became clear to us that there was another issue at stake, the kind of issue that touched us as citizens of a democratic country. It is one thing to buy into a community knowing that you are going to live near a busy commercial airport, and another thing to be surprised by the transformation of that modest general aviation facility into a potential LaGuardia. It is one thing for a community to make a deliberate choice for development, and another for it to be exploited and blindsided by developers.

Over the years, through many public documents and statements, the state of Massachusetts has deliberately lulled the locals into believing it would maintain Hanscom Field at its status quo. Only gradually have citizens understood that, in reality, our state agency, Massport, has been acting as a development organization for the aviation industry. Citizen participation in planning has been primarily a sham.

How has Massport succeeded in misleading the community about its plans for Hanscom? Its deception is a case study in clandestine development.

Until the summer of 1999, when it allowed commercialization, Massport had repeatedly told the four towns that Hanscom would remain a general aviation airport. Former Massport director Peter Blute, a former state legislator and member of the House of Representatives, had made this promise publicly at a community forum as recently as 1997. Even in December of 1999, after the airline began to fly, Massport denied plans for commercial development at Hanscom. For example, on its Web site at that time it asserted that Hanscom's role as a reliever airport was sufficient:

> How does Hanscom Field fit into [the New England] regional plan? Hanscom is the second busiest airport in New England in terms of operations. As a general aviation reliever for Logan, Hanscom handled 183,000 general aviation and training operations in 1998. Arguments to develop Hanscom as a commercial service airport do not take into consideration this critical "reliever" role. Corporate jet traffic, charters, pleasure users and flight schools are important aviation functions that need to be accommodated. . . .
>
> Why doesn't Massport make more use of Hanscom instead of building another runway?

> . . . To use Hanscom for commercial jet service would
> mean significant investments in baggage systems, terminals,
> gates, etc.
>
> Rather than reinvent the wheel, Massport is in the process
> of establishing an operating agreement with Worcester Airport.[10]

Despite these assertions, worried activists in the four towns
had been working to clarify the status of the airport for some
time. In 1997 local legislators met with then Massport director
Blute to work out a mutual agreement about the future of the airport. Subsequently, a proposal by the grassroots organization
ShhAir to Blute resulted in an ad hoc committee to draft a memorandum of understanding, which is a document of some legal
standing, among all the parties. By the late spring of 1998, the
committee, consisting of ShhAir, the Hanscom Area Towns
Committee, the Minute Man National Historical Park, the
Hanscom Field Advisory Committee, and a group representing
the business interests at the airport, had completed draft number
eleven of a memorandum of understanding that included a summary of the commitments Blute had made in 1997.[11]

In the memorandum, the mutual objectives for the future of
Hanscom Field were itemized as follows: "Massport desires to
maintain Hanscom Field available for use as 'the premiere general
aviation airport in the New England region.' This entails keeping
Hanscom available for general aviation uses of the type and character
it presently serves and not to provide commercial passenger service
[a footnote added: including such operations as commuter operations, certificated passenger service, and large passenger charters
that sell tickets] or heavy cargo or containerized cargo service."[12]

Also as stated in the memorandum, Massport was to agree not
to solicit commercial aviation services for Hanscom and would
only consider infrastructure development that would support general aviation purposes. It was to continue to actively promote
regional aviation development at nearby commercial airports that
were operating at less than full capacity.

Unfortunately, the memorandum of agreement was never signed. After eighteen months of talks and drafts, Massport suddenly stopped the process, citing criticism by a Boston television station that the process had been secret (in reality, it had been fully public) and by neighbors of Logan Airport who saw Hanscom as a more desirable site than Logan for future airport expansion. When the chair of the ad hoc group that had drafted the memorandum subsequently met with Blute and then acting governor Paul Cellucci, the governor stated that he did not want to put planes where people did not want them, and he agreed that the towns could meet with him again once the matter of Logan expansion was settled.

As commercial airlines became a reality at the airport, even the legislators for the four communities were not permitted to know the truth about Massport's plans. In the early spring of 1999, during a meeting of the Massachusetts state legislature's Joint Committee on Transportation, Massport officials presented their plan for regional air service and reiterated that Hanscom was serving its purpose as a general aviation airport. State Senator Susan Fargo, who was herself a member of the transportation committee and had been present at the meeting, learned only later, in June, and then only through a reporter for the *Boston Globe* who had obtained information under the Freedom of Information Act, that talks between Massport and the new airline had taken place as early as May.

When Fargo confronted Massport and asked whether conversations had also occurred with the airline even earlier that spring, she was told that her question was "offensive." In an interview for this book, Senator Fargo characterized these events as only the most recent in Massport's "pattern of deception."

Subsequently, the airline's vice-president wrote in the *Boston Globe* that its representatives had first visited Hanscom Field in May of *1998*.[13]

Again, even after the airline started flying, in late September of 1999, a Massport spokesman interviewed by the *Globe* asserted,

"The fear shared by many local residents that the number of commercial flights from Hanscom will grow exponentially is unfounded." There was little empty space at the terminal, he said, and the airfield would remain primarily "the corporate reliever to Logan." [14]

But the truth was, and is, that there is no cap on the expansion of commercial service at Hanscom Field. For that matter, with but a handful of exceptions, there is no cap on the expansion of commercial service at any small airport in the country.

To deflect public criticism about the expansion, Massport argued that it was forced by the federal Department of Transportation to allow any certified air carrier access to Massport facilities. Local activists countered by pointing out that while the air is the FAA's jurisdiction, the ground is the airport proprietor's. According to legal experts, a state agency such as Massport might voluntarily impose any number of restrictions to access on the ground that would maintain the airport's general aviation status, or in this case its status quo. Airport owners and operators elsewhere have in this way maintained some local control.

But soon after the airline started service, Massport adopted a new role: as cheerleader for commercial aviation at the airfield. An op-ed piece by its then director Virginia Buckingham, successor to Peter Blute, in the *Globe* on January 8, 2000, cited the airline's Thanksgiving "successes" and effused that "business is already booming" at Hanscom.[15] Her remarks flew in the face of a *Globe* article a month earlier that said just the opposite: that the airline was flying at about 52 percent capacity, not breaking even.[16]

Furthering the state agency's divide-and-conquer strategy to pit urban and suburban communities against each other, Buckingham also pointed out that, "[The Hanscom passengers] didn't trek to Logan." [17]

Of course, the communities affected by Logan Airport learned to distrust Massport long before the suburbs did. They have been fighting expansion there for years, and most recently their civil organization CARE (Communities Against Runway

Expansion) has been fighting the proposed new runway there. Massport claims that the proposed 5,000-foot runway, to be built on land reclaimed from Boston Harbor, is needed to reduce delays, while CARE's view is that it is merely one more profit-making venture for the airline industry and an initiative that will bring Massport closer to its stated goal of 120 operations per hour for Logan Airport. Massport insists that the purpose of the runway is to reduce delays caused by northwest winds, while CARE points out that about 80 percent of delays are due to other causes and that, even with the new runway, delays will reach or surpass current levels a few years after the runway is built. Massport also describes the runway as unidirectional and over the water, while the truth is that the FAA controls this and refuses to make a commitment as to where the planes will actually fly. Often, planes that start out over the water divert and fly over the city of Boston.[18]

One evening, I was telling my friend Dede, who has a wide acquaintance with state government, about all this: that the airline started out with what they called four flights, which were actually eight. That within less than two months there were ten flights, which actually meant twenty planes overhead. That the airline started out using turboprops, but that the planes were leased and the standard in the industry is even louder regional jets. That Massport deliberately misleads communities and never lets them in on what is happening until it is too late for them to do anything about it.

Dede interjected, "Oh, yeah, a salami strategy."

"Salami. Is that a term of art?" I asked.

"No," she laughed. "It's a term of Italian. You let them have one sliver of the salami, and then another. And pretty soon they've got the whole salami."

Westchester County, New York

The case of Westchester County Airport (WCA), located twenty-five miles north of New York City in White Plains, demonstrates

how one community has already climbed the learning curve on
airport development only to discover that there is no relief in
sight. This is the airport that Hanscom activists point to as the
negative model for the future growth of small airports. It is the
community whose activists counsel that it is essential to fight back
before too much growth has occurred—before airport owners
invest in improving their airport infrastructure and before too
many airlines have developed a local market upon which individuals and corporations depend for jobs and transport.

In the 1940s, Westchester County Airport consisted of
503 acres operated by the United States Army.[19] After the war,
Westchester County and Gulf Oil Corporation began participating in the airport's operation and a small number of commercial
flights began. Later, the airport was managed by Johnson Controls
World Services, a private company under contract to Westchester
County.

Until the 1980s, commercial traffic was relatively infrequent at
Westchester. Then, from 1990 to 1994, commercial jet flights more
than doubled, while private, general aviation flights decreased. By
then the airport had grown to 692 acres, although its character as
a small-town airport had been maintained: the main terminal was
still an original 1947 army Quonset hut. In 1980 the county had
proposed to expand the airport facilities, and this proposal was
debated and developed for the next decade. It was not until 1995,
following a close public referendum, that the county completed a
new passenger terminal, access road, and parking lot.

In a 1988 county environmental impact statement, residents
were told that future noise levels in the surrounding communities
would decrease because, even though the total number of operations would go up, quieter aircraft would be used. This was the
federal rationale for aviation expansion that was promoted in
communities nationwide at the time. However, according to a
study by the nonprofit Natural Resources Defense Council,
growth at WCA significantly outstripped these projections and,
furthermore, most of the growth was in noisier airplanes: In

1994 there were 11,867 of the relatively noisy commercial jet operations, a figure that exceeded the environmental impact statement's prediction for the year 2006.[20] From 1990 to 1994, annual commercial jet operations increased an average of 30 percent a year, including a mere 14 percent increase from 1993 to 1994, and the total increase for the period was 145 percent.[21]

Noise complaints from local households soared. In 1990, 650 Westchester County households registered 2,071 complaints, while in 1994, 1,329 households filed 4,762 complaints. Westchester at that time had 187,064 operations annually, which was 53 percent of the traffic of John F. Kennedy International Airport and 56 percent of the traffic of LaGuardia International Airport.[22]

Several plans to prevent the growth of the airport simply failed. To begin with, the Airport Noise and Capacity Act of 1990 had reassured communities that growth would not alter their quality of life. This federal law required all airlines to convert their jet aircraft from noisier Stage Two aircraft to quieter Stage Three aircraft, either by buying new planes or "hushkitting" the old ones—that is, equipping Stage Two aircraft engines with noise reduction devices.

The law also stripped communities of the right to regulate curfew hours for Stage Three aircraft without FAA approval.

Theoretically, moving the fleet toward more Stage Three aircraft was supposed to solve noise problems, but in practice it has not. According to the 1998 testimony of the National Organization to Insure a Sound-controlled Environment (NOISE) before the House Committee on Transportation and Infrastructure—Subcommittee on Aviation, "An impression has been created in some circles that with the passage and implementation of the Airport Noise and Capacity Act of 1990, which required the phase-out of Stage Two aircraft and the attainment of an all-Stage Three fleet mix by the year 2000, airport noise has ceased or will soon cease to be a concern. This is highly inaccurate."[23]

It is inaccurate for several reasons. First, there are degrees of quiet within the Stage Three category, and some aircraft barely make the threshold. Second, the expansion of regional and reliever airports and the conversion of former military bases to civilian airports brings noise problems to many communities not formerly exposed to them; air cargo operations, especially, tend to occur at smaller airports and mainly at night. Third, citizens experience significant annoyance from aircraft noise at levels below the standard the FAA uses to determine if federally funded noise reduction and mitigation is required.

Fourth, even under the current minimally useful definition of adverse impact, funding for noise mitigation (such as soundproofing homes) does not come close to meeting current community needs. In the end, a quieter fleet mix is just one tool that might be used to reduce aircraft noise. Others include land-use restrictions; takeoff, landing, and run-up procedures; land and building acquisition; sound insulation; and overflight controls.

Importantly, even though some aircraft are quieter, there are now more aircraft. The NOISE representative pointed out that, "While noise contours* are shrinking at some airports due to the phase in of the Stage Three fleet, an expected increase in the number of flights will expand these contours again in many instances. Noise contours will also increase with the introduction of the next generation of larger aircraft."[24] At WCA, older Stage Two aircraft operations were more than three times more likely to generate a complaint than newer, quieter, Stage Three operations.[25] However, it was commercial jet aircraft operations that were responsible for a disproportionate share of the aircraft noise complaints.[26]

The reduction in decibels with Stage Three aircraft does not meet even the FAA's own noise guidelines—that is, the level at which abatement and mitigation are triggered—let alone the more rigorous EPA recommendations or the World Health

---

*The official FAA standard is a 65 dB DNL noise contour; a noise contour is a pictorial representation of the pattern of noise around an airport. For a complete description of how the FAA determines an acceptable noise level, see pp. 103–6.

Organization recommendations.[27] And the European Union has argued (even in the face of American retaliation) that hush-kitted Stage Two aircraft are still too noisy and are major polluters as well.

In summary, as the study by the Natural Resources Defense Council (NRDC) put it:

> The DNL metric used at Westchester County Airport, and by the FAA throughout the nation, was virtually useless in predicting when and where noise complaints would occur. NRDC's study shows conclusively that annoyed residents complained in response to specific, single aircraft noise events rather than to high average noise levels. We found no relationship between the DNL noise contours at WCA and the distribution of community noise complaints. The FAA's threshold of 65 dB DNL for residential land use compatibility is an inappropriate threshold for WCA. Virtually all WCA noise complaints came from residences with noise levels below 65 dB DNL (over 99 percent), and even below 60 dB DNL (over 90 percent).[28]

Several creative community initiatives to slow development also failed. Westchester County established one of the country's first Noise Abatement Offices, whose job was to compile noise data from fourteen remote monitoring stations in communities around the airport and to communicate with aircraft operators new to the airport or whose aircraft generated complaints. The county instituted nighttime voluntary curfews and in the early 1980s attempted to make these mandatory, but the courts prevented this remedy. Finally, the county entered into a unique, voluntary agreement with the airport's commercial carriers limiting them to four airport gates, with a cap of 240 passengers and four commercial flights per half hour. In the mid-nineties the airlines and the county extended this agreement until December 31, 2004, but only under pressure from the communities and the NRDC.

Today the case of Westchester County Airport serves primarily to illustrate that well-meaning, cooperative community efforts are worthless in the face of the federal standards that have been designed primarily to grow airports.

Stuart, Florida

In 1999 a community just starting up the learning curve on airport expansion was Stuart, Florida, a small residential and commercial city about an hour's drive north of Miami. In that year the director of Witham Field reported that his airport was running at about a third of its maximum capacity of 36,000 operations, and that by 2012 their number of operations was expected to reach 145,000. In the fall of 1999 a new $850,000 control tower and a $470,000 administration building opened at the airport.[29]

Stuart's situation is remarkably similar to Hanscom's, albeit with its own regional accents. What follows is a glimpse of the day-to-day struggle of the local community as told in the local newspapers. For the short two-month period in 2000 during which we trace their story, it focuses on the challenge issued to the community by a prominent lawyer who wants to fly his jet out of the airport without restriction.

April 7, 2000: Attorney and businessman Willie Gary wants to land his new Boeing 737, a 100-foot jet purported to include a thirty-two-seat cabin, a bedroom, a dining room, and a conference table, at Witham Field. Gary, a prominent soft money contributor to Democratic committees, hosted a fundraiser for President Clinton in 1999 that raised about $500,000.[30]

Technically, Gary's 737 can land on the current runway, but the county can fine him if he does.

"I have a constitutional right [to land the 737]," Gary says. "The county can get into a whole lot of money fighting me and end up losing. I hate to step this up to a showdown, but I plan to land my plane in Stuart."[31]

The director of the airport reports that it would cost more

than $3 million to upgrade the runway and taxiway to accommo-
date aircraft like Gary's, which weigh over 105,000 pounds. He
denies that upgrading the airport would open it to commercialization. "In no way would we open ourselves up to passenger
aircraft service," he says.[32] Local activists are wary. One says, "We
want to see exactly what they have in mind."[33]

April 11: Willie Gary's publicist issues a press release announc-
ing a new pro-airport group called "Friends of Witham Field."
The press release attacks the Witham Airport Action Majority, a
civil group opposing airport expansion, saying, "The WAAM
group has used scare tactics and armed the public with misinfor-
mation concerning the airport . . . [alleging] that the airport will
turn into a large commercial airport."[34]

April 12: About 475 people attend a meeting on the future of
the airport. One resident says, "I'm disappointed that we even
have to deal with this in Stuart—that we have to try and benefit
two or three individuals." Another points out that, "When the pas-
sions run is when you're having your cup of coffee in the morning
and it starts rattling when a plane flies by. We want a say in this."[35]

April 13: The headline in the *Stuart News* reads, "Gary Vows
Fight for Landing Rights," and the story quotes the attorney
promising to fight "all the way to the Supreme Court" for the right
to land his 737 at Witham.

"They're just using this as a way of punishing someone with
a 737—I don't think it's fair," says Gary. He vetoes the idea of
landing at another airport: "I would have to get in my car and
drive 40 minutes every time I wanted to get on my plane."

And he rejects the idea of using a helicopter to shuttle him to
another airport. "I don't think I should have to do that. I don't like
helicopters."

Gary warns that famous people such as billionaire Wayne
Huizenga and golfer Greg Norman would also like to use the airport for larger aircraft and suggests any legal action against the
county might become a joint effort. Gary says, "They're not going
to stop me. I challenge [WAAM] to put up the legal fees that

they're going to have to spend to fight my efforts to exercise my constitutional rights—if they feel it's worth costing the county $5 or $10 million in legal fees, which is what it will be.

"Because I'm not taking a back seat. I'm not taking it laying down, and they might as well get ready for it." [36]

A second article in the same edition of the newspaper notes that county officials think the problem is not really weight, but noise. The county commissioners discuss a possible "Part 150 study," and the airport director points out how noise would be measured in such a study—by averaging noise and silence over an entire year. One citizen's reaction is, "So, in other words, the noise levels are averaged in with no noise levels. That's just great," and the audience responds with "peals of laughter." [37]

April 17: In a letter to the editor, a local resident writes:

Why do people leave beautiful, tropical Miami and Fort Lauderdale for the supposed peace and quiet of Stuart, and then show no understanding when we protest our airport turning into a busy, noisy facility? We now have the tremendous noise of private jets taking off—isn't that what Southern Florida residents are trying to escape when they move up here? Instead they are bringing their problems of traffic and noise pollution to us and insisting this is the way to go. Progress!

My home . . . [was] established when the airport was only a gleam in the eye of [a man who] used a grassy field for his small plane. . . . These people are saying that it was our choice to live by a noisy airport. . . . These rude people who write "if you don't like the noise go back up North"—why don't they go north and stop interfering with the citizens who have lived here before the airport and would like to return to a little of the former peace and quiet that made these beautiful rivers such a paradise? [38]

April 20: A local paper quotes a citizen at a public meeting on the expansion as saying, "Here's your data—the noise is too loud!" [39]

April 21: A local Stuart lawyer declares a "Not So Quiet Protest" to include a fleet of boats and vehicles sounding their horns outside Willie Gary's house. "I live in the community and have to listen to this noise every single day. I'm not going to sit around and let him turn this area into Willie world." The Friends of Witham Field suggest a plan to work with the FAA to reduce the hours of louder jets by establishing voluntary curfews from 10 P.M. to 7 A.M.[40]

May 3: The county commissioners hear a consultants' report on noise measurement and mitigation that recommends following FAA guidelines. One commissioner responds, "If this is going to be done, [the data compiled] just isn't going to make it. What can be done? It's getting worse. . . . How can we correct it?" The consultant, who worked for the FAA from 1990 to 1999, recommends a Part 150 study, and the county commission unanimously accepts his report.[41]

May 19: The county committee charged with updating the "Airport Master Plan" receives a consultant's report, part of a $407,000 contract, that recommends extensive upgrades to the airport. These would include improving, resurfacing, extending, and adding runways and taxiways, adding hangars, constructing a parking area, and identifying sites for helipads.

WAAM members accuse the consultants of conspiring with airport officials and businessmen in an attempt to make Witham Field a metropolitan airport. Says one WAAM member of the airport study committee, "It almost looks like you sat down . . . and came up with a wish list intended to completely change Witham Field . . . into a Cadillac-class modern jet airport. . . . You have known since day one that the types of proposals you are now making were inconsistent with the desires of . . . thousands of residents."

The airport director says he is surprised at this charge. "Members of WAAM sat down and helped us come up with the scope of the study," he said. The WAAM activist retorts that one of the goals in the scope of the study was "to provide for airport development which will satisfy aviation demands and be compatible with the environment, the community, other modes of transportation, and other airports." [42]

May 20: A county commissioner moves to suspend the consultants' study. "My understanding was that the study was supposed to analyze airport operations, but not make a case for expansion," she says. "I think it's absolutely outrageous!" [43] Later the proposal to suspend the study dies on a 2–2 vote.

May 25: After Gary's jet wakes and frightens his eleven-month-old son and his wife at 1:30 in the morning, a thirty-seven-year-old man runs to his pickup truck—without shoes, shirt, or identification—and races to Witham Field. There, according to a sheriff's report, he threatens two pilots of Gary's plane, and then takes off to pursue Gary and his wife, who are driving home in their Rolls Royce. Although still upset by the airplane noise, the man later denies making the threats and apologizes to Gary. [44]

The community reaction in 2000 to the impending expansion of Witham Field is especially colorful, and I present it here to illustrate the human side of the expansion drama. In Stuart in 2004, WAAM had 5,000 members and was engaged in a sophisticated, complex struggle to influence Martin County policymakers to control airport growth by reducing the airport infrastructure. Based on a county study of possible future scenarios for the airport, WAAM believes that the viable local alternative is to de-federalize the airport: it must stop taking the federal grants that tie it to FAA policies. [45]

Government and industry keep communities busy while inexorably expanding their airports. Secrecy is part of their strategy. For example, it was reported that "Chicago officials may have hidden plans for new runways at O'Hare while publicly stating they had no intention to expand runway capacity." [46] And at El Toro Airport in California, the county has been accused of withholding documents that demonstrated that noise impacts, including sleep disruption, were greater than had previously been disclosed. [47]

Unfortunately, as the mayor of one town has observed, "Most people are trusting. They don't believe government bodies would deliberately skew their numbers." [48]

The truth is that airport communities have already compromised. Even setting the lies and half-truths aside, communities near airports are being asked to swallow an awful lot in the name of commercialization and the common good. It was one thing in the 1940s to give up five hundred acres and tranquility for the war effort, as we did at Hanscom Field. It was one thing in the 1970s, during the Vietnam War, to live with air traffic that was as noisy as it has been at Hanscom Field. It was one thing in the 1990s to sacrifice peaceful afternoons so our neighbors could have fun flying their small planes, or so local businesses could be more efficient, or so government authorities could use the runway for emergencies.

It is quite another thing to be told to sacrifice our property, our peace, and our health so that a select group of customers and businesses may enjoy personal and corporate convenience and profit—which profit, not incidentally, they often export to other states. [49]

It is one thing to be caught up in a long-term transportation plan that has been fairly developed with community involvement. It is quite another to be dictated to by organizations that are so powerful that, with virtual impunity, they make a mockery of citizen participation.

Our communities are caught up in a fatal process. We have lost the right to local determination. A citizens' master plan for airports would look quite different from a master plan created primarily to boost commercial traffic. It would, for instance, give priority to local determination and needs assessment.

Applying the assumption that politics is the art of the possible, such a plan might simply react to the current situation. Here is what it might look like at Hanscom Field: Instead of merely fining planes that fly between 11 P.M. and 7 A.M., all flights except emergencies would be eliminated between 7 P.M. and 8 A.M. on weekdays and between 6 P.M. and 8 A.M. on weekends. This would allow for differing sleep patterns among workers (although not shift workers) and their children, and it would let residents have a peaceful breakfast.

Instead of permitting a mix of jets and propeller planes emitting a variety of noise levels, a true citizens' plan would allow only quiet planes at an airport. The plan would have no tolerance for air and ground pollution. It would cap traffic at current levels, or reduce it, out of concern both for residents and for existing business interests. The state or other agency that runs the airport would be required to pay a sum to the community approximating the difference between what it currently yields to the towns and what the towns could earn from taxes were the land available in the free market.

Yet even these modest proposals would be remarkable achievements given the current pro-expansion laws.

Applying the quite different assumption that politics is the art of *imagining* the possible, here is a stronger plan:

Airports should be built only in rural or industrialized areas. Excellent rail transportation should connect them to urban centers. We do not want any airplanes whatsoever flying over homes or schools, or indeed, over any congested area, anywhere.

Airlines should be required to consolidate flights instead of increasing them. Some airports should be restricted to traditional general aviation (recreational) and emergency uses. Some airports should be closed. In Lexington many would like to see the airport turned into an industrial park or a high-technology campus that would create high-level local jobs and revenues. One option is to turn the land into open space that complements the green spaces of the adjacent national park, preserves the local wetlands, and maintains the quality of life that has attracted so many companies here in the first place.

Author Richard Goodwin summarizes precisely what it is that powerful special interests today are taking away from communities. "Money establishes priorities of action, revises . . . legislation, shifts

income from the middle class to the very rich. Money restrains
the enforcement of laws written to protect the country from the
abuses of wealth—laws that mandate environmental protection,
antitrust laws, . . . and many more." He concludes, "We need to
take the money out of politics before money takes the politics out
of politics."[50]

Unfortunately, at developing airports nationwide, the master
plans have already been written, and not by local residents. In the
age of globalization, powerful business interests have extended
their tentacles into our very bedrooms.

We didn't expect them so soon.

5

Massport: The Aviation Industry's Model Organization

Mankind are more disposed to suffer, where Evils are sufferable, than to right themselves by abolishing the Forms to which they are accustomed.

—The Declaration of Independence

People want to live in a community, not merely work in a market.

—Progressive Governance in the 21st Century,
an international manifesto signed by the United
States, June 2000

My INTEREST in our local airport grew in direct proportion to the number of hours of sleep I lost. When you are awakened at 2:30 A.M., never to return to blessed oblivion, you have a lot of time, and pointed energy, to think.

I had many questions, the sorts of questions local groups nationwide are asking. Why should a state agency risk the ire of the local communities by commercializing an airport without studying the effects on ground transportation, noise levels, or other pollution? Why couldn't the citizens' legally constituted advisory group (in our case, the Hanscom Field Advisory Committee) get the planning information it needed to do its oversight job? For example, why couldn't it obtain the copies of the operating agreement between Massport and the airline? Why couldn't it get a planning document from Massport stating how much commercial traffic is planned, or possible, at the airfield? These sorts of questions touch on crucial issues of government accountability.

I turned researching our situation into a grim hobby. From interviews, meetings with our representatives, and Internet and newspaper accounts, I gleaned details in my spare time. Each day my neighbors and I would gather at the school bus stop with our kids, and I would bring them a new tidbit. Do you know that our state agency, Massport, is in this to make a profit? Can you imagine that a national group of pilots wants to abolish even the small penalty for flying over us between 11 P.M. and 7 A.M.? In the wee hours I wrote letters to editors.

I learned that the type of commercial aviation that involves unscheduled passenger flights (not the more recent, more threatening type) has some limited history at Hanscom. Before 1999, the most recent such commercial flights at the airfield were in 1991, when Mohawk Air suspended operations after three years.[1] Mohawk had been running two flights on weekdays, with up to fifteen passengers per flight, to underserved Rome/Utica, New York, and to Providence, Rhode Island.

In 1990 Continental Express proposed commercial service to Newark, New Jersey, with connections to Denver, Cleveland, Florida, and Guam, using thirty- and forty-six-passenger aircraft. At that time the community, through their grassroots civil organization People Against Hanscom Expansion (the forerunner of ShhAir), hired a law firm and demanded an environmental review. The lawyers noted that state regulations intended that developments in the state not be "segmented" or "phased"—that is, introduced gradually—to evade environmental review, and that there were numerous indications that the Continental project was merely the first phase of future commercial expansion at Hanscom. (These regulations on segmentation were subsequently rewritten under Republican Governor William F. Weld's administration to exempt the cumulative effects of air transportation from such review.)

The communities requested that an environmental impact review cover, at the very least, traffic, air quality, noise, water quality impacts on historic and recreation sites, and ecological effects. They further requested that both Continental and Massport be ordered to address the issue of available transportation alternatives as well as to commit to explicit limits on future expansions.[2] When the expensive review was granted, the airline withdrew.

During the economic slowdown of the early nineties, commercial interest in Hanscom was scant. One small airline applied to start service but did not follow up. An organization called Corporate Air Service, Inc., applied to fly passengers to Washington, DC. Later, cargo airlines considered access. Strong community opposition defeated all of these efforts.

The startup of the new commercial airline in 1999 coincided with a strong economy and a significant increase in the number of private jet flights out of Hanscom. Since 1997, private jet traffic had increased 40 percent. The new airline's planes were among the loudest, and because they presaged even more growth, they were the most worrisome.

In 1999, as fall turned toward winter and the holiday season grew near, air traffic grew even louder. I made half a dozen noise complaints. Neighbors commiserated together. Should we sell our homes? Should we stay and fight? Was it already too late?

I wrote more letters to the editor.

In December of 1999 Massport announced that next it would expand corporate aviation facilities at the airfield. It planned to review a proposal for a new 40,000-square-foot hangar sited next to the current 32,000-square-foot terminal, and it would also review a proposal for what it claimed was a 92,000-square-foot office building. ShhAir believed the building would be a terminal annex.[3]

I decided that I wanted to know with some certainty whether I could actually tolerate living in my home during the coming years, so I sought everything I could find about the state's plans for Hanscom Field. If there is a state clearinghouse for public documents, I could not then find it, so I called up Massport directly to obtain its plans for Hanscom Field. After a few phone calls, I reached the right person. In January I sent off $31.80 payable to the Massachusetts Port Authority to cover the cost of photocopying and mailing 159 pages at 20¢ per page. Two documents were forwarded to me, with a polite cover letter, by Massport's senior legal counsel for litigation.

Meanwhile the airline had added a flight each day to Buffalo, New York, and another flight each day to Trenton, New Jersey.[1]

The 1956 Massachusetts Port Authority Enabling Act is one of those egregiously dull documents that makes for fascinating reading. It is instructive because it established one of the most powerful state agencies in the country, creating a model for those who would consolidate power in government while relegating citizen accountability to the sidelines. It is a model for privatization that many special interests admire, one that the aviation industry hoped to emulate in its 1999 plan for restructuring the FAA (for more on this, see chapter 6).

Massport was created as a "public instrumentality" to serve the "essential governmental function" of managing a diverse set of properties, including Logan International Airport, the Tobin Bridge, and the Port of Boston.[5] It consolidated three separate authorities—the Port of Boston Commission, the State Airport Management Board, and the Mystic River Bridge Authority.

According to the act, since Massport is a part of the state government, the exercise of its powers must be "in all respects for the benefit of the people of the commonwealth, for the increase of their commerce and prosperity, and for the improvement of their health and living conditions."[6] This having been said, it is also true that when it established Massport, the state legislature was eager to dispose of politically charged, time-consuming transportation decisions.

Massport is not subject to supervision or regulation by the department of public works or any department, commission, board, bureau, or agency of the state. Its only administrative connection to the state is that the seven-member Massport board is appointed by the governor.[7] Not more than four members of the Massport board may be of the same political party, and one must be a representative of a national or international labor organization. Generally, the executive director of the agency keeps that position only as long as the board remains in the same political party as the governor.[8]

The Massport board members serve for seven years without salary, but with all expenses paid.[9] A Massport credit card for meals and entertainment is issued to each of the members, who regularly participate in foreign trips to attract trade. The Massport board members vote on millions of dollars worth of contracts and thus have enormous power in the business community.

Illustrating how important their role is, with no public notice, in 2000 Governor Cellucci reshuffled his appointments to the Massport board to ensure that his appointees—who cannot be fired by a new governor except for malfeasance—would survive his term in office. Two members got extensions of their service by writing letters of resignation, allowing Cellucci to replace them. They themselves then accepted the appointments to the two newly vacant seats with full seven-year terms.[10]

Massport has broad powers as a state agency. These include the power to issue revenue bonds and the power of eminent domain. Because the operation and maintenance of its projects constitute the performance of essential governmental functions, Massport is not required to pay taxes. Although it obtains its revenues from issuing bonds and collecting user fees, its profits are available to the state government for such projects as underwriting the cost over-runs on Boston's Big Dig highway and tunnel reconstruction project. In fiscal year 1998 its profit was about $49 million.[11]

Massport also claims to be exempt from local zoning ordinances.[12] Its police force has "all the powers of police officers and constables of the towns of the commonwealth" except the power of serving civil process.[13]

At the same time, according to its vice-chairman, Massport is "as close to a private business as a quasi-public agency can get."[14] Indeed, Massport's Web site goes so far as to state that it is *not* actually a state authority: "It is not part of the state government, although its board is appointed by the sitting governor of Massachusetts."[15] In fact, Massport refers to itself as "an independent public authority."[16]

It is interesting to consider that in Ireland, similar independent organizations comprised of business, government, and labor have been carefully, even laboriously, labeled "quasi-autonomous nongovernmental organizations"—quangos—to emphasize their mix of stakeholder controls. Even in New York, the Port Authority, which runs LaGuardia Airport, describes itself as "a financially self-supporting *public* agency." (Italics added.) Meanwhile, here in Massachusetts the contradiction inherent in using simultaneously the terms "independent" and "public" has gone largely unchallenged.

One way Massport makes good use of its so-called independent authority is through its exemption from civil service regulations. It employs consulting engineers, accountants, attorneys, superintendents, managers, and construction, financial and other experts, and it independently determines their compensation.[17] Among state employees, it is well known as a haven for political appointees.

Just like a private corporation, it routinely donates money to local charities, including such groups as the private Lexington Education Foundation,[18] the Charlestown Boxing Club, and the Chelsea High School Science and Technology Fair.[19] A state auditor's report noted that during the period July 1998 through April 2000, Massport contributed $600,000 to a number of groups with no apparent ties to transportation, including two western Massachusetts arts organizations that were pet projects of former governor William F. Weld.[20] Other organizations to which it donated during this time were the Azorean Earthquake Relief Fund and the Vienna Classic Gala.

Massport has also been criticized for classifying more than $1 million in expenses, such as $4,863 spent at a local restaurant, as "employee relations," and for purchasing business-class tickets for board members and employees ($563,000 over a twenty-two-month period) while letting frequent-flyer miles go unused.

With all its power, both public and private, does Massport do a good job? I asked an acquaintance, a high-level aviation manager with twenty years experience in the industry, to comment. Of course, he said, no one in the industry will say a word against them, because they all depend totally on Massport to approve and oversee their operations. But, he continued, everyone in the industry knows that the worst airport authority in the country is Miami-Dade, and second only to them is Massport.

With its highly paid legal staff, an agency like Massport can pull the wool over people's eyes even in a public document. Such a document is the Hanscom Field Master Plan and Environmental Impact Statement the agency published in 1978. In it, Massport, as proprietor of the airport, wrote that the airport plays "a significant role in the environmental and open space plans of each community." It recognized that "these communities offer high quality residential environments with low levels of pollution, ample open space and other attractive characteristics. The area is also a regional historic resource, with [Minute Man Historic National Park], among others, located in the Hanscom vicinity. Compatibility with and enhancement of these historic and open space areas has been and will continue to be an objective of the policies developed for Hanscom Field." [21]

This is the kind of statement that citizens find heartening.

The report goes on to note that numerous wetlands lie within the boundary of Hanscom Field, and that the existing storm drains deliver runoff water to surface drainage ditches, all of which terminate in the Shawsheen River and its tributary, the Elm Brook. According to Massport, fuel spill control was designed to intercept and contain a spill before it enters the storm drainage system. Moreover, at that time, it asserted that de-icing chemicals and other potential contaminants were not being used for snow removal at the field. They are now.

In 1978 the air quality near Hanscom was comparable to rural areas, Massport reported. The agency observed that noise levels from nonaircraft sources varied, from those similar to rural areas to those found in denser urban areas. It also pointed out, "Individual aircraft noise events by jet and other noisy aircraft can be above the ambient level, particularly in neighborhoods under or near flight tracks. These *individual* noise events, are the source of greatest community concern rather than the noise levels resulting from total Hanscom operations." [22] (Italics in the original.)

This recognition was also encouraging to our community.

The noise problem having been noted, Massport went on to suggest that the community should not worry about it. If the airport grows and higher noise levels result, it said, "As subsequent aircraft replacement with quieter equipment occurs, these levels would presumably decline to levels near or slightly above current levels." [23] Noise prevention through quieter equipment was the mantra of the day.

The 1978 master plan states that while passenger commuter carriers (that is, unscheduled commercial traffic in smaller planes) would be allowed, certificated air carriers providing civilian passenger air services would not be allowed to operate at Hanscom Field except in an emergency, or when diverted due to weather or other unforeseen conditions. [24] (Unfortunately, the document did not add, "Or unless we want them to.")

Finally, Massport wrote, "Proposals for these operations will be thoroughly reviewed with the Hanscom Field Advisory Committee for their economic, noise emission and ground access implications." [25]

The Hanscom Field Master Plan and Environmental Impact Statement was published in what was temperamentally a different era. To develop the plan, Massport employed in an advisory capacity a task force consisting of a subcommittee of Massport's own board, a consultant, and the governor's Hanscom Task Force—a group representing neighboring towns, airport users, the state legislature, and public interest groups that had been working since 1974 to review the transfer of surplus air force properties at Hanscom Air Force Base to Massport. It asserted that the plan evolved from joint efforts to establish a consensus for the future. Certainly at that time many members of the community believed that it did.

However, when the plan was published in 1978, President Ronald Reagan had not yet busted the air traffic controllers union. Frank Lorenzo had not yet run Eastern and Continental airlines into the ground. Globalization of our economy had not yet kicked in. Airlines were still regulated. Growth in demand for aviation services at Hanscom was projected to be slow through the late 1980s.

The plan was adopted by Massport as its official policy statement regarding the future development and management of Hanscom Field. That is its strength, and its weakness, as a legally binding document.

As I have indicated, over the years area communities have taken comfort in many of the statements made in this document. For example, when Massport wrote, "Hanscom Field . . . plays a significant role in the environmental and open space plans of each community. . . . Compatibility with and enhancement of these historic and open space areas has been and will continue to be an objective of the policies developed for Hanscom Field," [26] the communities deduced from this language that Massport would protect them from such dangers as environmental pollution, noise, and traffic.

Massport also said that their policy of not allowing certificated air carriers providing civilian passenger air services to operate at Hanscom Field except in an emergency "was established in recognition of the excellent air service already available at Logan and of the inappropriateness of a general aviation airport such as Hanscom serving large aircraft and large numbers of passengers associated with these operations." Their ensuing policy was, "The

Massachusetts Port Authority will preserve Logan International Airport as the high quality certificated air carrier service airport for the region. Certificated passenger air carrier operations will not be allowed at Hanscom Field, except in an emergency." [27] From this the community deduced that development at Hanscom would be limited, and that certainly certificated air carriers would not be allowed.

Massport wrote, "De-icing chemicals are not currently used for runway snow removal, and their use is not planned in the future." [28] Thus, the community believed that de-icing would not be used at the airport, and that de-icing chemicals would never run into the water table. Massport wrote, "Massport determined that no major construction would be undertaken at Hanscom Field which would increase the capacity of the existing airfield." [29] Again the community took this at face value.

Massport went on to say that the establishment of the permanent Hanscom Field Advisory Committee would assure that proposals for new operations would be reviewed and that noise abatement procedures and other environmental factors would be considered in future decision-making, [30] and thus, the community believed that Massport would take its needs into consideration.

The community has been wrong on all counts.

A different reading of the same document reveals its hidden agenda, the legalese to permit Massport to do in the future whatever it wants to do. The so-called plan relies on tentative declarations of intent while masterfully avoiding firm commitments.

For Massport also wrote, "Even if growth in Logan activity should require an effort to divert traffic, aircraft would first be diverted to off-peak hours at Logan. Only if this effort were unsuccessful would some diversion to other airports be likely. . . . Even if a high estimate of 30 percent of [Logan's general aviation and commuter activity were] diverted to other regional airports, the increase in Hanscom operations would be less than 5 percent over current Hanscom levels, assuming one half went to Hanscom." [31] This is hardly a promise to limit growth.

Indeed, the subsequent policy statements in the document leave Massport's options open: "The Massachusetts Port Authority is committed to maintaining Hanscom Field for the uses it now serves. The Authority seeks to preserve and enhance the economic utility of Hanscom Field while minimizing environmental impacts resulting from operations at the field."[32] It goes on, "The existing runways at Hanscom Field are adequate to serve expected aviation demand for the foreseeable future. Should future economic or other factors alter projected aviation demand substantially, the adequacy of the runways would be reassessed in a public review process including the Hanscom Field Advisory Committee. *At this time,* the Massachusetts Port Authority will take no action to expand airport capacity."[33] (Italics added.)

When the consultants for the plan performed their studies, in early 1975, there was concern that the high rate of growth they projected would result in a significant rise in noise in the local communities. The consultants offered as one alternative that Massport consider limiting activity at the airport to 250,000 operations, but "This alternative was not recommended by the Governor's Hanscom Task Force."[34] (By the time of the actual writing of the report, this growth had slowed.)

When Massport said that Hanscom would not support certificated passenger air carrier operations, it also said, "it does not *presently* support and will take no action toward the development of a second air carrier airport in the Boston region."[35] (Italics added.)

The plan allowed for "passenger commuter operations," which differ from certificated passenger air carrier operations in that they do not require certificates or rate approvals from the Civil Aeronautics Board. It said that the Civil Aeronautics Board at that time defined passenger commuter carriers as those operating scheduled aircraft with up to thirty seats or seventy-five-hundred-pound payloads, but that this was going to change considerably. Indeed, by the time that Massport issued its General Rules and Regulations for Hanscom, effective on July 31, 1980, the number of allowable passengers on passenger commuter carriers had doubled to sixty. Ultimately, the regulation was worded, "No person . . . shall conduct at Hanscom an operation in commercial air passenger service in an aircraft with a seating capacity of greater than 60 seats."[36]

As to noise, Massport's plan concluded, "It is possible, however, that if an unexpectedly high rate of growth or a slower rate of aircraft replacement were to occur, then higher noise levels would result. As subsequent aircraft replacement with quieter equipment occurs, these levels would presumably decline to levels near or slightly above current levels."[37] Throughout its analysis, Massport asserted it was attempting to balance its concerns for operating a viable airport to meet regional needs with the need to safeguard environmental quality. Yet, at the same time, its conclusion was that further efforts to restrict growth, such as limiting heavier aircraft, would not allow the airport to meet the economic needs of the region. It further asserted that the imposition of an evening curfew at Hanscom would provide few additional noise reduction benefits.[38]

The duplicitous message that Massport would protect the communities was repeated in a little-remembered 1986 Massport report entitled "Hanscom Field: A Delicate Balance." In this twelve-page public relations document Massport predicted that growth at the airport would include more "origin and destination commuter operations" (basically, chartered flights), more corporate aircraft, and "some" cargo activity. Specifically, it said, "Governed by the Master Plan, Massport has minimized adverse environmental impacts by its decisions not to expand the airfield facilities. *Commercial carriers, major sources of noise, air pollution, and increased traffic congestion, have not been allowed to operate at Hanscom Field.* And, Massport continues to reject any options that would cause environmental harm."[39] (Emphasis added.) This is as close as Massport came, and it is very, very close, to promising no commercial airlines at Hanscom.

If area communities today have any illusions as to whether the published plans for Hanscom Field protect them, they should compare the statement in the master plan that "certificated passenger air carrier operations will not be allowed at Hanscom Field, except in an emergency,"[40] with actions taken the day before the new airline commenced operations in 1999 at Hanscom. That day the FAA issued a full "Airport Operating Certificate" to Hanscom Field.[41]

In issuing the certificate, the FAA changed the status of the airport from one which permits only casual, unscheduled passenger commuter operations to one which now permits "certificated passenger air carrier operations," flights with regularly scheduled, ticketed operations for passenger planes over thirty seats. Thus, the FAA officially turned Hanscom into a full commercial airport allowing airplanes of any size. The communities complained and sued, to no avail.

From the outset in the spring of 1999, the airline and Massport had asserted that no legal changes were required for the start-up. Despite its own assertion in 1993 that the 1978 Master Plan and subsequent 1980 Noise Rules generally prohibited scheduled, noncommuter jet carrier service, Massport asserted in 1999 that the issuance of the new Airport Operating Certificate was a "technicality."[42]

In days gone by, our masters the British taxed us without consulting us. When significant local resources were exported to England, we were advised that we were contributing to the greater good of the commonwealth, and that the king, in his infinite wisdom, knew what was best for his subjects.

Because they sought to overturn such a regime, the people of Lexington literally stood up for their beliefs and were gunned down. They then fought a war to obtain self-determination.

Why did the colonies ultimately refuse to sacrifice for king and country? Because compromise was not part of the king's vision. Because the king was arrogant. Because the citizenry was exploited continually, and at every turn. The colonists were prospering. Under the king they could have gone on living decently for a very long time, and even improving themselves. But they wanted to be free, free to protect their homes, their families, and their livelihoods.

Today the imperial argument is that the free market knows better than we do what's good for us. Protection of interstate commerce and serving a market are much more important, we are told, than protection of individual property rights.

We are advised that for the common good, the principle of freewheeling capitalism must be allowed to hold sway. A corollary of this principle is that government for the people is best understood as government for markets. It follows, we are told, that individual citizens must sacrifice for these markets and, of course, for the special interests that run them. Today government-by-special-interests is our king.

When we look for help from our civil organizations—our mostly volunteer, mostly privately funded entities that express community values and needs—we discover that they fail to give the community the power it needs. They inspire and inform and organize—wonderfully, at times—and these are essential functions to be sure, but in the end they rely on voters and government to advance their agendas.

Of all the civil organizations involved in fighting the expansion of Hanscom Field, the Hanscom Field Advisory Committee has the greatest legal standing because it was legitimized by the 1978 Hanscom Field Master Plan. Yet, despite HFAC's oversight responsibility, in the fall of 1999 Massport refused to show HFAC its operating agreement with the new airline on the grounds that the four towns were suing Massport. They asserted this despite the fact that HFAC and the four towns are distinctly separate public entities.

I was there at the HFAC meeting when Massport denied that document request. I watched a brave back-and-forth about registered letters being received and not being received, HFAC claiming to have requested the document in writing, Massport alleging that they had not received the request. The bottom line was that HFAC could only request, not require, even those documents that were essential to doing its job. Turning over documents was not in Massport's best interest: revealing even after the airline had started flying that the airline had no cap on its flights would have damaged its salami strategy. And all that the community representatives on HFAC could do was get angry.

Is there an argument for the existence of an organization as powerful as Massport? There is no doubt that citizens can benefit from a government agency's autonomy. If citizens were to protest every move made by an agency, some projects would never get off the ground.

Yet even in our own Commonwealth of Massachusetts, some state agencies are designed to include real citizen participation. For example, the board of directors of the Massachusetts Water Resources Authority, a state public authority established in 1984, includes three voting members who are representatives from customer communities.[43] The MWRA philosophy is that "active citizen participation is a good investment, ensuring publicly supportable, cost effective and environmentally sound solutions." Their citizens' committee also has a full-time staff.

In contrast, while the governor appoints the Massport board, communities have no representatives there. If the citizenry does not like what Massport does, they cannot penalize them, and they cannot turn them out. The board members serve out their seven years (and, as we have seen, sometimes longer), no matter what the citizenry thinks, and the organization itself is impervious.

One has to ask the question why in one agency, Massport, power has become highly centralized, while in another, MWRA, it is more decentralized. The answer is profit. The resources of the port and the airport serve a lucrative private enterprise sector, while water resources are primarily a public holding. Special interests want to control Massport because in their jurisdiction there is a great deal of money to be made. Of course, there is money to be made in water services as well, and so it should come as no surprise that in the late 1990s Massachusetts governor Cellucci initiated a study aimed at privatizing MWRA.[44]

It may be tempting to argue that sacrificing a few communities for the greater good of the people of the state, or the region, or the world, for that matter, is for the best, and if the powerful state agency and the airline make that possible, perhaps how they do it does not matter. It can be tempting to think that the outcome is more important than the process, and that market power should prevail over preserving the decent quality of life in a few communities.

But we know better than that. To preserve our democracy, process has to matter. Meaningful citizen participation matters. Property rights that protect individuals from the tyranny of the majority matter. Trust in government matters.

Today, in our very large democracy, political process is more convoluted than ever before. There are many spheres of influence—industry versus government versus communities. There are many layers of influence—individuals; civic organizations like ShhAir and Save Our Heritage; voluntary government watchdogs like the Hanscom Field Advisory Committee; local, state, and federal governments; quasi-independent government agencies like Massport; and small, medium, large, international, and multinational companies.

Therefore, citizens have to work harder—perhaps harder than at any time in history—to become informed not just about the issues but about the political and social systems that frame the issues. They have to plow through spheres and layers of influence to get to the truth about the business and government systems that frame their communities.

Comparatively, King George was an easy target.

6

How the Air Transportation
Industry Pursues Growth

*As minister for aviation [in Great Britain], Chris Mullin
learnt, he says, two things: that the demands of the
aviation industry are insatiable, and that governments
usually give way to them.*

  —Economist, 2003

*"Capitalism" requires privatizing profit but socializing
cost and risk.*

  —Noam Chomsky

UNTIL SEPTEMBER 2001 the air transportation industry generated
well over $775 billion annually in commercial and retail buying
and selling, and it paid more than $30 billion each year in federal
taxes alone.[1] It directly contributed more than 9 percent of the
U.S. gross domestic product. In recent decades it has amassed
market, regulatory, and institutional power unprecedented by any
industry except oil. It remains one of the most powerful special
interests in our country, and like any business, it wants to grow.

In 1999 there were about 50 million operations at towered
airports across the country, a number that was projected to rise
about 28 percent to nearly 64 million operations by 2010, according to the FAA.[2] Passenger growth was predicted to rise from
600 million passengers on U.S. scheduled carriers in 1998 to

900 million in 2007. Sixty of the one hundred largest airports in the country were proposing to build new runways.[3] If at some point the industry returns to this growth pattern and the projections prove accurate, the added passengers might require ten new airports the size of Dallas–Fort Worth Airport.[4]

Nationwide, airline companies have been trying to grow their businesses by expanding airports. From 1995 to 2000, federal money for airports almost doubled.[5] Arguing that their profits are hurt by delays and congestion, leaders in the air transportation industry assert that the solution is even more government investment in runways and airports.

However, airport delays have been exacerbated by overscheduling, and flights are delayed for such reasons as labor and maintenance problems, adverse weather, and equipment malfunction. None of these factors, which account for the "vast majority" of delays, are addressed by new runway construction.[6] Even the head of the FAA, Jane Garvey, has noted that solutions to the congestion problem may require challenging some long-held assumptions. "We are not losing sight of technology. We are not losing sight of concrete," she said in 2001. But, she continued, "scarce resources must be rationed."[7]

To a great extent airlines themselves have been responsible for airport congestion. Industry critics point out that airlines have created more flights using smaller planes to cater to the demands of business travelers for more convenient flight times. Also, airlines concentrate flights during those times of the day that are most popular with business travelers, thus increasing congestion.[8]

A related factor is use of the hub-and-spoke system, which increases total number of takeoffs and landings for any given route.

Finally, though bigger airplanes are more fuel efficient, smaller planes are simply easier for airplane manufacturers to sell. All of these business factors add up to significantly increased congestion.

An air traffic controller and commercial pilot writing in the *San Jose Mercury News* in California summarized the situation: "Delays stem from the government sponsored inefficient use of our resources by a disjointed transportation system, driven by industry's (including airports') profit motives that serve only themselves, not transporting us."[9]

Whether the industry really needs more infrastructure has been challenged. As the *Economist* points out, "The case for expansion is less than clear cut. Predictions of passenger demand are based on falling airfares, faster growth by low-cost airlines, and a big hidden subsidy from the taxpayers. Challenge those assumptions and things look very different."[10] (In Britain, the fact that aviation fuel is tax-free gives the industry a £6 billion subsidy annually, while the fact that there is no VAT—value-added tax— on tickets yields another £2.4 billion per year.)

Even the major trade publication for the airline industry has questioned the need for more infrastructure. The editors of *Aviation Week & Space Technology* note that while the industry argues that passengers will disappear if more runways are not built, it has not substantiated what delays and congestion cost now. They quote one Wall Street airline analyst who put it, "Maybe delays increase everybody's aggravation, contribute to air rage and degrade the national psyche. But there's no indication it hits the airlines' bottom lines."[11]

Aviation Week editors note that the industry calculates the cost of delays and congestion in a curious way. The Air Transport Association (ATA), which represents twenty-eight major U.S. and international airlines, estimates that airlines spend about $32 for each minute a flight is delayed. Based on this figure, the ATA concludes that the total cost of delays to airlines and their customers in 1999 was $4.5 billion. Yet, of this figure, only 44 percent consists of actually increased operating costs. Part of it—$850 million—is based on the ATA's rough estimate of the added cost of handling passengers grounded by delays. A factor called "passenger time" is also included. Based on the Bureau of Labor Statistics calculation of the standard income for an American, a passenger's time is figured in at $20 per hour and amounts to $1.6 billion.

FAA estimates of the cost of delays and congestion are

even higher, with passenger time figured in at $44 an hour and comprising almost 74 percent of its estimate. Its loss estimate for 1994 was $9.4 billion.[12]

While lobbying for more infrastructure, the industry also wants to fuel its expansion by adding more flights at currently existing airports. It is well known that more flights have put a great deal of pressure on current systems, especially air traffic control systems. Despite airline deregulation, the FAA had to step in and institute a lottery system for slots at LaGuardia Airport in New York because the airlines there failed to adequately self-regulate the number of flights.

In addition to seeking more state and federally funded infrastructure, the industry continually explores other ways to enhance its power. A prominent voice for aviation is calling for a partitioning of the FAA into two organizations, allegedly to move forward solutions to the congestion problem, but certainly to grow air transportation.[13] The editor-in-chief of *Aviation Week* has argued that one organization should provide aviation safety and regulatory oversight, while a different, operations organization would provide air traffic services, including management of air traffic infrastructure. The air traffic operations organization would be run by a chief operating officer and would be "performance-based." Its board of directors would reflect the interests of "general and business aviation, regional carriers, controllers, airports, the military and the flying public—not just the major carriers."[14] Needless to say, communities are not listed as stakeholders.

The Aircraft Owners and Pilots Association (AOPA) is a major backer of these proposed changes, and AOPA supports turning the FAA into an independent agency. It argues this would free the FAA from "the grip of the politically-oriented, bureaucratic Department of Transportation." AOPA also supported the 1996 Transportation Appropriations bill in which Congress granted the FAA freedom from federal personnel and procurement rules, but now asserts, "The final piece of the puzzle is to free the agency from the grip of the Department of Transportation."[15]

In this restructuring, presumably community interests would be attended to by the proposed separate regulatory organization. But that group would have far less money and power than the operator of the traffic system, and citizens would be even further removed from meaningful input into FAA policies than they are now.

Aviation Week also suggests that the $10 billion Airport and Airway Trust Fund should be separated from the federal government's discretionary spending budget, to be used solely for the air transportation system, that is, that the money should be controlled by the new air traffic operations organization.

"Unfortunately," writes *Aviation Week* about the current design of the FAA, "safety trumps all other priorities in the FAA's modernization agenda. . . . The new business structure . . . would keep safety as the highest priority, but it also would run as a business, providing a responsive service for the users." [16]

"Unfortunately"?

What is truly unfortunate is that in the air transportation industry, the tradeoff between safety and profit is a daily reality. Today the same growth that is putting pressure on consumers and communities is also putting pressure on airlines' operations. More flights, cheaper flights, and more smaller airlines strain the availability of top-quality equipment and trained pilots.

As inspector general of the U.S. Department of Transportation from 1990 to 1996, Mary Schiavo audited the FAA's efforts to achieve airline compliance with safety rules. She says it is a fallacy that once certified by the FAA, an airline is always safe. "No one at the FAA or in the aviation industry wants to acknowledge that vast differences exist among airline maintenance facilities, the age and quality of aircraft, the caliber of spare-parts inventory and programs for screening bogus parts, the qualifications and experience of pilots and crew, and security practices." [17]

Indeed, Schiavo observes that, for years before the ValuJet crash that killed 110 people in the Florida Everglades in 1996, the FAA insisted that all airlines were equally safe, whereas it now says merely that airlines flying today meet the agency's minimum safety standards. It refuses to rank airlines or to assess how much an airline exceeds the minimum.

At the same time, pressures to produce pilots quickly have caused some airlines to reduce their training standards. Skyway Airlines in Milwaukee, for example, over a period of two years reduced its required flying time for new pilots from 2,500 hours to 700. Its new pilots start flying turboprops and small jets for salaries of about $17,500 a year.[18]

The FAA has always had a dual mandate to promote aviation and safety, but according to its critics, in practice, safety has often taken a back seat. In her book *Flying Blind, Flying Safe,* Schiavo writes, "When times were bad, the FAA didn't want to add to aviation's burden. When times were good, it didn't want to hobble growth. As a result, the FAA regularly reduced safety issues to their operating costs. . . . At its core, safety isn't cost effective."[19]

Recognizing such concerns, in the 1996 FAA budget reauthorization, Congress modified the agency's mandate by charging the FAA with "assigning, maintaining and enhancing safety and security as the highest priorities in air commerce."[20]

Nevertheless, the airline industry has sought to redefine the FAA as an operations business and development agency for aviation. It wants to separate safety from profit, while emphasizing profit. It seeks an organization that is maximally independent from public input, an organization with an extraordinary combination of public and private powers. In short, it wants to turn the FAA into a federal version of Massport.

On the international front, in a further attempt at a power grab, the industry has created a lobbying organization to develop a new worldwide aircraft noise standard.[21] In July 2000 the chairman of the newly formed Coalition for a Global Standard on Aviation Noise asserted, "The noise issue has the potential to disrupt not only the aviation industry itself but the entire global economy if it is not addressed." The coalition seeks to protect the airline industry's investment in the Stage Three aircraft, to preserve "the international principle of a single global certification standard for noise reduction," and to develop an "effective and technically feasible aircraft noise certification standard."

From the citizens' view, this effort is actually aimed at forcing powerful groups like the European Union to stop monitoring and regulating aircraft noise pollution and to accept instead the FAA's engine-based methodology—what it refers to as the "certification standard." In plain language, accepting such a standard would mean that, once a government accepted Stage Three aircraft, the community would have to accept whatever noise emanates from those aircraft. This approach would reduce, eliminate, or make ineffectual the actual measurement of noise in communities not just in the United States and Europe but worldwide.

The coalition has named to its advisory board the following list of business and government organizations:

Aeromexico	General Electric
Aeroports de Paris	Iberia
Airbus Industrie	LanChile
Air France	Lufthansa
Air Line Pilots Association	Massachusetts Port Authority
All Nippon Airways	Metropolitan Washington
American Airlines	Airports Authority
The Boeing Company	Minneapolis/St. Paul
BAA, plc	International Airport
British Airways	Northwest Airlines
County of San Bernardino	Qantas Airways
Airports	Rolls-Royce, plc
Coalition of Airline Pilots	Snecma Moteurs
Associations	South African Airways
Delta Air Lines	TACA International
FedEx	United Airlines
United Parcel Service	United Technologies

Once again, there is no representation of the communities damaged by air transportation pollution.

Who is it that wants to start commercial service at your local airport? A faceless corporation? A friendly pilot? Here in Lexington we attracted a notorious competitor.

In 1999, the new commercial airline at Hanscom was a start-up named Shuttle America, incorporated in Delaware in 1996. For a while, the only other thing we knew about it was that its president and CEO was David Hackett and its vice president for marketing was Gregory Aretakis.

On October 13, 1999, a short letter to the editor of the *Wall Street Journal* from a Lexington lawyer pointed out that the principals of Shuttle America had been longtime business associates of Frank Lorenzo's. Frank Lorenzo is remembered for his union busting in the airline industry in the 1980s. Barbara Walters once asked him whether he realized he was the "the most hated man in America." [22] In 1989, *Fortune* magazine listed him as one of American's toughest bosses, whose subordinates thought of him as a "loose cannon." [23]

Owner of Texas Air Corporation, Lorenzo pursued business strategies predicated on low prices that were made possible by bringing unions to their knees. Unfortunately, instead of responsibly improving the companies he acquired, he ruined them. He led Eastern Airlines into bankruptcy and weighted down Continental Airlines with so much debt that it too eventually went bankrupt. The financial details of these bankruptcies are less relevant here than the virulence with which Lorenzo pursued his strategy. After Eastern had been in bankruptcy for more than a year, its creditors asked for a trustee, complaining, "There should be no mistake that it is the unsecured creditors of this estate who are being asked to fund the continuing fantasies of Eastern and Texas Air." [24] Fantasies? About what?

It appears that Lorenzo was at least as obsessed with busting the unions as he was with making money. In the White House at the time was Lorenzo's alter ego. As author Aaron Bernstein observed in his book *Grounded: Frank Lorenzo and the Destruction of Eastern Airlines,* "Union officials charged that Lorenzo was getting help from inside the White House. . . . Lorenzo had struck gold. The White House not only favored Texas Air to begin with, presidential strategists also saw a chance for [President George] Bush to come out a hero. After all, Ronald Reagan had dealt a devastating blow to labor by firing the striking air traffic controllers [in 1981], and had emerged as the victorious tough guy, the toast of corporate America and the scourge of the greedy labor unions. Here was a chance for Bush to imitate his mentor."[25]

For a letter I was writing, I interviewed Susan Fargo, the state senator representing the town of Lincoln and nine other communities. She pointed out to me that our Republican governor at the time, Paul Cellucci, was hoping to go to Washington with President Bush's son George W. Bush.

I did an Internet search for "George+Bush+Frank+Lorenzo," and I was transported to the George Bush Presidential Library and Museum in College Station, Texas. There I learned that on March 7, 1989, at the president's news conference, a reporter had posed to George Bush the question: "The head of Eastern Airlines, Frank Lorenzo, is from Houston, Texas. Is he a friend of yours? Did he give money to your campaign? And one of his vice presidents is on your staff as head of congressional relations. Is he giving you advice?" President Bush replied, "He has recused himself, as I understand it, from the Eastern Airlines; and he's not giving me advice. I know Frank Lorenzo, and in all probability he gave money to the Bush-Quayle campaign. Now, follow-up?" A reporter asked, "Does that influence you in any way?" Bush: "No, it does not influence me in any way."

The Scandinavian airline that in 1990 bought what was left of Continental insisted that Lorenzo leave, and furthermore that he sign a pact to stay out of the airline business for seven years.[26] In 1990 an article in *Air Transport World* entitled "Say Goodby, Frank," labeled Lorenzo an abuser of capitalism and the free market system who profited from his company's troubles.[27]

In 1993 Lorenzo attempted to get back into the airline business by creating a shuttle airline in the Washington-Baltimore area.

He planned to start with four planes serving Baltimore, Boston, and Atlanta.[28] That venture, ATX, Inc., was turned down by the U.S. Department of Transportation after an extraordinary public outcry in which more than one hundred members of Congress petitioned against Lorenzo,[29] and after Lorenzo attempted to mute criticism by diluting his stake in company ownership from 74 percent to under 50 percent.[30] In 1994 the Department of Transportation declared Lorenzo "unfit to run an airline in accord with the public interest," noting that although ATX had adequate financing to start an airline, it lacked the "managerial competence" to ensure a sound operation. It cited Lorenzo's problems managing labor, maintenance, and operations at Eastern and Continental Airlines as "among the most serious in the history of U.S. Aviation."[31] The Air Line Pilots Association held Lorenzo personally responsible for the loss of jobs and the human misery of hundreds of thousands of airline workers and vowed to fight Lorenzo's efforts to start up ATX "at every venue, at every government office, and in every marketplace."[32] That ATX venture was squashed.

Lorenzo was undeterred. In March 1995 a start-up carrier in Georgia called Nations Air began operations in Pittsburgh, Philadelphia, and Boston. Four months later the FAA grounded the airline for a week after regulators found problems with its training programs and with cockpit and cabin crew proficiency.[33] In September the U.S. Department of Transportation requested that Nations Air supply additional information on the current and proposed involvement of ATX, Inc., and its founder and controlling shareholder Frank Lorenzo.[34] Nations Air had entered into an equity investment agreement with ATX, Inc., involving advisory services and loan agreements.[35] This agreement, said the Department of Transportation, called into "serious question Nations Air's continuing fitness to hold its authority."[36] Lorenzo had loaned money to Nations Air through his own Houston-based investment-banking firm, Savoy Capital, Inc., which invests in aviation and other businesses.[37]

In 1996 a reporter for *Financial World* asked Lorenzo about his future in aviation. He replied, "How long can [the Department of Transportation] keep us from making investments in a business we love and know? Why should we be denied making money providing what the public wants?"[38]

In Shuttle America's application to the FAA for permission to fly out of Hanscom, I learned that David Hackett had begun his job as the airline's president and CEO in January of 1996, the same month that he left his position as managing director of Lorenzo's Savoy Capital, Inc. As of May 20, 1998, Hackett owned 40.5 percent of Shuttle America's common stock.[39] Prior to his job at Savoy, Hackett was senior vice president for planning for ATX, Inc. (1993–95), managing director/associate of Savoy Capital, Inc. (1991–93), an independent consultant in air transportation and financial advisory services (1991), director of financial planning for Continental Airlines Holdings (1990–91), and manager of capital planning and director of financial planning for Continental Airlines, Inc. (1987–90). Hackett listed his address as Friendswood, Texas, near Houston.

Gregory Aretakis, Shuttle America's vice president of marketing, hailed from Humble, Texas, also near Houston. He worked as managing director of Savoy Capital, Inc. (1995–96), vice president of marketing at ATX, Inc., (1993–95), staff vice president of market planning for Continental Airlines (1991–93), vice president of planning and marketing for Continental Express Airlines (1988–91), and staff vice president of Texas Air Corporation (1987).[40]

Shuttle America's vice president for finance, William R. Schriber, of Houston, was formerly an independent aviation and financial consultant whose primary client was ValuJet Airlines, Inc. (1994-96). He was also formerly director of special projects at Continental (1989–90).[41]

The International Association of Machinists and Aerospace Workers that had opposed Lorenzo's ATX venture issued a statement that it would oppose Shuttle America even if Lorenzo were not involved. It noted, "Lorenzo has attracted criticism in the aviation industry since his use of the bankruptcy courts to kill union contracts at Continental Airlines in 1983 and at Eastern Airlines in 1989. The executives formerly involved with Lorenzo, comprising David Hackett, Bill Schriber, and Greg Aretakis, maintain there is no connection between Shuttle America and Frank Lorenzo."[42]

One thing is certain: our communities are up against hard-driving companies. Understanding the realities behind the airlines' carefully crafted image is one of our communities' continuing challenges.

7

How Noise Laws Fail Communities

We control airspace. Cities don't control airspace.
　　—John Clabes, FAA spokesman

What we are about is fighting tyranny. They have made a mockery of the Constitution.
　　—Susan Fargo, state senator,
　　　Lincoln, Massachusetts

THE EVOLUTION OF LAWS on noise pollution is the prime example of how the air transportation industry has stolen power from local communities.

Interestingly enough, early decisions in aviation noise law interpreted the Constitution in favor of community-friendly noise regulations and local control of noise problems. Originally, such decisions were left to the states. Indeed, the Tenth Amendment to the Constitution says, "The powers not delegated to the United States by the Constitution, nor prohibited by it to the States, are reserved to the States respectively, or to the people."

In 1958 the Federal Aviation Act consolidated in one agency in the executive branch aviation controls that had previously been diffused within that branch, but the act was not concerned with the problem of aircraft noise. At that time it seems that Congress did not intend to take the power of noise regulation away from the states.[1] Indeed, a report of the House Committee on Interstate and Foreign Commerce of the period noted:

Until Federal action is taken, the local governmental authorities must be deemed to possess the police power necessary to protect their citizens and property from the unreasonable invasion of aircraft noise. The wisdom of exercising such power or the manner of the exercise is a problem to be resolved on the local governmental level.

Airports in the United States, as a general rule, are operated by a local governmental authority. . . . These airport operators are closer, both geographically and politically, to the problem of conflict of interests between those citizens who have been adversely affected by the aircraft noise and the needs of the community for air commerce.[2]

The first congressional legislation to deal nationally with the problem of aircraft noise was the 1968 noise abatement amendment to the Federal Aviation Act of 1958. Even then, according to an opinion by four justices of the U.S. Supreme Court, neither the House nor the Senate committees that commented on this amendment had argued that the federal government should control noise regulation. Here is what the House Committee on Interstate and Foreign Commerce said about the type of federal regulation that the act sought to impose:

The noise problem is basically a conflict between two groups or interests. On the one hand there is a group who provide various air transportation services. On the other hand there is a group who live, work, and go to schools and churches in communities near airports. The latter group is frequently burdened to the point where they can neither enjoy nor reasonably use their land because of noise resulting from aircraft operations. Many of them derive no direct benefit from the aircraft operations, which create the unwanted noise. Therefore, it is easy to understand why they complain, and complain most vehemently.[3]

The congressional view at that time was that technical solutions were the answer to the noise problem. Although land-use planning was also mentioned, subsequent federal legislation would aim primarily at regulating aircraft engines:

> The possible solutions to this demanding and vexing problem, which appear to offer the most promise are (1) new or modified engine and airframe designs, (2) special flight operating techniques and procedures, and (3) planning for land use in areas adjacent to airports so that such land use will be most compatible with aircraft operations. This legislation is directed toward the primary problem; namely, reduction of noise at its source.[4]

Still, the Congress did not seek federal control over noise regulation. Rather, the House committee further observed:

> The committee expects manufacturers, air carriers, all other segments of the aviation community, and State and local civic and governmental entities to continue and increase their contributions toward the common goal of quiet.[5]

Along the same line, here was the view of the Senate Commerce Committee on the federal preemption of states' rights:

> It is not the intent of the committee in recommending this legislation to effect any change in the existing apportionment of powers between the Federal and State and local governments. . . . The proposed legislation will not affect the rights of a State or local public agency, as the proprietor of an airport, from issuing regulations or establishing requirements as to the permissible level of noise, which can be created by aircraft using the airport. Airport owners acting as proprietors can presently deny the use of their airports to aircraft on the basis of noise considerations so long as such exclusion is nondiscriminatory.[6]

Other early decisions also interpreted the Constitution in favor of the local landholder. The Fifth Amendment states, "nor shall private property be taken for public use, without just compensation." A 1946 Supreme Court decision found that military aircraft that passed repeatedly over a farmer's land at eighty-three feet constituted a taking by the airport proprietor, in that case, the federal government.[7] A 1962 decision declared that a county was required to pay just compensation when it required aircraft to fly regularly and frequently at very low altitudes over a residential property, causing a family to move from their home.[8] A Supreme Court decision in 1980 held that a law authorizing a state or local government to condemn lands does not authorize them to do so simply by physically intruding on them first.[9]

As the national aviation noise problem escalated, courts increasingly debated whether states or the federal government should control it, and the battle between communities and commerce was joined. In 1972, Congress, dissatisfied with the FAA's progress with noise abatement, passed the Noise Control Act. This amended the Federal Aviation Act by involving the Environmental Protection Agency in the regulation of noise. Pursuant to the act, the EPA created the Office of Noise Abatement and Control. Its responsibilities included setting noise emissions standards, requiring product labeling, facilitating the development of low-emission products, coordinating federal noise-reduction programs, assisting state and local abatement efforts, and promoting noise education and research.[10]

In the pivotal 1973 Supreme Court decision *City of Burbank et al. v. Lockheed Air Terminal, Inc.,* the majority held that the federal government should monitor noise at airports. The decision concerned an ordinance that made it unlawful for aircraft to take off from the Hollywood-Burbank Airport between 11 P.M. and 7 A.M. The only regularly scheduled flight affected by the ordinance was an interstate flight of Pacific Southwest Airlines departing every Sunday night at 11:30 P.M. In a 5–4 decision, the Supreme Court affirmed a district court ruling that found the ordinance to be unconstitutional on two grounds. First, the Court found that the ordinance violated the Supremacy Clause that gives the power to control aviation to the federal government, and second, it agreed with lower courts that one of the FAA's responsibilities is to manage air space to promote interstate commerce. The Court concluded, "The pervasive control vested in EPA and in FAA under the 1972 Act seems to us to leave no room for local curfews or other local controls. What the ultimate remedy may be for aircraft noise which plagues many communities and tens of thousands of people is not known. . . . The Federal Aviation Act requires a delicate balance between safety and efficiency . . . and the protection of persons on the ground." [11]

At the same time, the dissenting opinion by Justices William H. Rehnquist, Potter Stewart, Byron R. White, and Thurgood Marshall was vigorous. In their view the 1972 act was not intended to alter the balance between state and federal regulation that had been struck by earlier congressional legislation in this area. They argued that the 1972 act had established exclusive federal control of the technological methods for reducing jet aircraft noise at its source, "but that is a far cry from saying that it prohibited any local regulation of the times at which the local airport might be available for the use of jet aircraft." [12] In fact, the four dissenters believed that the history of congressional action in this field demonstrated an affirmative congressional intent to *allow* local regulation.

The dissenting justices also dismissed in one paragraph the majority's finding that such a curfew put an undue burden on interstate commerce. They pointed out that the lower court's decision had appeared to be based at least in part on the notion that interstate commerce would be damaged if all municipal airports in the country enacted ordinances such as that of Burbank, but that such a determination was improper based simply on the case in front of them. Further, they wrote, "The Burbank ordinance did not affect emergency flights, and had the total effect of prohibiting one scheduled commercial flight each week and several additional private flights by corporate executives; such a result can hardly be held to be an unreasonable burden on commerce."[13]

In the end, however, the majority opinion by Justices William O. Douglas, Warren E. Burger, William J. Brennan, Henry A. Blackmun, and Lewis F. Powell held:

> In light of the pervasive nature of the scheme of federal regulation of aircraft noise, as reaffirmed and reinforced by the Noise Control Act of 1972, the Federal Aviation Administration, now in conjunction with the Environmental Protection Agency, has full control over aircraft noise, pre-empting state and local control.[14]

In 1981 the Office of Noise Abatement and Control established at the EPA by the Noise Control Act of 1972 was defunded by the Reagan administration. As a result, a thousand community noise abatement programs dependent on federal funding were shut down.[15]

The office has not been funded since.[16]

In the next decades, the classic Tenth Amendment conflict between states rights and federal preemption of noise laws plowed on in the courts, with the states losing ground. But the FAA and the industry wanted closure, so they went to Congress once again.

A 1990 federal survey of 140 airports found that only 3 airports had local bans on noisier (Stage Two) aircraft, but estimated that by the year 2000, 77 airports, including a large portion of the nation's largest airports, would likely ban Stage Two operations.[17] At that time, about 60 percent of the U.S. fleet was composed of Stage Two aircraft. The federal survey asserted that local noise restrictions caused airlines to alter their schedules or curtail service to many cities, and that unresolved noise disputes "threatened the continued growth of airports."[18] It asserted that noise problems could be solved through noise abatement, such as a ban on Stage

Two aircraft, and noise mitigation, which it defined as lessening the impact of noise on the people who are exposed to it by such means as soundproofing homes and schools and improving land-use planning.

The Airport Noise and Capacity Act of 1990 (ANCA) was the legislative outcome of these views. The trade-offs it makes between business profit and human suffering was never fully or publicly debated in the Congress. Rather, the bill was inserted into the Omnibus Budget Reconciliation Act of 1990, the federal budget bill for fiscal year 1991. Sponsored by Wendell H. Ford (D-Kentucky), John McCain (R-Arizona), and John C. Danforth (R-Missouri), it states that henceforth the federal government alone will control noise pollution.

ANCA asserted that community noise concerns had led to uncoordinated and inconsistent restrictions on aviation that could impede the national air transportation systems, and that these noise concerns could be alleviated "through the use of new technology aircraft, combined with the use of revenues, including those available from passenger facility charges for noise management." When Senator Ford introduced ANCA, he reported that more than four hundred airports had adopted local noise regulations.[19] His view on the noise issue was, "The greatest obstacle to expanding airports and increasing air carrier service is the opposition to aircraft noise and not the cost of building more runways and establishing more technologically advanced air traffic control. . . . Delays and congestion are the result of the noise problem and airline passengers are the victims. . . . The solution is to establish a National Noise Policy. Since a vast number of airport operations are classified as interstate travel, it is appropriate for Federal aviation leaders to end the noise debate."[20]

The aviation industry was tired of fighting noise restrictions case by case, state by state, often losing, and it wanted to reduce them. ANCA, in concert with the Aviation Safety and Noise Abatement Act of 1979, mandated the FAA to manage noise planning. Henceforth, to receive certain important federal funding, airports could not change their noise compatibility programs without prior approval of the FAA.

After the passage of ANCA, any noise problems that rose to the level as defined by the act could be ameliorated only by using different planes or using federal monies for mitigation.

From the airline industry's point of view, ANCA worked swiftly and effectively: as a result of new FAA rules and procedures, "the rush of communities to propose and adopt restrictive aircraft rules has virtually stopped," crowed the National Business Aircraft Association in a 1995 report.[21]

From the community's point of view, ANCA has been a disaster. The level of noise defined by the act is unrealistically high, and mitigation is a cruel deception.

Most importantly, the act was written, and further interpreted in FAA regulations, so as to make it extremely difficult for communities to claim their noise levels are high enough to trigger either abatement or mitigation. Under the ANCA implementation program developed by the FAA, called a Part 150 Program, in areas with land uses that are incompatible with high noise levels, such as residential areas, airports are required to prepare maps showing noise levels. Airports then may propose a program to reduce this incompatibility. If the FAA accepts their program, airports are eligible for federal funding to implement such projects as land acquisition (for demolition of homes) and soundproofing. *Funds may not be used to encourage reduction in aircraft operations.*

The most controversial part of a Part 150 Program is its reliance on a particular noise assessment process called the Day-Night Average Sound Level (abbreviated DNL). The formula for the DNL yields a measure of noise called the Ldn, which is the average noise level per day at a given place, incorporating a factor that accounts for different existing levels of noise during the day and night. Since noise levels can vary enormously, Ldn is measured using a logarithmic scale.

To obtain Ldn, detectors located throughout a community continuously measure noise levels. The six Massport sound detectors near Hanscom, for example, measure sound in decibels (dBA) eight times per second, around the clock. When obtaining an Ldn level, daytime and nighttime noise are treated differently: 10 decibels are added to noises occurring between 10 P.M. and 7 A.M. to account for the facts that little background noise exists to mask noise during this period and people are more sensitive to noise when they are trying to sleep.[22] The noise data used to calculate the Ldn include average noise contributions from both aircraft fly-overs and all other normal sources of community noise during that period at that location.

The Ldn was originally developed by the EPA as a metric of environmental noise to be used to protect public health and welfare. While it is a reasonable measure for noise sources that produce a relatively constant noise level, such as highways, it is a poor measure for noise events that vary significantly from the background or ambient noise—that is, the noise that exists in the absence of an airplane.

It is common for airplane noise to alter the sound environment enormously from one moment to the next. For example, if the ambient, or typical, sound in a community is 40 dBA, and a plane flies over at 100 dBA, the 60 decibel difference describes an acoustic power that is one million times that of the ambient sound. (Fortunately, this difference in acoustic power translates into a human annoyance factor that is numerically somewhat less.) Ambient sound varies significantly by locale. Thus, the quieter the community, the more it is harmed by a flyover. Even as far as fifty miles from the Denver International Airport, when a single aircraft passes over, the noise level rises from the ambient Ldn level of 20 dBA to a one-time event level of 77 dBA.[23]

Clearly, using a formula that averages intense noise events with the quieter periods of normal community sound does a disservice to the human beings exposed to airplane noise. The effect of a plane that wakes someone up because it yields 100 decibels is essentially discounted when it is averaged in with quiet times.

Using the DNL formula to gauge airport noise is like measuring how hot a stove is by averaging it over a twenty-four-hour day—and then concluding that if you put your hand on the red-hot burner for a few seconds you won't be burned. Or, as Les Blomberg of the Noise Pollution Clearinghouse so colorfully puts it, it is like taking a punch from Mike Tyson averaged over an hour and calling it a love pat.

Obviously, such calculations protect the air transportation industry, not the citizen. Virtually every citizens' report on noise points out that managing single-event noise levels (known as SENLs) is crucial to effective noise control, but Congress has not required the FAA to consider them.

Although many scientists have argued that for the purpose of measuring human reaction to noise the Ldn measure should be discarded entirely, the reality is that it is the primary measure in use. And yet even by the standards of this measure, the FAA guidelines raise concerns. Since 1974 the EPA has asserted that 55 dB Ldn—or 55 decibels as measured using the Day-Night Average Sound Level formula—provides adequate protection of public health and welfare outdoors in residential areas.[24] Originally, this level was not developed as a standard but rather as a threshold below which there is little reason to suspect that the general population will be at risk from the effects of noise. However, according to the chairperson of the United States delegation to the International Organization for Standardization Acoustics and Noise committees, for urban residential areas and other similarly sensitive urban land uses, noise impact becomes significant at 55 dB Ldn. In suburban areas where the population density is between 1,250 and 5,000 inhabitants per square mile, noise impact becomes significant at the level of 50 dB Ldn.[25]

In addition, neither the EPA nor the FAA takes into consideration *annoyance,* which here is a formal term referring to a negative subjective reaction to noise on the part of an individual or group, such as being startled or fearing a crash. Annoyance depends on such factors as the abruptness of noise change from the ambient sound, the magnitude of change relative to the ambient sound, noise duration, the number of noise events over a given period, and individual differences. The EPA has pointed out, "Although it is important to understand the importance of annoyance as a concept, it is the actual interference with activity on which the levels . . . are based."[26]

Although the EPA had long recommended the 55 dB Ldn guideline, the FAA dropped it in favor of the current higher noise guideline of 65 dB Ldn, citing the need to take into account economic considerations as well as citizen protection. In other words, using the more stringent guideline would have required them to assist the impossibly large number of citizens impacted by airports, so the 65 dB Ldn was adopted for policy purposes as the limit for outdoor noise levels in residential areas, including schools and hospitals. It is only when the 65 decibel threshold is exceeded that the FAA considers land to be adversely impacted by noise and thus eligible for financial assistance. The government's argument is that we cannot lower this threshold because we cannot afford it. Even in 1979, for example, the EPA estimated that while 5 million people lived in areas of 65 dB Ldn or greater, 45 million people lived in areas between 55 dB Ldn and 65 dB Ldn.[27] Even at that time, the FAA said nothing could be done for residents outside the 65 dB Ldn noise contour area; the average noise they were exposed to did not entitle them to federally funded relief.[28] Of course, this is still true today.

Yet, as one noise consultant put it, "We judge it as folly to stand before a room full of concerned citizens, show a map with noise contours of only 65 dB Ldn and above, and say there is no adverse effect outside the contours. Any citizens who live outside the 65 dB Ldn contour and judge the noise as too loud or as unacceptable will have trouble believing the analysis. Additionally, they may all know that the levels at their house are often well above '65 dB.' Both the inappropriate use of Ldn and the confusing nature of the Ldn metric serve to hinder the establishment of public trust and confidence in the noise analysis."[29] It is not the dead periods that bother people, it is the noisy periods, and these are not being factored in appropriately when the federal government monitors airport noise.

The Ldn levels are published on maps that indicate noise exposure areas around airports. Because people who buy property near an airport are presumed to have had knowledge of the noise exposure map, the liability of airport proprietors for noise pollution is reduced. The only way a property owner can challenge this presumption is by showing there has been a significant change in the type or frequency of aircraft operations at the airport, airport layout, or flight patterns, or an increase in night operations, and that the damages resulted from this change. The Aviation Safety and Noise Abatement Act of 1979 also prevents property owners from using the noise exposure map against an airport in a civil suit seeking relief from aircraft noise.[30]

Massport's 1978 Hanscom Field Master Plan is typical of the spin on noise regulation that has been given by government to communities nationwide. In the late 1970s the noise levels in "most of the area" near Hanscom were within or below the 55–65 Ldn range. At the time, the plan asserted that in the future new jet aircraft might be 5 to 15 decibels quieter than existing aircraft. "Hence there will be offsetting effects between increased aircraft use and a quieter mix of jet aircraft," it declared, and even with 320,000 operations there would be only a slight increase over the existing noise levels. This estimate was based on the Massport consultant's own estimate that quieter planes would result in a 4 to 6 decibel reduction in the Ldn.[31] The plan asserted that, "Noise experts estimate that most activities including residential are fully compatible with noise levels up to 60 Ldn, and are not incompatible until the Ldn reaches 65 or higher."[32] Of course, back in 1978 even Massport was willing to recognize that individual aircraft noise events by jet or other aircraft could be above a reasonable level, particularly in neighborhoods under or near flight tracks.[33] It even pointed out that although a high average noise level is annoying, it is not what stops conversations or wakes people up.

Consider a suburban neighborhood, like mine in Lexington, in which the ambient sound is 40 dBA. If in one twenty-four-hour period only ten planes fly over that neighborhood, but each creates 80 dBA for four seconds, the resulting Ldn is a mere 47.5 dB. The fact that the community may have been disturbed ten times is not recognized by the metric. Furthermore, it is not until seven hundred planes have flown over the neighborhood during a twenty-four-hour period that the Ldn will equal 65 dB, the FAA threshold for harm. Imagine living near National Airport and Dulles Airport in Washington, DC, where in 1997, 31 to 53 percent of noise monitoring stations reported readings greater than 65 Ldn.[34]

To show just how worthless the Ldn levels are for communities, consider how they reflect the recent changes at Hanscom Field. In one year, from 1998 to 1999, total operations at the airfield grew from 183,184 to 197,302, a 7.7 percent increase. Night operations grew from 1,390 operations to 1,622, an increase of 16.6 percent.[35] Noise complaints grew from 1,552 to 3,672, an increase of 139 percent. *And the Ldn, the only number that matters legally, actually went down, from 62.3 to 61.6.*[36]

If a community were to be so unfortunate as to reach the standard of noise set by the 1990 Airport Noise and Capacity Act, what would be the remedy? One thing we are promised is abatement. The term abatement, in general usage, is any procedure used to alleviate suffering caused by aircraft noise. Technically, however, abatement is *removal* of the noise source.

Massport predicted that the airport noise at Hanscom would be abated by quieter aircraft. Yet, there are limits to this noise abatement strategy.

How much change will we see when only Stage Three aircraft are used? ANCA forbids the operation of Stage Two aircraft in the United States after December 31, 1999 (with the exception of a small portion of the fleet that could take waivers until December 31, 2003). Stage Two noise limits are 93 to 108 decibels at takeoff, depending on the weight of the aircraft. Stage Three noise limits are 89 to 106 decibels,[37] still well above sane and safe limits, still putting that lawnmower next to your bed.

Furthermore, according to a 1990 federal study, aircraft manufacturers do not believe it is possible to make aircraft significantly quieter than the quietest aircraft already being built, while also retaining fuel efficiency. Even relatively quiet aircraft expose people who live close to the airport to a high level of noise. In 1990 the FAA estimated that 1.1 million people would continue to be exposed to excessive noise levels (as based on their own much-criticized guidelines) even after Stage Two planes were banned.[38] In the year 2000, it estimated that half a million people were exposed to "significant levels of aircraft noise."[39] Such numbers are indeed estimates. In his introduction for ANCA, Senator Ford reported that the number of impacted Americans is about 3.2 million. On the other hand, the Quiet Communities Act introduced in 1997 by twenty-three members of the House of Representatives has asserted that nearly 20 million Americans are exposed to noise levels that can lead to psychological and physiological damage, and another 40 million people are exposed to noise levels that cause sleep or work disruption.

While the very newest aircraft do show improvement, their noise levels are still objectionable. For example, in November of 1999 Congress permitted a 6 A.M. shuttle flight at Washington's Reagan National Airport because the aircraft met the noise limits required of early takeoffs there. Such new aircraft yield 75 decibels at takeoff, and they attain altitude quickly.[40] At that time, twenty-four new flights per day were added (Senator John McCain of Arizona had pushed for forty-eight). The *Washington Post* opined, "Congress has [disregarded] carefully negotiated flight schedules set by the regional authority." And they added, "The congressional flight plan now includes a breaking of the 1,250 mile limit on flights in or out of National; 12 of the additional flights could go beyond the limit to hub airports such as Phoenix, home base of America West Airlines in Senator McCain's home state."

As a reporter for the *Washington Post* put it, "With no choice in the matter, local officials are saying that they can live with the new plan, that they're happy that at least it's for 24 rather than 48 more flights a day. But how happy will they be when Congress calls for still more flights to still more cities? And what difference will it make what they think?"[41]

Communities so besieged by noise that they meet ANCA's threshold have also been promised mitigation—*management* of existing noise. At first glance, mitigation sounds pretty decent, like a fair trade. Uncle Sam takes something of yours (sorry about that), but here is something in return. When it comes to airport pollution, however, mitigation includes things like putting double-glazed windows in people's homes (god forbid they should want to open them) and putting noise burrens at the end of runways to deflect jet blasts into the sky. Sometimes, although rarely, the airport buys the homes in the flight paths.

Massport has used millions of dollars in federal grant money to alter homes in the Logan Airport neighborhood. T. F. Green Airport in Rhode Island, where passenger counts more than doubled between 1996 and 1999, plans to buy out 260 homes. Taxpayers are footing these bills. And while residents may get a fair price for their homes, their communities will lose in property taxes. State officials in Rhode Island are asking for a federal law that would make airports responsible for reimbursing localities for the tax revenues lost.[42]

Nationwide, airport authorities typically suggest mitigation as the ultimate remedy because the government pays for it and naïve communities are assuaged by it. But generally it does not come close to replacing the value of the homes and the quality of life that were lost.

In Lexington we could lose key residential neighborhoods that comprise at least two fine school districts, and even then the homes that would be newly close to the runway would still be impacted. Today we understand that Massport's long-term plan is to develop Hanscom Field until it reaches full capacity, whatever that is. The Hanscom Field Master Plan suggested in 1978 that ground traffic levels would not be likely to increase significantly even if total aircraft operations increased to 320,000.[43] Similarly, it predicted, "Even at 320,000 operations the air pollution emissions . . . will increase only slightly."[44] So the community has imagined that the state's target could well be at least 320,000 operations, a 60 percent increase over current usage. Massport's director publicly confirmed this in April of 2000, when she wrote that, "The airport itself can accommodate up to 320,000 operations a year before capacity issues arise."[45] If past is prologue, the state will find a way to circumvent even these targets, just as in the spring of 2000 the limit on the number of slots available at LaGuardia Airport in New York was circumvented by new legislation.[46]

Yes, our government holds out mitigation to communities as the ultimate solution, and for once, it is correct. The airport is a cancer, and mitigation is death to healthy communities.

In recent years the battle over noise reduction has gone international. Many foreign airports have stronger noise restrictions than we do.[47]

For example, in the Netherlands, the Dutch Aviation Act of 1978 set the legal noise limit around all airports at the equivalent of about 50-55 dB Ldn. Beginning in November 1995, Amsterdam Airport Schiphol increased its noise restrictions every six months. It now forbids landings between 6 P.M. and 8 A.M. of all Stage Two aircraft and has doubled landing fees for these aircraft. Many other restrictions apply, including various curfews and limitations on runway use. Unfortunately, the airport's practice of putting a quota on the annual number of operations has been replaced by another system that sets no specific limit but instead measures total noise volume and maximum noise levels.

In general, the European Union has tougher noise laws than the United States. For example, in legislation passed in 1998 the European Union banned the use of "hushkits" on older U.S.–made aircraft. The European Union argued that the kits do not reduce noise enough around European cities, and that they prolong the life of obsolete, polluting aircraft. According to Jonathan Howe, managing director of Geneva-based Airports Council International, U.S. certification of hushkits that consist solely of changes in throttle and flap settings and do not modify the engine was damaging U.S. credibility overseas.[48] The American industry countered that because of the ban on hushkitted planes, American airlines had to sell their older, noisier planes to third-world countries, and the company that manufactures the kits, Pratt and Whitney, lost sales.[49] The United States claimed the aviation industry lost more than $2 billion as a result. The industry put pressure on Congress to retaliate against the European Union by banning flights of the Anglo-French Concorde, stripping the European Union of its role in the International Civil Aviation Organization, and/or denying European carriers access to the U.S. market.[50]

In 2002, the European Union hushkit legislation was modified to apply only to urban airports, defined as being in the middle of a built-up area, with no runway longer than 2,000 meters, and serving only domestic or European traffic. Berlin's Tempelhof and London City Airport are examples. The legislation also established an international framework for airport noise management.[51]

In a case that will have wide implications for environmental law in Europe, citizens living near Heathrow Airport in London have argued in the European Court of Human Rights that night flights violate their "right to private life" and respect for their homes. Although citizens have complained for many years about the noise and pollution from Heathrow, in 1993 the British government instituted a night-flight program, which even after many noise reports and opportunities for citizen feedback, resulted in more rather than fewer flights between 4:30 and 6 A.M. One citizen described their plight:

> I joined HACAN [the Heathrow Association for the Control of
> Aircraft Noise] because the nuisance of aircraft noise was much

greater than I had expected, having been misled by official
assurances that a new generation of quiet aircraft was to replace
old technology, and that a limit of 275,000 movements was to
be implemented.[52]

After the HACAN ClearSkies group and local authorities lost
their battle against the night flights in Britain's House of Lords
and in the courts, they took their case to the European Court of
Human Rights, which in 2001 settled in favor of the communities.[53] In effect, the court ruled that people have a fundamental
right to a good night's sleep.[54]

In 2003, upon appeal by the British government, this ruling
was overturned. However, the European court encouraged the
communities by ruling that, because of inadequate legal procedures in Britain, the residents had been denied the right to an
effective remedy, and it awarded them costs and expenses. One
activist concluded, "This is a part victory for us. We have been
told we should be able to sort this out in British courts. The fight
goes on."[55]

Public debate on the merits versus the problems of air transportation has been minimal. ANCA was never debated on the floor of
the U.S. Congress—it was slipped into a thick budget bill proposed by a joint congressional committee. No national champions
have come to the aid of communities.

One reason may be that such a debate requires a substantial
examination of the value of communities versus the value of commerce, and in the heyday of laissez-faire capitalism and powerful
consumerism, this debate is politically difficult.

It is also not a simple fight of us against them. Yet, as a citizen
of my community, I find it ludicrous that so frequently the over-
riding value of commerce is simply assumed in the law without
examining the actual costs on either side. Too often the argument
that interstate commerce will be jeopardized by airport restrictions of any kind is simplistic and unsubstantiated. For instance, in

Burbank v. Lockheed the Supreme Court in its majority opinion
quoted the solicitor general as arguing that the imposition of curfew ordinances on a nationwide basis would cause, in the hours
immediately preceding the curfew, a "bunching" of flights that
would aggravate congestion and worsen the noise problem by
increasing flights in the period of greatest annoyance to surrounding communities.[56] And yet the fact is that air carriers themselves
bunch flights to meet the demands of consumers for early morning and late afternoon departures—so who is the Court protecting, and how much worse would the bunching have been?

The Court also quoted the chairman of the House
Committee on Interstate and Foreign Commerce as saying, "We
have evidence that across America some cities and States are trying
to pass noise regulations. Certainly we do not want that to happen. It would harass industry and progress in America. That is the
reason why I want to get this bill passed during this session." In an
argument that could be plausible if data were presented, the Court
held, "If we were to uphold the Burbank ordinance and a significant number of municipalities followed suit, it is obvious that frac-
tionalized control of the timing of takeoffs and landings would
severely limit the flexibility of FAA in controlling air traffic flow."
However, in clinching its argument, the Court majority relied on
a 1960 FAA statement that read:

> The practice of prohibiting the use of various airports during
> certain specific hours would create critically serious problems
> to all air transportation patterns. The network of airports
> throughout the United States and the constant availability of
> these airports are essential to the maintenance of a sound air
> transportation system. The continuing growth of public accept-
> ance of aviation as a major force in passenger transportation and
> the increasingly significant role of commercial aviation in the
> nation's economy are accomplishments which cannot be inhib-
> ited if the best interest of the public is to be served. It was con-
> cluded therefore that the extent of relief from the noise

problem which this provision might have achieved would not
have compensated the degree of restriction it would have
imposed on domestic and foreign Air Commerce.[57]

Communities required to jump through hoops like measuring
Ldn levels and commissioning private health studies to prove they
have been harmed are insulted by policy based on this level of
reasoning.

Yet it seems that whenever the growth of the air transportation industry is threatened, it trots out the restraint of trade argument. This practice is not limited to American soil. When the
citizens of London complained to the European Court about
night flights, their government argued that the fifteen flights that
arrive at Heathrow between 11:30 P.M. and 6 A.M. were vital to
the British economy.[58]

American companies typically claim that the European Union
restrictions are trade barriers disguised as environmental protection.[59] Of course, that could be a factor. Competition certainly
exists. On the other hand, the American argument flies in the face
of the fact that Europeans have routinely passed more sensitive
noise policies than we have.

Communities deserve laws that are based on sound analysis of
the economic and environmental effects of commercial aviation
and aviation growth. In Boston the argument would include the
tradeoffs between the jobs and commerce created by our airports'
growth and the costs to our quality of life. It would recognize that
our quality of life is what has attracted many companies to locate
here in the first place and what allows companies to retain high-
tech workers. It would be sensitive to the fact that millions of
tourists visit Boston and its historic sights every year.

Business interests that would be negatively impacted by
airport growth tend to be silent on these issues: business is, in the
final analysis, a community. Nevertheless, it is commonly accepted
knowledge that in determining the location of a new business,
entrepreneurs say that the most important factor is quality of life

in their community. A report by BankBoston examining the effects of the Massachusetts Institute of Technology on local innovation noted it is of "critical importance" that "scientifically oriented entrepreneurs like living in the Boston area. Absent the symphony, the parks, the ocean, the universities, the art museum, and other cultural attractions that make Boston unique, the city would fail to hold these entrepreneurs and would grow more slowly." [60]

We also need analysis of exactly how air traffic patterns are restricted by noise regulations. Where are the arguments demonstrating these impacts?

Most importantly, we need to figure out exactly how the state and federal governments should be discharging their duty toward their citizens. How is Massport meeting their charter to improve "our health and living conditions"? [61] How is the EPA helping communities with noise? Government's duty to develop viable transportation systems must be balanced, in law, against the data that the health and welfare of millions of citizens are being damaged.

In the meantime, while the federal government has taken the legal high ground, there are still lots of skirmishes in the foothills.

In 1992 the Sixth Circuit Court of Appeals held that the methodology used by the FAA to estimate noise impact areas is not arbitrary and capricious and that the FAA is not required to use estimates based on the impact of individual noise events. This ruling was made in response to a suit brought by a community surrounding the Louisville, Kentucky, airport, where an expansion plan included buying out three complete neighborhoods. [62] On the other hand, in 1993 the Tenth Circuit Court held that the FAA's finding that a proposed airport construction project had no significant noise impacts on a public recreational area *was* arbitrary and capricious. [63]

Airlines are working to have airport restrictions on heavy aircraft eliminated. A 1996 decision held that the FAA has not resolved the issue of whether ANCA applies to any restriction affecting heavy Stage Three aircraft or only to restrictions designed to limit airport noise. [64]

By the early 1990s, five hundred noise-related cases had been fought in federal courts, and seven hundred more cases had been brought in state courts.[65] Today the headlines highlighting the plight of helpless communities continue: "Arizona Residents Sue Town for Airport Noise Damages"; "Vancouver Residents Plan Legal Action to Fight Airport Noise"; "Van Nuys Airport Exceeds State Noise Limits But Gets Permit to Continue Operations"; and so on.

What will be the legal resolution to the problem of aircraft noise?

In the short haul, legal analysts have called for reactivation of the Office of Noise Abatement and Control within the EPA. Although it has been defunded, ONAC retains authorization and a mandate to oversee and coordinate federal activities on all types of noise, including aircraft noise, from a public health perspective.[66] The Natural Resources Defense Council suggests that ONAC should be reauthorized at an appropriate level of funding and should conduct a case study of airport noise and its effects on surrounding communities. Others suggest that ONAC as originally structured in the 1970s will be inadequate to the task because, while it made important contributions, the FAA often disregarded them in enacting regulations.

Legal writer Kristin L. Falzone has suggested that an independent commission composed of ONAC, the FAA, and Congress should be established to ensure equality of power among the various federal agencies.[67] She points out that the FAA is highly influenced by the air transportation industry lobby and that its resources are primarily devoted to its air traffic and safety responsibilities. "Thus, without an order, or at least encouragement from an independent source, the FAA will continue to address inefficiently the growing airport noise pollution problem."[68] Certainly the administrative mechanism for change will be a less powerful FAA rather than a privatized FAA.

The Quiet Communities Act of 1997[69] would reactivate ONAC, and calls for a study on how aircraft noise affects health.

With a budget of $5 million per year (increased to $8 million after three years), ONAC would be directed to examine the FAA's selection of noise measurement methodologies, the threshold of noise at which health impacts are felt, and the effectiveness of noise abatement programs at airports around the nation. The act points out that because the EPA remains legally responsible for enforcing the Noise Control Act of 1972 even though not funded to do so, and since the Noise Control Act prohibits state and local governments from regulating noise sources in many situations, "noise abatement programs across the country lie dormant."[70] Sponsored in 1997 by Senators Robert G. Torricelli, Frank R. Lautenberg, Alfonse M. D'Amato, Daniel Patrick Moynihan, Paul Wellstone, and Charles S. Robb, the bill was tabled (that is, defeated) in the Senate by a vote of sixty-nine to twenty-seven (four members did not vote). That House version had twenty-three sponsors. Reintroduced in 1999, the bill had twenty-nine cosponsors—twenty-three Democrats and six Republicans.[71] Today the bill continues to be revised and reintroduced.

Others believe that involving the FAA in the regulation of pollution is a conflict of interest, and that they should have no hand whatsoever in monitoring noise. For example, activists in both Chicago and Boston believe that the FAA-drawn noise contours for their cities are inaccurate and have called for independent agencies to create impartial monitoring devices and systems.

The Natural Resources Defense Council suggests that under the National Environmental Policy Act and other federal laws, Congress should incorporate a comprehensive set of single-event and other factors into FAA noise reviews. Reliance on the Ldn metric underestimates the number of people affected and annoyed by aircraft noise, it believes, and single-event noise levels should also be monitored. At a minimum, a newer metric called the CNEL (community noise equivalent level) should be added to noise regulations. The CNEL is used in California and many European countries, and adds a 5 dB penalty during the hours of 7 P.M. to 10 P.M. to the Ldn's 10 dB nighttime penalty. Furthermore, a 55 dB CNEL threshold should be set for residential noise levels.[72] In many cases night flights should simply be banned.

One hope for legal action may be in the more generalized scheme of environmental law. At their foundation, federal pollution laws are based on both technology-based controls and health risk–based controls. Noise pollution laws have emphasized technology-based controls (such as updating aircraft engines), but federal environmental statutes contain "a number of provisions calling for the imposition of more stringent requirements when it is evident that application of technology based requirements alone will cause violation of an environmental standard or will create an unacceptable health risk."[73] The Clean Air Act, for example, directs the EPA to impose stricter limits on technologies when there is a cancer risk greater than one in a million. This precedent may suggest an avenue for curtailing airport operations.

Falzone also points out that liability for aircraft noise should be shared. In *Griggs v. Allegheny County,* the Supreme Court established in 1962 the rule that airport proprietors rather than the federal government are responsible for damages resulting from aircraft noise.[74] Furthermore, since under airline deregulation air carriers have more ability to choose their routes, they can increase pressure on airport proprietors to reduce their noise abatement activities. Airlines, local governments (other than the airport proprietors), states, and the federal government are all exonerated from responsibility for noise. Just compensation in proprietor liability suits, Falzone observes, might reduce the level of political controversy around airport growth and lead to more efficient decision-making about airways.[75]

Looking at the situation more broadly and longer term, our representatives should revisit the idea that local communities are in the best position to make the tradeoffs among such issues as quality of life, jobs, and noise. This is not to argue that we should necessarily return to local control. Certainly on the face of it one can sympathize with the air transportation industry when it finds a variety of local regulations to be an annoyance and an impediment to their business. A certain level of standardization for safety, security, and pollution is responsible.

On the other hand, national control has meant putting irresponsible power in the hands of the industry, and as we have seen in the goals of the industry's Coalition for a Global Standard on Aviation Noise, there is more of this ahead. Curbing the power of this industry must be part of the solution. One component will be to push airlines and airports toward paying more of their fair share of the actual costs of airline travel by reducing government subsidies.

8

How Will Citizen Involvement
Solve These Problems?

*Community environmentalists are regarded as irresponsible
and dismissed with the tired cliché "not in my backyard."
In fact, the movement for environmental justice has
embraced a public-spirited goal that is more positive and
ambitious than the government's—to stop the corporations
from dumping their stuff in anyone's backyard.*

    —William Greider

*To tell you the truth, I am thrilled if I have time to brush
my own teeth.*

      —Working parent, when asked whether
      she calls the noise complaint line

In LEXINGTON, as the threat to our community has escalated
dramatically, our residents have experienced the gamut of emotions that is typical of airport communities.

We are angry. Among those who know only a few details
about our case, there is generalized anger at the situation in which
we find ourselves, and acute anger when the airline, or a loud jet,
or a helicopter, flies overhead. Those who understand the case
in more depth are angry at our state and the governor; they are
angry at being duped.

We are afraid. Obviously we fear what will happen in the future—to our children, our environment, and our property values. But, unaccustomed as many of us are to dealing with such a controversy, we also fear speaking out in front of neighbors who may disagree. Some of us fear taking on the public role of activist. We fear retaliation. We fear being seen in our workplaces as antibusiness.

We are ashamed, embarrassed that this is happening here, among people who because of their education, their professions, the very town in which they have chosen to live, might have known better.

No doubt we have at some level assumed that our competence as professionals translates into competence as citizens. We have freedom of religion, of speech, of assembly . . . all these and more, and still we have let the quality of our community slide. Yet, as my grim hobby grew into a part-time Web and media project, it took me eight months, from June until February when I acquired the Hanscom Field Master Plan, to document that the Hanscom Field Advisory Committee has no power. People like me are embarrassed that we have not been better informed, and that we cannot readily command the information we need. We are embarrassed that although we work for powerful organizations, the reality is that we do not have powerful organizations working for us.

Some feel guilty. "I am sorry I haven't been involved, but my family has to come first," they say. "I want to be involved but I haven't had time." We feel, especially, liberal guilt. "Maybe it really is fair to the suffering communities near Logan that we take on a share of their problems."

Some people are in denial, for which there are many forms. One is belligerence: "If you didn't want to live near an airport, you shouldn't have moved here in the first place." Another is rationalization: "My property value has increased so much that if it goes down some, I don't really care." Yet another is wishful thinking: "We always got rid of them before."

In a related psychological strategy, some are deliberately "forgetting" about the airport in order to protect themselves or their children. "I can't afford to worry about it because my stress level is already so high." "I have to focus on keeping my home peaceful for the kids; I don't want them to be aware of the problem."

Recent history tells us that we are not alone. Our experience mirrors that of other communities at home and abroad. Consider the British citizens exposed to the noise and pollution of Heathrow Airport in London. Community activists there surveyed residents house to house and discovered they were often reluctant to admit their problems. The researchers concluded, "There is a rational belief that to acknowledge an environmental problem affecting the place you live will either diminish the value of your greatest asset, or in some way reveal a foolishness on the part of the resident for living under such conditions."[1] They noted that several householders in one town deeply resented aircraft noise but would not complain for fear that their *relatively* low noise burden would be increased by a change in policy intended to spread the noise problem more evenly.

The study concludes: "For some people, acknowledging a problem with aircraft noise leads them into a downward mental spiral and reduces their ability to function effectively. These are the people who are annoyed, upset and become tired and anxious, who then get further upset by the feeling of being powerless to stop the problem. Now, conscious of the debilitating nature of the problem, they are even more sensitive to the next day's flights. An internal compromise is often attained by trying to ignore the problem, by never discussing or admitting it, and existing with the subconscious knowledge that this is the only way to survive."[2]

Charles Derber in his book *Corporation Nation* has observed, "The breakdown of community is so transparently related to the new corporate economy that the dead silence of most communitarians about the subject is truly remarkable."[3] Part of the explanation for our silence is that we are ashamed to admit that we have lost control of our own destiny. Part of the explanation is that we are angry—and feel helpless to assuage that anger. Part of the explanation is that we are afraid—and afraid to admit it.

These emotional effects of our situation must be reckoned with.

Involvement alleviates our pain, but is it effective? We picket, we write letters, we call the noise complaint line. Do we imagine that these actions are accomplishing something? Some of us believe that if enough of us do these sorts of things, we will be heard. Certainly it can be true that large numbers can turn into political clout, and at this point political clout may be our only avenue to protection.

Yet I wonder whether we are primarily making ourselves feel better. If effectiveness is the measure, the reality seems to be that our gestures of activism are little more than a primitive rite, raising the talisman of our involvement to ward off evil spirits in an act of ego that is no more effective now than it was in the face of a mastodon attack.

Noam Chomsky has pointed out that it is ironic that we Americans send advisors to Haiti to teach the people about democracy when the indigent people there already have such a vibrant civil society. There, in the poorest country in the American hemisphere, the culture is rife with grassroots movements and associations and unions and ideas and commitment and hope and enthusiasm.[4] What differentiates Americans from Haitians?

What are the modern prerequisites to citizen involvement and the practice of democratic skills?

Certainly real need galvanizes. Psychologist Abraham Maslow and his followers suggest that before individuals will attempt to meet their needs for friends, self-esteem, or self-actualization, they will focus on meeting their needs for safety, food, clothing, and shelter. The development of an airport in a residential community threatens citizens' ability to fulfill their most basic needs. Property values, a keystone of personal financial stability, are affected. Noise causes sleep deprivation and stress, threatening residents' psychological stability and their jobs. More development brings a higher risk of plane crashes in neighborhoods, and the attendant congestion brings more risk of vehicle accidents on the ground.

Yet unlike the citizens of Haiti, the citizens of our community are not practiced in dealing with such threats. In fact, like any peoples unaccustomed to dealing with big government power, we have problems even imagining the possibilities.

We are not unlike the group of inexperienced women in a remote village in Guyana who sold seventeen exquisite hammocks for a thousand dollars apiece on the Internet, turning the economics of their community upside down.[5] When controlling that much capital brought the group to the attention of regional officials, one of the officials convinced the women to put him in charge of their affairs, and although the group was a nongovernmental organization funded by international aid organizations, he took it over. In the ensuing power struggles, the workers quit and the business declined. Perhaps the people of Lexington are more sophisticated about the threats posed by exploitive leaders, but for many years we have nevertheless lived under the illusion that our civil organizations were adequately representing us to a responsive government. Even more importantly, we believed we could trust our government to negotiate in good faith with its citizens.

Kay Tiffany, longtime Lexington ShhAir and community leader, describes community awareness this way: "The activists themselves have never been naïve. I don't think they have simply trusted their civil organizations to get the job done—they have been pushing them for years. But we have been up against absolute power that none of us wanted to acknowledge exists in America."[6]

It may be that privileged Americans are not in a position to believe in the reality of exploitive authority. Our pretty homes and towns, our nation's continued world hegemony, our civil protections, our free press, our very democracy, all conspire to create our complacency. Nor can many of us point to having received an enlightening civil education. How many of us could describe in detail even one modern case of a citizen movement's success, especially a local one? How many of us could be said to know "how the system works"? We do not understand the limits of our government and our civil society in part because they have not done the job of educating us, and in part because concerns that do arise are camouflaged by effective public relations campaigns mounted by rich, smart organizations like Massport and the airline lobby. Furthermore, political parties today are more beholden to the wealthy few than to average citizens. As Thomas Ashley, the former liberal Democratic congressman from Ohio, puts it, "The American system is no longer a democracy because democracy is based on accountability and it's not there now."[7]

Research has shown that the better educated are somewhat more likely to challenge authority than the less educated. Those in the "moral professions" like teaching, medicine, and law are somewhat more defiant than those in the more technical professions like physical science and engineering.[8] Ironically, since we here in the Boston suburbs are a community of educated, confident, assertive achievers, we should be among the nation's top activists.

Yet, activism must be based on conviction, and my guess is that individually we have not sorted out our beliefs about the key causalities in our situation. In the Hanscom Field controversy, for instance, we observe a particularly hardened and determined management team starting an airline, and we may think: Well, that's OK, isn't it? Isn't that part of the free market and all that? Isn't what's good for business good for America? And then there's our out-of-control state agency—isn't the government not to be trusted, anyhow? We knew that already, right? And the community . . . well, the community is just caught in between. Can't do much about that.

Or a person may think: I'm moving up, or out, in a few years, so it doesn't affect me. It's not my problem.

Maybe I am being too cynical. But to be honest, until my recent experiences, my own sophistication about these issues was not much beyond this level, and I am a professor who has spent a good portion of my time studying business–government relations.

I suspect that my neighbors who are not specialists in economics or politics or law are in a similar place to where I have been.

Scholars who have studied citizen involvement confirm these personal impressions and provide a context for them. Of America's failure to develop effective political involvement, Charles Derber has written: "The moral development and empowerment of the individual has often been disassociated from political change and become an end in itself. This is the great failure of the new politics on all sides of the political spectrum. It confuses moral development, community building, and personal empowerment with political change—or takes one as a substitute for the other."[9]

And Professor John Ehrenberg has suggested, "Democracy . . . requires public supervision of the market, and this necessitates sustained public action, vigorous state activity, and broad political thought. . . . The economy is not just another sphere of association like a book group. . . . It is no longer possible to theorize civil society as a site of democratic activity and counterpoise it to an inherently coercive state without considering how capitalism's structural inequities constitute everyday life. . . .

"In the end, reviving civil society requires the breadth of thought and action that only politics and an orientation toward the state can provide."[10]

In other words, when it comes to bringing community values to bear on powerful special interests and government, we have not done the personal values clarification and learning about fundamental issues of capitalism and democracy that is required, and so we have not developed personal strategies for actively engaging our political system.

This is not surprising. When, exactly, should we have done this kind of personal development? In college, perhaps? In the evening, after commuting into the city and back, working hard all day, and helping our kids with their homework? At the bus stop? While cleaning out the guppy bowl at school?

It is also true that most of us, like employees everywhere, are not independent financially. A few, yes. The vast majority, no. As

self-starting, assertive people, we do not like to admit our financial
dependency and what it does to us in our world, yet a part of our
reality is that as employees it is difficult to speak out.

If we are working in a company or a law firm, if we are a
supplier or a service, we fear appearing to be anticorporate. Not
only do we risk going against the specific values of our
employer—which we may or may not actually know but which in
the absence of other cues we assume to be in favor of laissez-faire
capitalism—we risk appearing to be antibusiness to the wider
community. And being antibusiness is not conducive to getting
our next job, or to keeping the job we have.

It is also likely that when issues are complicated, it may be
difficult to feel that we have adequately informed ourselves. It may
be also be true that we are simply too busy, working at jobs that
we need, to find the time.

Forty years ago, in the wake of the rise of totalitarianism that
led to World War II and of the German society that allowed and in
some respects fostered it, Yale psychologist Stanley Milgram inves-
tigated how people react to authority. His results give us some
ideas about how U.S. citizens today can begin to feel powerful
enough to take on our current system of government by special
interests. Milgram conducted famous experiments in which a
teacher was ordered to use increasingly painful shocks to punish
an errant learner; these suggested that most human beings are
susceptible to commands and coercion delivered by legitimate
authorities.[11] Milgram also suggested a set of conditions that will
increase obedience to authority. These are the presence of a legitimate authority figure, the context of a prestigious institution, personality factors such as passivity and the belief that one is not in
control of one's fate, the issuance of direct orders, and monetary
incentives.

Prerequisite to resisting authority, to developing into citizen
activists, is a set of social-psychological skills that in placid times
are largely unpracticed. Based on Milgram's theory, here is what
we as a community need:

To begin with, citizens must understand how authority works. Individuals must be exposed to the gamut of ideas about how corrupt authority can be resisted, from psychological research like Milgram's to political science research on citizen activism, civil society, and special interest power.

Further, we must grasp, fundamentally, that authority can, will, and does exploit. We must understand that just as Milgram's man in the white coat pushes the teacher to shock the learner, so the ruthless individuals among us will assume power if they can. Accepting this reality may not be as easy as we think. The experience of history suggests that individuals will cling to their belief in the rationality and beneficence of their government despite overwhelming evidence to the contrary. If there is one lesson to be learned from the victims of Nazi terrorism, to cite the most extreme example, it is that they continually denied the disintegration they saw around them. Famed Holocaust diarist Victor Klemperer admitted that even as the Gestapo searched his home, he clung to his belief in the rationality of his world and the government under which he lived. In his diary he wrote: "Eight-man squad . . . vilest abuse. . . . They rummaged through *everything*, stole . . . half a pound of margarine (legitimately bought with ration coupons)." [12] Later Klemperer wryly observed that people could say to a woman whose husband was arrested by the Gestapo, "But your husband *must* have done something; they don't just kill someone for no reason!" I cannot help but think that in similar fashion people outside of our Lexington communities must be saying, "But you *must* be wrong (or arrogant, or dumb). The state doesn't ruin people's lives and property for nothing." Maybe, to some extent, we are even saying this about ourselves.

Clearly, another truth is that when facing up to a prestigious institution like Yale, or governmental agencies like Massport and the FAA, supporting each other matters deeply. Not only are individuals alone ineffective, they are also likely to doubt their own judgment. Yet, when supported by even one or two others, they will stand fast. For this reason, it is essential that neighbors find time to consult with one another and that communities organize together.

Another important factor that supports resistance to authority is personality. People who have a strong belief in their own abilities, and who have developed an assertive style, are more likely to say no. Also, people who have examined their own beliefs inoculate themselves against the confounding beliefs of others.

Finally, being financially secure also gives individuals the courage to resist.

So what is the real potential for resistance to authority that exists in our communities today?

This is how our particular Lexington community measures up on empowerment: We have the ideal educational level and the personality profile to want to confront the powerful special interest system that we are facing. However, our collective knowledge about how citizen movements confront exploitative authority is limited. Our conceptualizations of community, democracy, and capitalism are concerns to us, certainly, but so far many of us haven't had the time or the resources to clarify what we really believe so that we can confidently take a stand. Finally, the sad truth may be that, whatever our convictions, our ideas will go nowhere because we may be reluctant to speak out for fear of disrupting our livelihood or our otherwise delicately balanced lives.

Another prerequisite to citizen involvement and the practice of democracy is a system that is accountable to individual citizens. Accountability is both a political and a psychological concept. When citizens experience, or learn, or intuit, that the system is not accountable, they tune it out. It is also a fundamental tenet of human behavior that if the system is not accountable—if it does not give feedback to people—people will turn elsewhere for their psychological gratification. For example, they will turn to charity work, or entertainment, or their jobs. This is the psychological nature of human beings. This is the nature of Americans.

Today the erosion of people's belief in government accountability strains American democracy. To bolster citizen confidence in government, our country badly needs citizen successes. Critics have pointed out, for example, that we need to make broadcasting companies accountable to the citizens who own the airwaves, and that we need to make mining and logging companies accountable to the citizens who own the lands and the forests.

While many of the citizens in towns near airports are rallying against their airport's expansion, others remain concerned but inactive. A few support expansion, and some do not much care. The picture today may not be all that different from that of the Revolutionary era, when the country was split about evenly among those who were for revolution, those who were against it, and those who just wanted to be left alone. It is popular in political writing about America's inactive citizenry to label those who are not involved as cynical or apathetic. As a psychologist, I believe we emphasize these psychological labels because we have become comfortable with them and because our audience relates to them, yet they hardly begin to characterize the problem. By calling our citizens apathetic we interpret only individual beliefs and attitudes, while in reality it is the system in which individuals exist that is the more powerful determinant of their behavior.

Focusing on individual American citizens and their psychology is a shorthand approach that is both misleading and dangerous, a Lone Ranger fallacy that must be replaced with a clinical look at human systems. We focus on the individual at our peril. Rather we must learn how each individual operates within an organization and, crucially, how organizations operate within the world of organizations.

If institutions are not accountable, that is, if citizens cannot effect change in them, there is no motivation—no reason, no reward—for citizens to stay involved. In Lexington, we have seen that an individual's power in the case of Hanscom Field is limited to informing others, informing the community, voting every four years for the governor, and asking one's busy representative, who is not always fully informed, to represent one's interests. While citizens pursue the problem in these limited ways in their spare time, the airline, aided by the state and federal governments, establishes a brand name, grows larger, seeks new routes, and every day in every way seeks to grow bigger and stronger.

Naturally, if the only community involvement available is to vote once every four years, citizens will tune out the system until a short time before the election. Obviously, if they believe their leaders are taking care of the problem, citizens will wait for the results. Certainly, if they cannot be fully and accurately informed, many people will choose not to be informed at all.

Focusing on individual apathy is merely blaming the victim. Instead we must reconceptualize the problem of citizen participation. Every time we hear about individual cynicism, we should deliberately turn our attention away from the individual to search for some weakness in the design of the democratic organizational system of which each person is a part. When we ask how a problem like unlimited aviation expansion could happen in our community, we must focus on how we have designed civil society in its relation to special interests and government. Worrying about individual apathy deflects our energy from more important truths about institutions and their connections. The more effective approach is to focus on an individual's power to act within the system—the person's ability to know it, engage it, and influence it.

Obviously, I believe that a good place to start retaking our democracy would be to make the airline industry accountable to citizens in airport communities.

9

The People Play Defense

Tyranny is always better organized than freedom.
—Charles Péguy

We are not the enemy; we are your neighbors, family, and friends who need your help in protecting our neighborhoods, communities, and the globe. Please support our initiatives.
—Jack Saporito, American Working Group
for National Policy

Imagine an early conversation that might have taken place in Lexington between the startup airline and our state agency.

"So you want to start an airline," says Massport.

"Not exactly. We want to run our planes in your jurisdiction. We are already flying in other markets," says the airline.

"Good for you. Tell us how your company is positioned in the market."

"We are currently operating in a projected high-growth era for the industry, as you know. Under our regional rollout strategy, we have started small and hope to capture market share with low fares. Later, of course, once we are established, we can increase our fares and deepen our profits."

"I can see you have studied Porter's competitive strategy. We have an underutilized airport in Worcester, Massachusetts, west of Boston. We would be happy to welcome you there."

"Thank you so kindly. However, we would prefer to start up

at Hanscom Field in Bedford, as it is more convenient for our passengers and we would have no competitors there."

Says Massport, "But Worcester is an established commercial facility, into which we have sunk millions, and it is actively seeking airlines, while we have been telling the people around Hanscom for some time now that their airport would not be commercialized. Not that they have it in writing, mind you."

"Yes, you certainly do have a crack legal staff. Well, our view is that offense is easier than defense. Worcester already has another airline, far better capitalized than we are. Of course, as we grow, we would expect that you would develop the infrastructure at Hanscom, and we could not expect that would be exclusively for us. In the meantime, we would perform the essential service of pioneering commercial flights, facing down the locals, and opening up the market for other airlines."

"You know, of course, that there is strong community resistance to commercial aviation at Hanscom."

"As we say down in Texas, they are all hat and no cattle. Our motto is 'get the routes and they will come.' And with Massport's political, financial, and public relations backing, how can we go wrong?"

While these negotiations are going on, the citizens are enjoying a lovely spring.

"Heard anything about anything lately, Harry?"

"You bet, Greta. They're going to move the entrance at the high school from one wing to another, and they actually expect us to pay for it."

"Do tell."

"Gotta defeat that."

"A-yup."

Meanwhile, down at the town hall, just as they have for many years, the citizens' elected representatives are talking with Massport about the future of the airport. And down at the State House, their representatives are being told that nothing new is going on out at Hanscom.

In business, strategic thinking is an integrated perspective on the future of a company, a vision derived through synthesis, intuition, and creativity. Typically a company's goal is to enhance profits by gobbling up market share. It studies its competitors, strategizes an attack, and moves in. To a large extent, the more predatory a company is, the more likely it is to succeed. Companies are sharks, and proud of it.

Contrary to its carefully crafted public image of friendliness and solidity, aviation is among the more cutthroat industries. In his book *Hard Landing,* author Tom Petzinger, Jr., a veteran reporter for the *Wall Street Journal,* writes, "The marginal economics of the industry—the proximity of success and failure to every decision—breeds executives who love risk, who crave victory, and who are ruthlessly averse to defeat. . . . Calling them men of ego would be like calling Mount McKinley a rise in the landscape." [1]

That's business. Or, at least, the highly competitive type of business that airport communities are up against.

Robert Reich, former U. S. secretary of labor, notes that corporate executives do not necessarily behave irresponsibly when they ignore the social consequences of their actions. "In the absence of laws and rules that tell corporate executives where the public interest lies, they should be under no obligation to guess. They are neither trained nor selected to make such choices," he writes. [2] However, he further points out, companies have an obligation to obey the law, and they pay their lawyers well to discover legal loopholes and technicalities. Such investment in legal expertise is useful to corporations, Reich observes, because "it buys the firm at least temporary relief from a regulation, enabling the company to profitably continue doing what it was doing before. . . . American lawyers . . . cultivate reputations for their elegant pirouettes around statutes. The art of Washington practice is to stake out an area of government regulation and then become expert at outwitting those who administer it. Talented people have been known to spend entire careers circumventing a single, arcane area of regulation for the benefit of a few corporations."[3]

Now a community is a mind-your-own business kind of creature. Not particularly competitive, but rather peaceful and complacent, it is prepared to zap its enemies only if they get too close. Communities are skunks.

The skunk's idea of strategy is fundamentally different from that of the shark's. A community's plan, if it has one, derives from collective values about what it represents, and although it is something of a romanticization, there is some truth in the notion that communities see themselves as realms of peace and quiet, as refuges from the cares of the commercial world. Certainly they are arenas in which citizens exhibit their most positive energies through volunteerism, civility, and family life. Improving the quality of life for all is a value that is still cherished.

No doubt today there is among our citizens a realistic recognition of the interplay of these traditional values with the more competitive values of commerce. Still, unlike a business, a community targets no competitors and monopolizes no market. Although it has to manage its growth, it does not need to grow in order to survive. Although it is occupied with the day-to-day business of running itself, strategically it takes a long-term view, looking to leave a legacy—environmental, educational, commercial, and historical—to successive generations. It is what business is for, not business itself. Although its solvency is valued, a community's effectiveness is measured not in dollars earned but in contented citizens and educated children.

Typically a community's strategy is conservative. Yes, it hopes to develop social and financial resources to deal with unforeseen disasters, improve its schools and maintain its infrastructure. But fundamentally it hopes to continue on as before. While it competes with other communities for external funds, this competition is held indirectly, through mediating state agencies. Because it is not attempting to put other communities out of business, and because it is a member of a larger state, a community generally seeks compromise and the common good.

Business plays offense while communities play defense. Obviously, the shark and the skunk are very different animals.

When the shark and the skunk go out to play together, a favorite game is called planning.

Planning, thinks the shark, is any bureaucratic directive that helps me to grow my business and make more money.

Thinks the skunk, planning is a process that provides stability and fairness to our community. The skunk takes a long-term view that considers growth in the context of the needs of all stakeholders, including our citizens, businesses, the environment, and other communities. Planning should emphasize local control because local people understand local needs, a principle that is at the foundation of our democratic system.

Now consider the differing views of the shark and the skunk specifically in terms of the aviation industry. From the airlines' point of view, transportation planning should help the aviation industry to grow. From the community's point of view, transportation planning should take into consideration any mode of transportation that best serves people's transportation and other needs.

Let us examine what has happened in Massachusetts when the shark and the skunk go out to play at planning and invite their friends Massport and the FAA to come along.

Massport has repeatedly cited the need for "regionalization" as their reason for commercialization of Hanscom Field. What does regionalization mean? The communities think it has meant unfettered growth. In an editorial in the *Boston Globe* entitled, "Thinking Regionally about Logan Airport," Massport's director Virginia Buckingham reported on "the first-ever New England Regional Transportation Summit," held in November of 1999.[4] (The skunks thought it should have been held a decade or two earlier, but no matter.) Buckingham described the conference this way: "Governors from three states agreed that New England airports must cooperate and not compete." (Asked the skunks: Where were New England's other three states? Where was the powerful, contiguous state of New York?) "Following the summit, the governors approved several immediate action steps: posting signs on their highways directing drivers to all of the regional airports; establishing a comprehensive rail plan for New England; and creating a joint marketing program that will promote each New England airport through brochures and a Web site. Finally, the governors agreed to meet again and continue their commitment to regional transportation solutions." (The skunks observed that Massport has no jurisdiction over rail, and that no binding document emerged as a result of the meeting.) Buckingham concluded, "So we have heard the concerns of families and businesses that live and work next to America's seventeenth-busiest airport [Logan]. And we have responded to those concerns. Massport has developed a regional strategy that incorporates Worcester, Manchester, T. F. Green, Hartford Bradley, and Hanscom." Four months later, when the airline at Hanscom sought to open more new routes and further increase flights by pursuing slots at LaGuardia Airport in New York, Massport's spokesperson continued along the same line: "Massport has an obligation to the residents of Logan's impacted neighborhoods to pursue regionalization. We have consistently said Hanscom is not going to be the next LAX [Los Angeles International Airport], but it does have a role as a niche commercial facility."[5]

What is Massport really doing in terms of planning? Consider the plight of the citizens of Hull, a seaside community four miles south of Boston that will be significantly impacted by Logan's new runway. In a meeting with Massport, a resident of the town asked the agency why it did not divert to other airports and use rail before impacting the 1.7 million people who live in the seventeen communities near Logan and as far away as Hingham and Cohasset. The resident argued that the FAA has already invested $600 million in T. F. Green, Manchester, and Worcester airports and that using these airports along with rail could reduce the burden on Logan by 5 million passengers per year. Massport's response, their mantra in the pro-runway campaign, was that they would still need the runway for wind-related problems.[6] Plainly put, even if some traffic is diverted, they will still need to expand.

Communities Against Runway Expansion (CARE), the civil organization representing the concerned citizens affected by Logan growth, has called upon Massport to develop a real regional strategy rather than "quick-fix, feel-good 'solutions' such as Runway 14/32." CARE has argued that, "while the runway may provide some transient relief, it will inflict irreversible harm on the quality of life of thousands."[7] Its argument received significant support in a report requested by the runway opponents and funded by Massport, in which consultants from Florida-based Montgomery Consulting Group criticized the runway review by Massport and the FAA as "a significant misinterpretation or misrepresentation of reality."[8] Supported by the organizations fighting Hanscom expansion, CARE has suggested that the FAA create a New England regional task force to examine all modes of transportation for the next thirty to fifty years.[9]

Interestingly, transportation bond bills passed by the state legislature of Massachusetts have included a requirement for a regional transportation plan, but according to Senate Transportation Committee Chairman Robert Havern, recent administrations have simply ignored them.[10]

Why has planning failed here, and elsewhere? Because in many ways, at the state level planning is a moribund concept. The legal, political, and economic realities are that Massport, like all transportation authorities, is not empowered to do regional, multistate planning. And its airports do in fact compete not only with airports in nearby states but with other transportation modalities.

An independent agency like Massport is empowered to make a profit on its properties. Naturally, it will promote its own airports before it will encourage its customers to develop a loyalty to others. Naturally, when Massport speaks of regional planning, what it really means is planning for more profits in the region of Massport. In New England, the predominant reality is that Manchester, T. F. Green, and Hartford Bradley Airports are established commercial airports in nearby states that directly compete with the Massport-owned facilities. Together they account for about a third of passenger activity in the Boston area, while Logan Airport accounts for 63.4 percent and Worcester accounts for 0.1 percent.[11] Massport would be fiscally irresponsible to its own bondholders and the Commonwealth of Massachusetts to support the development of competing airports in any serious way.

Despite its statutory duty to promote the health and welfare of the citizens of the Commonwealth, Massport's operational goal is to attract business for its own properties to make a profit. The only aspect of Massport's charter that comes close to achieving the representation that might promote community health and welfare is the requirement that its board have a bipartisan composition that includes one labor representative. Otherwise, it is only in its relationship to state and federal environmental laws that Massport must consider pollution controls and community impacts.

Enter the communities, which are themselves powerless to develop a regional transportation strategy with which they could debate Massport. As much as they may appreciate the logic of planning, as much as they may wish for a long-range, community-friendly and multimodal view, they themselves do not have the essential resources—the information, staffs, budgets, mandate—to develop even the rudiments of a credible plan. Indeed, the idea of a plan has been used against the local interests. At one point when the communities asked Massport for a regional transportation plan that is multimodal and includes several states, their spokesman rebuffed them: "These activists are not interested in a plan. They are interested in choking our economy and our infrastructure."[12] This while, at the same time, the powerful agency was going to the media with its public relations campaign to prove that it is engaging in regional planning.

The fact is that it will take federal intervention to accomplish actual regional planning. Unfortunately, at the federal level as well there is minimal transportation coordination, and no multistate plan. Former governor and presidential candidate Michael J. Dukakis, as vice-chairman of the Amtrak Board of Directors, has repeatedly pointed out that in the Northeast there is no regional plan "at all."

In January 2003, forty-seven organizations, including twenty-two state departments of transportation, called upon the federal government to establish a national program for intercity passenger rail patterned after the existing federal highway, airport, and mass-transit programs.[13] Fortunately, it seems that the necessity of planning may at last be finding some support in Washington. At this writing, a new bill to enhance rail and multimodal transportation has been introduced in the Senate by a bipartisan coalition. The American Railroad Revitalization, Investment, and Enhancement Act (also known as the "Arrive 21 Act") is a $42 billion program that funds Amtrak infrastructure and includes the development of a "50-Year Intermodal Blueprint." Environmental organizations would have involvement in the development of the blueprint by way of their membership on an advisory board. A dozen high-speed rail corridors have already been designated, and others are possible (see appendix C).

The path to a national plan will not be easy. One obstacle will be entrenched resistance from aviation interests. As local and state governments have discovered, transportation planning is hindered by the 1978 Airline Deregulation Act that bars states and cities from regulating routes and other services. One impact of the act has been demonstrated in an important court decision in Texas. In a 1968 bond ordinance, the cities of Dallas and Fort Worth had assigned long-distance flights to their then-new, large joint airport and forbade them at the smaller Love Field. But a 2000 court interpretation negated their plan.[14] From a planning perspective, the bottom line is that for the moment the possibility of rationalizing the uses of smaller and larger airports for local purposes has been suppressed.

Despite obstacles, some examples of sound and even multimodal transportation systems have already been built.

In the United States in recent years the large newer airports serving Denver, Colorado, and Dallas–Fort Worth, Texas, have been located far from population centers. Many world-class cities now locate their airports well outside of their populated areas and build excellent ground transportation connectors to the center city. Chek Lap Kok Airport is thirty-two kilometers from Hong Kong and is linked to it by a rapid rail trip of twenty-three minutes. Charles de Gaulle Airport was located northeast of Paris in what was originally farmland, land that is now covered with light industry, warehouses, and trade-show venues. A train to the center of the city takes just thirty-five minutes.[15]

It is well known that Europe's high-speed trains ("TGV") are serving the public well, with an average departure and arrival punctuality of more than 95 percent on short-haul routes, including Paris to London, Europe's busiest cross-border city-pair.[16] Also in Europe, new intermodal transportation centers are beginning to appear in which the airport is also the high-speed rail station. Already, a passenger can link by high-speed rail directly from Charles de Gaulle or Lyon to various regions of France.

Of course, it is an inescapable fact that in Europe high-speed rail is now a major competitor to the airlines. In 2001 in its first six months of operation, France's newest high-speed rail line from Paris to Marseille captured 60 percent of all air and rail traffic, up from the 40 percent of market share held previously by the conventional rail line.[17] Two years after the TGV line opened, the number of passengers using the Marseille airport dropped by 700,000. ("High-speed rail" in France is defined as trains that run at speeds over 186 miles per hour.) Back in 1991 when Germany introduced high-speed trains, Lufthansa shut down its Hanover-to-Frankfurt route, and in 2001 Air France's route from Paris to Brussels was discontinued because of a new rail line. According to the chair of the rail company SNCF International, the shorter the journey time by train, the larger the rail market share is.[18] In general, the airlines have found it difficult to compete with trains for journeys up to three hours.[19]

Unfortunately, today polarized politics and good guy–bad guy scenarios all too often replace complex processes for determining the long-term common good for legitimate planning. In the cast of characters in our local drama it is easy to identify the stereotypes. If you live in Lexington, the good guys are the community, its civil advocates, and their elected representatives, while the bad guys are the airline and Massport. On the other hand, if you are the airline industry, the good guys are the entrepreneurs breaking into a new market and the state officials who support them in the name of "regionalization," while the bad guys are obstructionist communities who won't accept their fair share of suffering in the name of progress. As a Shuttle America spokesman said on a Boston television program, people opposing commercial development at Hanscom are "hysterical, not historical, and elitist, not environmentalist." [20] And so the level of debate declines.

As a matter of national policy, citizens have long expected that their government would keep powerful and monopolistic industries in check. We have seen here in Massachusetts that this is unlikely. Our elected state representatives are not powerless in the long run, but when it comes to aviation expansion today, our state executive office and Massport hold the trump cards. In a state in which the Clean Elections Law passed by the voters has been all but overturned by the legislature, the laws that govern commercial-community relations will continue to reflect the existing power structure.

To hope that the federal government will step in where the state has been co-opted flies in the face of many forces. Citizens faced with aviation pollution have turned to their government for answers and have been rebuffed. It is too expensive, they are told, to protect communities with effective antinoise laws. The country has come late to rail, they hear, and now population density makes it so difficult as to be impractical. As to clean air, or for that matter global warming, well, first you need to prove there is a problem.

Citizens have turned to civil organizations for help. When we have a problem in our community, we count on these organizations to significantly supplement the efforts of our government. A disaster, and they are there. An injustice, and they are speaking out.

Were government citizens' only voice, our only means of empowerment, our democracy would be less effective. American communities are grounded in their civil society, the population of
organizations that serve the dual purposes of service and advocacy.
A healthy civil society is essential to maintaining and enhancing
our participation and our well-being; it is a crucial building block
of a democratic nation.

Yet, activist groups that have been trying to contain aviation
expansion and pollution have learned that relying on civil organizations has significant limitations. For one thing, civil organizations
are designed to protest, not to compete. Volunteer organizations
tend to be reactive rather than proactive. Volunteers' time is
severely limited. Issues are complex. Activists burn out.

Again, while the aviation industry plays offense, communities
play defense.

While the industry focuses on only its own interests, communities handle many diverse problems.

While the industry can act quickly, communities operate
slowly.

While the industry can work secretly, communities must
work openly.

While the industry is on the job full-time, citizens volunteer
part-time and mostly on nights and weekends.

While the industry can direct its troops, communities operate
on hard-won consensus: Some citizens don't care about having an
airport in their town as long as it is not in their backyard. Some
citizens are hard of hearing. Some are indifferent to the next
town's water supply. Some work for the aviation interests. Some
prefer to vote with their feet.

For another thing, the aviation industry has far more, and
different, resources than the activist community organizations. The
ability to wage expensive public relations campaigns is one example.
Through their staff of public relations professionals, government
agencies like Massport have a broad opportunity to shape public
opinion, in part by defining "the public interest" in relation to

aviation. In Massachusetts, whenever the development of a third runway at Logan or of commercial airline traffic at Hanscom is mentioned, Massport repeats its case that by expanding airports they are serving the interests of customers. At one point, the agency even developed a public relations campaign supporting Logan expansion by inviting passengers who have experienced Logan delays to go to their Web site and "weigh in on this debate" by adding their name and comments below a prechecked box that says, "I support Runway 14/32."[21] Civil organizations, on the other hand, have small public relations budgets and rely heavily on local media.

The struggle to define the public's interest in aviation is an important one not just in our own country. It is playing out currently in Great Britain in a dispute over the value of landing slots (the right to land at a particular airport at a particular time). Airport activists in London believe that landing slots should be treated as a public asset just like the broadcast frequencies. They argue that the true value of the slots is not appreciated, and that the question of who actually owns landing slots has not been properly addressed legally. Meanwhile, the airlines argue that their property rights have been grandfathered in, and that to require any airline to give up slots would be irrational, unfair, and *against the public interest.*[22]

The airline industry also holds the public's attention with its classic free-market argument that its own development is essential to interstate commerce, ignoring the larger contexts of multimodal approaches and environmental accountability. The drive to laissez-faire capitalism has captured the minds, or the pocketbooks (we cannot be sure which), of national and international leaders, and of many citizens. In many quarters the globalization of commercial endeavors and the attendant disruption not only of labor and local markets but of communities is widely accepted as inevitable. So when powerful organizations argue that protecting interstate commerce is necessary for the greater good, even if some communities must suffer because of it, many citizens

acquiesce. For another thing, complex arguments about pollution
and global warming, about community participation and empowerment, have a hard time competing in the mass media with concrete, sound-bite concerns like flight delays, safety, and cheap seats.

Finally, paradoxically, our very confidence in our civil society
weakens it. Well-meaning citizens may assume that while they are
doing their part over here, others in the community are doing
their part over there. Citizens choose service over advocacy. In
Lexington and the three other towns that abut our airfield there
are at least four organizations concerned about airport expansion,
including two volunteer citizens groups and two legally constituted watchdog groups. Some may imagine that with all of these
organizations, someone is taking care of the problem, right? We
can count on them, and of course our government, to represent
the community, can't we?

Unfortunately, as we have seen here, this wishful thinking
belies the reality. As a community, as a nation of communities, we
have not quite grasped that to be involved is not necessarily to be
influential, or that to be wealthy is not necessarily to be powerful.
Our civil organizations do a lot of necessary, important work, but
they are less powerful than we believe, hope, or know. The problem lies not in the commitment of hearts and minds, and not in
leadership, but in how well they can muster resources to get the
job done.

Given the nature and goals of the aviation industry, what will it
take for communities to survive, to maintain their quality of life?
Is paying attention to the threat and having strong defenses sufficient, or is a more aggressive stance necessary?

In the natural ecosystem, real skunks and real sharks employ
different tactics for survival within different niches, while in the
organizational ecosystem sharks and skunks compete directly for
the same resources. The aviation industry's major trade journal
has characterized the environmental lobby (us) as "militant,"[23] and
the president of the American Association of Airport Executives

has said the battle to increase airport capacity and to expand major airports "will be like Guadalcanal."[24] In this context, to improve our community's chances for environmental survival, the shark's tactics may be necessary tactics. Can we really argue to the contrary?

Visionary scientist Edward O. Wilson believes that one day we will be able to synthesize the social and natural sciences on a foundation of ethics, that ethics is the fundamental organizing principle of society. "Human social existence, unlike animal society, is based on the genetic propensity to form long-term contracts that evolve by culture into moral precepts and law," he writes. "The rules of contract formation . . . evolved over tens or hundreds of millennia because they conferred upon the genes prescribing them survival and the opportunity to be represented in future generations."[25] A moral ecosystem, Wilson asserts, would be based on full-cost accounting. "Competitive indexes and gross domestic products . . . remain seductive, not to be messed up in conventional economic theory by adding the tricky complexities of environment and social cost. The time has come for economists and business leaders, who so haughtily pride themselves as masters of the real world, to acknowledge the existence of the *real* real world. New indicators of progress are needed to monitor the economy, wherein the natural world and human well-being, not just economic production, are awarded full measure."[26]

Which is correct—the gentler assumptions and outcomes of Wilson's ethical universe, with leaders in all civil and business organizations willing to account for environmental and other well-being concerns, or the harsher assumptions and realities of the sharks and the skunks? Is there a middle ground? What assumptions about survival does a community make, must a community make, and do we have the skills of empathy and civil debate to ferret these out?

Consider that communities exist within a worldwide ecosystem of organizations, an interlocking network of coalitions and connections that amass power through information and resources.

In this ecosystem, communities live side by side with other organizations of all kinds—a variety of other communities, businesses large and small, governments at varying levels, unions, law firms, multinationals, religions, and so on. All of these organizations compete for power on regional, national, and international levels. In this scenario, natural selection will favor communities that pay close attention to their environment. In particular, it will favor those that are especially alert to indications of threat and can be proactive.

A main reason why communities across America have failed to protect themselves from the major impact of commercial air traffic is that they were never designed to do so. Communities are not designed to defend themselves against special interests with global reach.

In a nation that prides itself on its individual freedoms, citizens in the path of aviation expansion are asking the question, "The freedom to do what?" Their ability to sleep in their homes has been preempted. If they choose to move, their ability to predict which places are secure from aviation expansion has been obscured. Their ability to protect their children's schools from noise, jet fuel pollution, and the threat of crashes has been preempted. Their voice in determining for themselves the balance between residential and commercial values in their communities has been preempted. The question communities face now is whether they can reinvent themselves sagely enough and quickly enough to fight back and to assure their quality of life and effective participation in government. As citizens we must get beyond our ignorance, get beyond our time constraints, get beyond our belief that we personally will win in the end, get beyond our preoccupation with concerns that are literally more visible, get beyond our own emotional reactions to power—in order to investigate, to communicate, to strategize and act together for more representation.

How do communities become more competitive? Being clear about assumptions lays the foundation. Is growth inevitable? Often local residents assume that the development of their airport cannot be stopped. The authors of the influential book *To Empower People: From State to Civil Society* advise:

> A strong argument can be made that the dynamics of moder-
> nity, operating through the mega structures and especially
> through the modern state, are like a great leviathan or steam-
> roller, inexorably destroying every obstacle that gets in the way
> of creating mass society. There is much and ominous evidence
> in support of that argument. While we cannot predict the out-
> come of this process, we must not buckle under to alleged
> inevitabilities. On the more hopeful side are indications that the
> political will of the American people is beginning to assert itself
> more strongly in resistance to "massification."[27]

Another assumption we must examine is the notion that the government sits at the top of a pyramid of power in which citizens and their civil organizations comprise the base and the fundamental force. Critics have long debated whether civil society really does pose a countervailing force to government. Many citizens assume that it does, yet certainly the story of aviation expansion shows that our civil organizations, from the self-organized and self-financed volunteers right on up to the legally constituted oversight groups, however strategically savvy and hardworking they may be, have so far failed to prevent the growth and/or commercialization of most airports, or indeed, to regain the legal powers that in recent decades have been lost.

In this struggle, local civil organizations have several clear tasks. One is to clarify, and to explicitly publicize, the links to power that citizens do and *do not* have. Citizens must know, for example, that an agency like the Hanscom Field Advisory Commission has no power beyond the power of informing. They must know whether calling the noise line is worth their time. They must know how federal laws regulating the airline industry get passed. Issues-oriented civil organizations must continue to do

their utmost to expose special interest influence on government to
public scrutiny.

Further, activist organizations can educate citizens about the
historic background of local issues. For example, much of the
story of Hanscom Field happened before many of us moved here,
and there is no accessible, written analysis of our local history.
We count on our newspapers to keep us informed, but even good
reportage is not enough to paint the full picture that we urgently
need. Daily newspapers do not systematically review history,
the evolution of community values, or the law, although perhaps
they should.

If in 1997 I had talked to more locals before I purchased my
home, I would have gotten such a mixture of viewpoints that I am
sure I would not have discovered any significant risks. Even had I
made a point of talking with local activists, I would have learned
that we had not had an airline for many years and that Massport
and the communities were actively working on an agreement to
limit airport growth. I would certainly not have learned that
commercialization of the airport was possible. Remember, even
the local state representatives, including the senator who sat on the
state committee on transportation, did not know that commercialization was imminent. There was no conceivable way that I, an
average citizen, could have predicted the sudden change. In fact,
before buying his home one local and enterprising lawyer had
looked up the state environmental impact statement and read that
there were no impacts from the airport. Only after moving in did
he learn the truth that he was in a noisy flight path. So communities desperately need a deeper level of information. We do not
need the local equivalent of the *Wall Street Journal,* which provides
good coverage of top events but seldom follows a story over time,
but rather the in-depth and background coverage provided in a
magazine like the *Economist,* and we need this information on the
local level.

Civil organizations must also be aware of their own processes
and impacts. Today solutions to environmental problems require

extensive technical and legal expertise, and in recent decades local groups have come to depend on national activist organizations that have become increasingly professionalized. This is itself a form of centralization that puts power into the hands of more affluent communities. We must move forward in our understanding of these phenomena, clarifying and nurturing the relationship between communities and professional environmental activist groups on the one hand, and on the other hand, strengthening and empowering not only affluent but all communities.

Finally, communities need to consider whether their mix of charitable and advocacy civil organizations is strategic. Gone is the luxury of assuming that any volunteer activity is a good activity. Historians, sociologists, and tyrants all agree that civil society is an essential component of democratic systems. When it is rendered irrelevant, a community faces great costs in quality of life, and in basic freedoms. Individual citizens need to reflect upon which volunteer activities are crucial and which are merely self-indulgent. Ultimately, this decision may prove to be just as important as selecting a voting lever.

10

Aviation with Representation

Freedom is participation in power.
　　—Cicero

No aviation without representation.
　　—Jay Kaufman, state representative,
　　Lexington, Massachusetts

Since we, the community, do not like the way things are, what is it that we want? What would *aviation with representation* look like?

In general, new airports will be placed where it makes sense to put them, far from urban and suburban centers, with easy access to public transportation. Growth of many older airports will be capped, and in some cases use will be rolled back to livable limits. Enforceable standards will be put in place to ensure that these limits will never be exceeded. Some existing airports in residential areas will be closed. Trains and other relatively environmentally friendly transportation will replace air traffic whenever feasible. When rail corridors are developed, procedures will be developed to ameliorate local impacts, including avoiding the growth purgatory experienced by airport neighbors.

We will adopt the policy to encourage investment in transportation modes based in part on their environmental sustainability. High-speed rail is superior to both planes and cars in terms of energy expenditure.[1] It will receive preferential funding by state and federal government. Nontransportation modes of access such as telecommuting will also receive incentives.

More specifically, the current incremental development of airports will be replaced by responsible long-term transportation planning. This means that we must encourage legislators to develop long-range transportation agendas. Communities need to know where they stand. They should not be subjected to decades of ambiguities, misrepresentations, and pollution only to discover that no remedy will ever be forthcoming. Having unambiguous, long-term plans lets everyone, not just the state agencies that hold the cards, not just the special interests pushing their agendas, make rational decisions about their property and goals. Of course, this is true for any transportation change that affects residential and community life, including the development of railroads and roads. When it comes to aviation, such planning is something our communities want, expect, and deserve, but currently have no legal right to.

Political and agency leadership will be in the hands of those who have demonstrated their ability to represent not just one but a diverse set of stakeholders. We should not forget that industry power structures impact businesses as well as communities. Some businesses receive favorable government treatment, and some do not. Some businesses are protected by state agencies and policies, and some are not. It is bad for business, particularly small business, when the responsibility of the state to the community is operationalized solely as responsibility of the state to the aviation interests in that community. At some point small-scale aviation operations are pushed out of airports by large-scale operations. At some point the need for extraordinarily large subsidies of one industry over another simply cannot be supported.

The leadership of our state governments—in particular governors and secretaries of transportation—have to be committed to transportation planning and competent to administer it. They have to be able to work with the federal government. The leadership of our state agencies should be able to balance community, environmental, and commercial interests. Public agencies sometimes eschew public planning because they believe projects can be stopped early by small groups of activists. Leaders need to be skillful enough to balance the community's need to know and the government's responsibility to tell them.

Planning will be based on clear assumptions about growth. The aviation industry's model of the future admires unfettered growth, while a community model does not. Yet if the community concedes that dumb growth is inevitable and the problems associated with it are intransigent, if it fails to aggressively assert its values, narrow business interests will define the plan and dominate by default.

Plans for transportation systems will be multimodal. This includes the possibility of direct links between modes. In New England, for example, the mayor of Boston has called for a commission to study this possibility, and former governor Dukakis has called for a summit of the region's governors, mayors, and transportation planners to discuss links between rail and air.[2] Two decades ago Dukakis spearheaded Amtrak's new high-speed Boston–New York rail service, which will be linked to T. F. Green Airport in Providence with a moving sidewalk. In eastern Massachusetts, other obvious intramodal links locally are a bus line that would connect the Worcester Airport with the Worcester railroad station, and Boston commuter lines that could be extended to Manchester Airport in New Hampshire.

Nationwide we will do much more with rail. Since approximately one-third of all flights out of American airports are for 350 miles or less, it would be reasonable to emphasize rail transportation on these, and indeed on other short hauls up to perhaps 500 miles, or any journey of three hours or less. Such a policy would be especially reasonable where population is dense. This planning innovation would also free up airport slots for longer plane trips, which would be a benefit as long as planes and airports are subject to appropriate pollution monitoring.

The economic reality is that the high-speed rail link between Boston and New York is a competitor to the airlines. Where our elected local leadership fails to negotiate reasonable tradeoffs, the federal government will mandate coordinated planning of these assets. The Federal Aviation Administration Reauthorization Act of October 1996 included new provisions that require the secretary of transportation to cooperate with state and local officials to ensure that airport planning is coordinated with other state and local planning. More should be done to strengthen this process.[3]

For at least some airports, growth will be capped. In those types of communities in which high human impact areas already surround their small airports, control of the airports should be returned to the local people and they should be allowed to say no to growth without dire federal reprisals like the loss of FAA funding.

More defensive powers should be granted to those communities that will be newly affected by the development of a large airport nearby. Instead of requiring communities to sit passively by and watch the pollution mount, the federal government should require the FAA and the air transportation industry to demonstrate that more flights will not cause harm. Laws that aim at preventing harmful effects of incremental growth should be strengthened.

As to the specific monitoring of environmental concerns, regulations will be written to protect communities instead of industries and the government. An independent EPA will monitor and control airplane emissions and ground pollution using regulations that do not change radically from administration to administration.

Noise laws will be rewritten. First, nighttime curfews will be adopted nationwide. At night any single event over 45 dB (indoors) should be prohibited. Second, we will adopt a new metric or metrics for measuring airplane noise. Replace the Ldn with a measure that more fully accounts for the disruptive influence of single noise events. As an interim step, instead of using the current decibel measure that is sensitive to low-level sounds (A-weighted), use the one that is more reflective of our hearing at the 80 dB range (C-weighted) and that is already on most sound-level meters. Eventually switch to the measure that best accounts for low frequency sounds like aircraft engines. Third, all pilots will be required to be instrument rated so they can be required to fly at a minimum altitude of 3,000 feet. Fourth, any notion of supersonic transport over populated areas—such as the idea of developing a fleet of private supersonic jets that would fly coast to coast—will be rejected. Finally, we will close the loophole for aircraft under 75,000 pounds: Stage Three sound-level requirements currently do not apply to these small planes, including jets.

Noise will be measured in terms that all citizens can understand. Average noise figures, for example, will not be presented in decibels, but in a new, simplified metric. Communities also want to know the amount of time during the day that aircraft noise exceeds a certain threshold (a metric known as "Time Above"). Modeling of noise contours will be a well-defined and open process; all parameters, assumptions, and data will be disclosed and justified. There are good arguments on both sides of the case for returning decisions about airport development to the state and community level. The central argument for co-opting communities' ability to limit noise has been that dealing with a variety of noise standards can be confusing and limiting and thus detrimental to commerce. On the other hand, noise regulations are only one component of an already complex set of factors that make up a flight plan or a delivery schedule, and many places in the world have managed both economic viability and noise curfews.

The issues surrounding air and ground pollution are similar to those of noise pollution. Responsibility for monitoring pollution should be taken from the FAA and returned to the EPA, assuming that the EPA will actually be directed by the current administration in power to do the job. The ability of states to monitor pollution varies widely, and many lack the resources—skills or budgets—to do it adequately. This does not mean there could not be local regulation, too, but the federal government must set a floor for standards.

It will be widely publicized and understood that proposals to shift funding for airport improvement projects to passenger facility charges and other user fees only lead to further disenfranchisement of communities. User fees will be rejected in favor of funding through government appropriations that all voters, not just passengers, can influence.

A demand management strategy will encourage the industry to use and develop more efficient aircraft and to use existing aircraft more efficiently. As the European Union is recommending, the industry needs financial incentives that would encourage airline companies to consolidate flights, reduce engine idling, and improve per-capita fuel efficiency.[4] For example, raising ticket prices for flights at peak times will encourage airlines to use bigger planes and encourage consumers to alter their travel plans. In addition, the purchase of fuel for aviation should be taxed. (This will require overturning an international agreement, the 1944 Chicago Convention, that bans this practice.) The ticket tax that individuals pay currently should be abolished, and taxes should be charged instead to companies on such polluting components of aviation as take-offs, landings, low approaches, and flying during sensitive hours. A middle ground would be to retain the ticket tax in the short term but use it only for FAA safety improvement and noise abatement, abolishing its current use to fund the expansion of airport infrastructures.

When agencies discuss aviation safety, they will routinely include the needs of people on the ground as well as passengers. All planes, including general aviation, will be under FAA flight controls at all times. To allay fears about planes flying low over homes and schools, student pilots will not be allowed to practice over congested areas. To give pilots time to react to emergencies, small planes will be required to maintain minimum altitudes of 3,000 feet.

In the wake of September 11, a major safety concern for communities is safety from attack. Given that a plane travels roughly 100 miles in twelve minutes, government should consider banning all nonscheduled commercial and general aviation within a 100-mile radius of such sensitive sites as nuclear power plants. It should also ban unscheduled commercial and general aviation over large cities. Passenger planes should carry no cargo other than people and their personal luggage. Not only will these policies protect, they will have the additional impact of reducing pollution in high-density areas. If the federal government fails to do these things, states should seek the power to do them.

Finally, public organizations will be held accountable for their implementation of any of these plans. Electing effective representatives is a step in the right direction, but hardly a solution. State representatives, in particular, handle a multiplicity of issues on meager budgets. In an ideal world, they would be able to assign a full staff to each pressing concern, but this is seldom possible. Moreover, our representatives are themselves embedded in a system, compelled to be loyal to their party's line on one issue so they can push forward the community's agenda on another issue. They must build coalitions over time. They cannot introduce bills with such frequency as to lose credibility. They literally must consider the common good. As predators go, they are slow and only modestly productive.

Today the plight of American communities near airports shows clearly that accountability cannot be left to the ballot box alone. By the time citizens and their elected representatives realize the gravity of an issue like the commercialization of their airport, much damage has already been done and momentum is in favor of the aviation industry. It is clear that to get the all-important lead on communities, government agencies will distort the truth. More accountability of state agencies to their legislatures is necessary. So-called "independent" state agencies like Massport will be redesigned to include citizen watchdog organizations. Legally constituted citizen oversight groups must have budgetary and policy-making powers. Agency members may be required to live in the areas their planning affects, just as municipalities often require their employees to live within their boundaries.

Government can be required to be more accessible, as well. Every representative, and every arm of the government, should be required to have a Web site concerned not merely with public relations and the administration of services but with presentation of essential data and discussion of the agency's position on wider transportation issues. Every citizen should be able to get fundamental information documents free with the click of a mouse.

Local advocacy organizations can do part of the job of generally informing citizens. Advocacy organizations with a national mission include the Noise Pollution Clearinghouse, United States–Citizens Aviation Watch, and NOISE. National environmental groups with strong legal resources and aligned interests include the Natural Resources Defense Council, Common Cause, the Sierra Club, and the Conservation Law Foundation.

In the end, as Robert Reich has pointed out, when every argument turns into a debate over the relative merits of centralized planning versus a decentralized market, "we lose the capacity to design the market in accordance with our values."[5]

After all, designing the market in accordance with our values is what no taxation without representation was about in the first place.

In our country it is risky to be labeled antigrowth. When our probusiness culture is at its knee-jerk worst, to be labeled a NIMBY is the highest form of mockery. The "not in my back-yard" phenomenon may have originated in real estate lore, in which city dwellers, having bought homes in the pretty countryside, try to preserve their open space by preventing further development. They do this by changing the zoning laws, or buying up land for public use, or challenging developers' permits. Who prevails depends on connections, money, knowledge, and power . . . in short, on politics.

The NIMBY label is a favorite bludgeon with which to hit airport communities, especially suburban ones. Let us take a closer look at it.

Suppose that a family considers buying a house in a new subdivision next to a large cornfield. They look out at the cornfield and think that some day it will become a subdivision, too, and that they will lose some of the open spaces that make their homes desirable, but they buy the house anyhow. Lo and behold, the field is indeed transformed, not into a subdivision, but into a foul pig farm. The homeowners complain: we don't want a pig farm in our backyard! NIMBY!

Do the homeowners have a right to complain because they never imagined the pig farm? Is justice served if they have to live next to the pig farm? Is it smart that a community should be designed with pig farms next to families?

While onlookers debate these abstractions, the locals are in an uproar. The new homeowners organize their whole subdivision, which pickets the farm and organizes a local boycott against pork. The farmer asserts that pork farming is essential to the local economy, citing how many people he employs and how much business he brings to local merchants.

Who is to blame for the problem in this community? Perhaps the bureaucrats down at the local planning board. Maybe they thought that having a farmer's field next to a subdivision was a reasonable usage mix, but failed to predict that such a valuable piece of real estate might actually be turned into a pig farm. Or perhaps one should blame the homeowners, who may have lacked sufficient imagination to predict such a dire change. Or perhaps the farmer is at fault for keeping his business plan to himself. Whoever caused the problem—and perhaps all were equally culpable—the upshot is that the community is now a miserable place to live, while the pig farm prospers on outside business.

All want a fair solution. Here are some choices. (1) Raze either the houses or the pig farm. (This solution depends on who has more political clout.) (2) Relocate either the homes or the pig farm to a more compatible setting, with government subsidies. (After all, the government's planning lacked imagination.) (3) Change the pig farm operation—make it smaller or better—so that it does not impact the homeowners. (After all, the farmer should run a nonpolluting operation.) (4) Leave things as they are, and let the homeowners suffer. (After all, they were dumb enough to move there in the first place.)

Those who dismiss the complaints of people who live near airports as mere NIMBY selfishness are choosing the last option: to simply let people suffer. And the notion that the homeowners should be forced to sacrifice for the greater good is no more than a rationalization for that irresponsibly simplistic choice.

Thankfully, in our country, for most issues, forums exist in which such local conflicts can be publicly played out. The homeowners and the farmer can battle it out at the local planning board. Unfortunately, in the case of airport expansion, such public forums do not exist, and such forums as there are are increasingly being neutralized.

The federal government, as demonstrated in its overwhelmingly proaviation laws and regulations, has taken the simplistic position that this community antigrowth stuff just has to be squashed, that in the face of the need for commercial expansion communities will be sacrificed.

Let us for a moment take a hopeful stance and consider what would happen if the communities were to prevail. Suppose all communities with airports currently in their midst were successful in containing the growth of that airport. What terrible thing would happen?

Market forces would kick in. There would be fewer choices in flight times as airlines worked harder to fly full. Probably the price of tickets would go up at first, and for their shorter trips people would seek cheaper forms of transportation. Trains and buses would see their ridership go up, and businesses and governments would pay more attention to developing them, earning them more government subsidies, lowering their prices, and improving their services. The United States would develop a good high-speed train system, as they have in Europe, and importantly, having this system in place would enhance the transportation security of the country.

In the face of competition from other modes, the price of airline tickets would drop to a competitive level.

Is this a doomsday scenario? Or is it a reasonable shifting of resources, a new and better vision for transportation in this country?

Back home in our communities we have to face the facts of urban sprawl and degradation. If the airport degrades our city or town, where are we going to move next? The frontier is gone. On average, individuals are not making any more money today than they did twenty-five years ago. We aspire to do so, we might do so, but statistically, on average, we won't. And our children won't either.[6] So in the future only a few of us will be able to escape our newly degraded town for a more exclusive suburb. Here in the inner suburbs of Boston, if adding airport traffic to an already clogged and degraded Route 128 corridor does not actually drive out high-technology companies, it will hurt them because none of their employees will want to live nearby anymore. Some employees who move out to the farthest suburbs will be able to stomach the commute back into the corridor, but they won't be likely to go there on weekends.

Former governor Michael Dukakis shapes these growth concerns this way:

> I cannot think of a worse place to put a commercial airport than Hanscom. I say this not because I am more sensitive to the concerns of people in the suburbs than I am about urban communities. On the contrary, anyone who knows me and has followed my career knows how deeply I feel about urban communities and their residents.
>
> That is precisely why I think Hanscom is the wrong place for commercial aviation and why a combination of the Providence, Worcester, and Manchester airports plus high-speed rail service to New York and Washington are so much better. Encouraging commercial flights out of Hanscom encourages sprawl . . . 128 is a moving parking lot at five in the afternoon. Providence, Worcester, and Manchester all hold out the

opportunity for air-rail connections that cannot only get passengers to and from those airports quickly and safely but can
dramatically reduce congestion on the already overcrowded
interstate system.

In short, promoting and expanding high-speed rail service in
the Northeast Corridor and encouraging growth at three regional
airports that serve three important older urban communities
makes all kinds of sense. Allowing or encouraging expanded
commercial aviation at Hanscom makes no sense at all.[7]

In the war against urban sprawl, airports in residential neighborhoods are a major battlefield.

I must admit that the powerlessness of communities in the face of
the air transportation industry concerns me beyond the issue itself.
Today I count myself a fortunate person to know a bit about how
important freedom really is. I have experienced elsewhere in the
world the less democratic direction in which our country could
go, and I worry.

Brian O'Connell, author of numerous books on civil society,
has observed:

> Here in our privileged setting we don't know what we've got
> or how much it takes to hold onto it. . . .[8]
>
> . . . Through all my hopefulness, I must still confront the
> awful question of whether this democracy will survive another
> century and maybe beyond. No other democracy has lasted as
> long as ours, so we cannot assume that ours will just keep
> rolling on. . . .
>
> I find myself worrying what the consequences would be if
> in the course of the new century we experience a worsening of
> such factors as selfishness, taking liberty for granted, govern-
> mental limits on citizen participation, the influence of special
> interests on public officials, separation between the haves and
> the have-nots, intolerance, and incivility. *How much deterioration*

of our civil society would it take to weaken democracy irreparably?[9]
(Italics added.)

In America today, if I observe that our citizens are apathetic,
I am "that learned professor." Yet, if I assert that our citizens are
powerless, I am "that radical." Such are our habits of mind. We
need to speak the truth more readily, and to apply our theories
more specifically, if we are to regain power for our communities.

Given the size of the world today—the sheer numbers of
people and organizations—civil society, from activist groups to
charities, is more psychologically important than ever before. It
has become a major mechanism by which individuals feel connected to humanity whether or not they actually achieve power
through that connection.

Our civil organizations have practical importance. Poised
between people and their governments, they have enormous
potential for influence, but their potential may be waning.

As I have worked on this book, we have celebrated here
in Lexington the 225th anniversary of the beginning of the
Revolutionary War. I could hear the guns going off in the distance
all through town, and I imagined what it must have been like to
sit here on a little plot of land as a farmer's wife, waiting, not
knowing whether my husband was alive or dead. Meanwhile,
overhead, great jets saluted the heroes of that war.

Today there is no standing army to fight. We are thankful for
this, of course. But at least throwing the bums out was an obvious
solution. As local people face up to a powerful interest like the
air transportation industry, their solutions are, at the very least,
less clear.

As I sit here in my garden, hoping to preserve local rights, this
is what I believe.

We citizens have looked away. The power brokers know this,
they know how to pull the levers of influence, and the stories of
airport development in communities across the country show
how much they can accomplish. Over the long term the game

is being set up to block the average citizen out of democratic participation through administrative and legal vehicles that work primarily for the industry.

Our democracy depends on an educated citizenry, capable of evaluating their own assumptions about what is workable and unworkable both socially and economically for the country and the world community. It depends on citizens who understand the system of business and special interests, government and civil society. It depends on citizens who know the law, who can detect the difference between good law and bad law, and who, through their representatives, can actually influence the law.

Aviation does many wonderful things, but being fair to its neighbors on the ground is not one of them. We must ensure that in communities basic human rights are established and protected. Among these must be the right to a peaceful, quiet, safe community and an environment free of pollutants. It is simply unacceptable to take unquantified risks with our lives and with the lives of our children.

Further, in a hostile organizational world, communities must be more than vigilant. They have to be aggressive. They have to be willing to focus on flawed laws and processes, on the country's governmental integrity, and what it takes to maintain it.

We must tend to our civil organizations—from grassroots activist groups to legally constituted watchdog organizations. We must know the limitations of their power. We must understand how they can be used and manipulated by larger, remote, and powerful governments and organizations. In general, the balance of local and corporate power to define community life, now tipped in favor of corporations, must be tipped back toward the community.

How will we know that we have succeeded?

Election campaigns will be funded more by citizens and less by industries. While today most charitable giving—almost 90 percent—comes from individuals, and most political giving comes from corporations,[10] these numbers will be reversed.

More citizens will use more of their volunteer time for advocacy.

Local aviation activists will become international aviation activists.

We will all be able to sleep through the night, untrammeled by dog, fowl, or flight.

11

How to Work for Sustainable Aviation

With powerful business interests on one side and citizens with a personal stake but little leverage on the other, success is surviving to fight the next battle.

—Peter D. Enrich, activist and law professor

The fight may be local, but the battle is in Washington, DC.

—United States–Citizens Aviation Watch

WHAT COMMUNITIES want is, simply, detection of, and protection from, the various kinds of pollution created by airplanes and airports. These include climate change, noise pollution, air pollution, ground pollution, and the loss of landscape, heritage, and wildlife. As a nation we will be better off if we face aviation pollution head-on rather than disguise the issue in arcane regulations that foster community cynicism and increase distrust of government.

The reason why pollution protections are not in place right now is because the aviation industry and those it supports in our legislatures don't want them to be in place. The industry wants to run itself without regulation, perhaps because it believes in unfettered competition on principle, because constraints are simply a pain in the neck, or because it has to compete in a world market in which pollution controls are unevenly applied. Another reason we lack controls is that some legislators have been persuaded that current policies are adequate. Another is that imposing controls would incur costs. Going forward, communities must meet each of these arguments more fully and clearly than we have to date. A variety of different perspectives can be tapped using the list of resources on aviation and the environment in appendix B.

This book has been an introduction to the environmental and political realities surrounding aviation expansion. The laws and the science surrounding aviation and transportation are enormously complicated, and it is indeed likely that some professionals will spend their entire careers on just one aspect. To get a further flavor for the administrative as well as the legal and scientific complexity, try reading *Controlling Airport-Related Air Pollution* by the Center for Clean Air Policy and the Northeast States for Coordinated Air Use Management.[1] What the states have the legal right to do, given federal curbs on their power, is nuanced and untried. The scientific measures of pollution that the EPA uses are debatable. Administrative coordination is complex.

In looking to the federal government for relief it will be important to push simultaneously for pollution controls and for more sustainable transportation alternatives like rail. Part of the challenge will be to publicize the realities of transportation subsidies. Rail is typically referred to as "subsidized," while aviation, which receives the lion's share of federal money, is seldom described as "subsidized." The fact is that in 2001, prior to September 11, Congress spent $33 billion on highways, $12 billion on airports, and only $521 million on passenger rail, and more than a third of the rail money went to a railroad industry retirement fund.

Depending on one's point of view, these subsidies may be seen as favorable treatment of a developing, strategic industry or as corporate welfare. In the history of our capitalist country, we have often determined that it is in the public interest to encourage one industrial sector for a while and later to rein it in. We are doing this currently with commercialization of the Internet, supporting it by not levying taxes now, while reserving the right to do so later. Some of the same political dynamics that have led to lax security at our airports have kept the important environmental impacts of aviation out of the national agenda. These include overdependence on private companies that are governed more by the bottom line than by the public interest; the enormous influence of the aviation industry in states, the Federal Aviation Administration, and Congress; and an unsuspecting public. We also know from experience that one outcome of laissez-faire capitalism is big business monopolies.[2] Today we are probably at that juncture when the aviation industry has too much power.

While continuing to pursue environmental controls at local airports, communities must avoid being caught up in day-to-day local protectionist tactics to the neglect of the national scene, where the most important laws are written. The National Air Transportation Association has called local communities "isolated groups of vocal airport opponents,"[3] and to some extent they are right. Citizens should act at the local level and the national level simultaneously.

At the local level, communities can learn from those few that have had success managing airport growth. Because the federal government has preempted the laws controlling air space, these communities have primarily used their right to control the development of the land occupied by their airport.

For a time it was thought that the agreement reached by the City of Chicago and the State of Illinois in 1997 to close Meigs Field Airport was such a local victory. A multistate coalition dedicated to preserving natural habitat and conserving land and water along the shores of Lake Michigan had recommended to the Chicago Park District that the land, aptly called Sanctuary Point, be converted into a nature preserve. Subsequently, this arrangement was undermined in a set of deals to expand O'Hare. Still later, the mayor of Chicago made Meigs Field famous by quietly ordering that it be bulldozed.

One success is the victory achieved in Florida eight years after a consortium of business interests attempted to develop Homestead Air Force Base into a major reliever airport that would have sent planes over Everglades and Biscayne National Parks. A political compromise brokered by the Clinton administration in 2001 stopped the development, and the air force offered Miami-Dade County 717 acres for nonaviation redevelopment while maintaining federal control over base runways and flights.[4]

Most recently, in March of 2002, the residents of Orange County in southern California rejected a plan to turn El Toro Marine base into a major airport. With 58 percent of the vote in a county referendum, residents ended an eight-year effort by their county to develop the site, which will now be sold off in pieces by the navy. They also turned the pro-airport county supervisor out of office.[5]

Yet, victories are few. If they do not own or administratively control their airports, communities must consider a variety of tactics, from micromanagement to strategic partnerships. At Westchester County Airport, to prevent Continental Express from abusing the voluntary curfew, which extends from midnight until 6:30 A.M., the airport simply closed its parking garage between 12:30 A.M. and 5:50 A.M. Here in Massachusetts, the National Park Service and the Advisory Council on Historic Preservation have entered into a published partnership with the U.S. Department of Transportation to protect Minute Man National Historical Park near Hanscom Field.

Communities should set ideal agendas for the future of their airports and strive to eradicate laws that are in their way. How large an airport is really sustainable? While working toward their ideal, they might pursue such specific goals as putting moratoriums on building more infrastructure, especially runways, until multimodal regional funding is a reality, and improving environmental laws and regulations that have failed to control incremental change, cumulative impacts, and urban sprawl. Looking to the future, states should consider instituting a plan for noise-free zones, areas in which there would be no overflights within ten miles and, on the ground, a ban on the use of noisy equipment. These zones might at first be our national parks and historic areas and other sensitive lands. Later, they could be residential and recreational areas.

Individuals can help in several ways. When choosing a mode of transportation, work to find an alternative to flying, which is the most polluting type. Remember that on a round-trip from New York to London, your Boeing 747 emits 440 tons of carbon dioxide, the same amount emitted by 80 SUVs in a full year of hard driving.[6] Try to limit your annual flying trips to two. Avoid flights that take off or land late at night or early in the morning when people are sleeping. Fly direct flights rather than connecting flights. If you have time to volunteer, consider advocacy.

We can support, and build on, efforts to protect national and state parks from noise pollution. As more Americans have become aware of noise in our national parks—from snowmobiles in Yellowstone to planes in the Grand Canyon to flyovers of Minute Man National Historical Park—the federal government has paid more attention to demands for regulation there. Natural areas that are currently under grave threat from airport expansion include, among many others, the Mammoth Lakes region of the Sierras, Grand Teton National Park, and Zion National Park. Susan Staples, an activist seeking to protect Minneskwa State Park and Reserve in New York, points out, "For us the issue has to do with having a reprieve from the noise and stress of metropolitan life. Here you hike three miles into this pristine place only to experience the relentless bombardment of jets approaching Newark, New Jersey, a hundred miles to the south. Natural quiet is a quality that has to be protected just like water or air."[7]

Certainly we must also pay attention to the power politics of the aviation industry. We have seen here that communities are hemmed in by national laws and practices. They are also outgunned by the industry's Washington lobby. In the period leading up to the 2002 elections, 65 percent of the money donated by the industry went to Republicans and 35 percent went to Democrats.[8] The influence of the industry's lobby was in evidence immediately after September 11, when the airlines used twenty-seven in-house lobbyists along with others from forty-two Washington firms to secure $15 billion in aid, $5 billion of which was in outright grants. Among the lobbyists were Linda Hall Daschle, wife of the Democratic Senate majority leader and a lobbyist for American Airlines, and Rebecca Cox, the wife of a Republican representative from California and a lobbyist for Continental Airlines. In crafting the aid package, "Pleas of organized labor to protect airline employees were pretty much ignored," according to the *New York Times.*[9] Later the industry came back for, and got, even more billions. Senator John McCain of Arizona opined, "If [the airlines] came back to the well a third time, they would not get my support no matter what the condition of the industry is."[10]

Given the environmental degradation in flight-path communities and the 130 percent rise in consumer complaints against the industry before September 11,[11] there are some indications that, at the federal level, the idea of more closely monitoring the industry is taking hold. In late 2000, the airline industry was subject to the first antitrust action brought against it since 1989 when the Justice Department challenged Northwest Airline's 55 percent voting control of Continental Airlines (the fourth- and fifth-largest American airlines) and examined the proposed acquisition by United Airlines parent UAL Corporation of US Airways Group (the first- and sixth-largest American airlines).[12] Reregulation— accomplished in the 1960s and again in the 1980s—has been suggested by several members of Congress.[13] In this context it makes no sense that the FAA should be turned into an autonomous profit-center like Massport, independent of regulatory agencies. Rather, the federal government should increase control of that agency to force it to focus on pollution and safety. To this end, it should close the revolving door between the aviation industry and the FAA.

Although it is beyond the scope of this book, it is not merely an afterthought that we should also oppose international efforts to impose ecologically unsustainable aviation standards and policies.

Internationally, subsidies for air transportation must be modified, and exemption from pollution controls must be ended.

We must do more to recognize that air space is a finite resource and to learn more about how to make aviation sustainable. We should encourage research—governmental, academic, and private—on the environmental costs of transportation. The report *The Plane Truth: Aviation and the Environment* asks the right questions. Authors John Whitelegg and Nick Williams challenge cherished assumptions made by both the aviation industry and aviation activists and suggest specific ways that the pollution costs of aviation can be made transparent and then carried by the polluter. For example, they point out that we need more data on aviation's hub-and-spoke system. While adding to airline profits, this system also doubles the number of landings and takeoffs for a given route. On the face of it, it would seem to be in the best interests of the public to create incentives for airlines to abandon this system, but more information is needed.

In the final analysis, people do indeed want to live in a community, not merely work in a market. In the next century, as the power of centralized, globalized businesses and governments increases, our ability to live in peace in our communities will be severely challenged.

As witnesses to the struggle of urban and suburban communities against the powerful aviation industry, we are also observing the development of an unprecedented power differential between individuals and governments, states and the federal government, and governments and corporations. Is this kind of centralization inevitable in a capitalist democracy, or will we be able to temper it in the interests of quality of life and our system of government?

Let us hope that, as a democratic nation of both corporations and individuals, we will find the wisdom to create balanced and enduring answers to our mutual concerns.

Epilogue

*It saddens me that, here in the twenty-first century, we
have to argue about preserving an area that includes the
first battlefields of the American Revolution, the celebrated
pond and woods that gave birth to the environmental
movement, and the homes of people who contributed to
our culture and literature in ways that still echo down the
corridors of our history. Massport says that the expansion
of Hanscom is "progress." But ignoring a historical legacy
is neither progress nor good economic development.*

    —Ken Burns, filmmaker

*If I were in your shoes, I would be doing exactly the
same thing.*

    —Comment to picketer from airline customer

IN APRIL 2000, the Federal Aviation Administration reauthorization bill—the Wendell H. Ford Aviation Investment and Reform
Act for the Twenty-first Century, signed by President Clinton—
opened up new slots at New York's LaGuardia Airport. Less than
seven months after the start of commercial operations at
Hanscom, Shuttle America applied to the federal Department of
Transportation for permission to begin flying to and from
LaGuardia with twelve flights a day and was approved. It initiated
service November 2, 2000, and soon had thirty-two operations
per day, four times the number of flights it had at the outset.

Next, US Airways announced that it would also apply for slots at Hanscom in order to service New York's LaGuardia Airport with seven daily round-trip flights.

The Aircraft Owners and Pilots Association, which represents the general aviation interests of 360,000 individual pilots and aircraft owners in the United States, asked the Hanscom Field Advisory Committee to send a letter to the FAA requesting that the FAA investigate Hanscom's nighttime user fee due to "the unreasonableness and unjustly discriminatory aspect of this airport access restriction."[1] The AOPA, which is often called the National Rifle Association of the aviation industry, argued that such restrictions should be based on noise, rather than weight. Their suit, if successful, would likely trigger an FAA Part 150 noise study, which will "discover" that, indeed, currently Hanscom does not meet the unreasonably high federal standard for abatement or mitigation. This would result in removal of all nighttime use restrictions at the airport. The AOPA has initiated a systematic national campaign to abolish the weight rule, filing similar suits at many other airports. If, in enough of these cases, weight as a criterion of exclusion is discarded in favor of noise, then weight itself will become suspect as a criterion for exclusion of an aircraft from an airport. It is entirely possible then that the courts would decide that larger, noisier passenger aircraft would have to be allowed.

Meanwhile, the superintendent of the Minute Man National Historical Park declared that despite her strong objections, the most recent state environmental impact report ignored the potential effects of airport expansion on the park. Indeed, the state's Generic Environmental Impact Report concluded that there would be no impacts on the park or to its rural character.[2] The communities near the Minute Man Park advised the FAA that under Section 106 of the National Historic Preservation Act, it must take into account the effect of Hanscom expansion on the historic properties. Save Our Heritage, ShhAir, and the local congressmen called for the secretary of the United States Department of the Interior to review under Section 106 any further increase in air traffic at Hanscom Field, and they now have taken Massport to court over this issue. While this lawsuit may be a seminal test of the effectiveness of the Historic Preservation Act, unfortunately, in the final analysis, the act mandates only that the federal government must follow certain reporting procedures. The regulations do not materially prevent Massport from going forward with its plans to develop the airfield.[3]

On April 18, 2000, the Hanscom Field Advisory Committee passed a resolution that would require Massport to give it ninety days to respond to any plans for the airport before implementing them. A committee member noted that it will probably take several years for this resolution to pass through the state legislature.

At the beginning of 2001, ShhAir received a letter from Joe and Vicky Bartolo (Joe is one of ShhAir's cofounders): "Today, January 29, 2001, we received your notice of the January 16 FAA presentation to extend the runway at Hanscom. We are sorry to read the bad news, but must confess, we got sick and tired of fighting the bureaucrats and so we decided to pack up and move. We had to move to regain peace and tranquility. After 35 years in Lexington, we feel we were forced out of the place where our family grew up, got educated and worshipped; and where the dream of a pleasant and peaceful retirement finally turned into a nightmare. . . . I feel we have fought these bureaucrats with peaceful means. Evidently that was not enough. I hope they remember history."[4]

In 2001, even before September 11, the national economy went into decline. On April 17, Shuttle America declared it was seeking bankruptcy protection but would continue to fly, and on the same day, Massport, in a blatant public relations effort, declared that three other airlines were also interested in flying out of Hanscom. Subsequently, one of the airlines also went bankrupt. US Airways, citing intense community opposition, decided not to start service after all but left its options open for the future. The third airline chose not to start service. At Hanscom the number of flights, and residents' noise complaints, temporarily declined.

Meanwhile, in Boston, the proposed new runway at Logan stayed on hold.

After the September 11 attacks, the air transportation industry went into an immediate decline, and at this writing is still recovering. Massport came under severe criticism for lax security at Logan Airport, and its security chief was reassigned to cover the Port of Boston. A gubernatorial commission was appointed to examine the design of Massport.

In October 2001, US Airways Express announced that Shuttle America would become one of its partnership carriers and would increase its flights out of Hanscom Field.

In 2002, the new runway in Boston was approved by the FAA, while the 1976 court injunction against it remained in effect. Late in 2003, a judge lifted the injunction, and Massport announced groundbreaking for spring of 2004.[5] The town of Hull is suing Massport for nuisance. As one citizen put it, "Hull High School is just bombed with planes."

In June of 2003, the National Trust for Historic Preservation, a government-mandated, privately funded organization that works to save historic sites and revitalize communities, named Minute Man National Historical Park and its environs near Lexington and Concord among the eleven most endangered historic places in the United States.

Late in 2003, the FAA reauthorization bill (Flight 100–Century of Aviation Reauthorization Act) signed by President Bush dramatically curtailed the role of the U.S. Environmental Protection Agency, the U.S. Fish and Wildlife Service, and the U.S. Army Corps of Engineers in monitoring airport expansion by requiring all federal and state agencies to be directed by the Secretary of Transportation whenever the acceleration of airport expansions is at issue. The Natural Resources Defense Council, Friends of the Earth, and others point out that the new law "shuts out other federal and state agencies with valuable expertise, weakens or eliminates essential checks and balances, and disenfranchises affected communities."[6]

In the end, there are two fundamental approaches to fighting aviation pollution. One is to play defense—to find out who owns the local airport and to analyze realistically what controls local citizens have over them. I hope this book has helped elucidate the issues that frame this approach, the most important of which seem to me to be incremental environment degradation, the hegemony of commercial interests, and the limitations of citizen involvement.

An additional, more far-reaching approach is to determine who controls the FAA and the EPA, indeed the federal government, and to determine how they can be influenced toward supporting sustainable transportation. This will require more resources, and greater national sophistication, than communities have at present. Yet, with homes and communities at stake across the nation, we shall find a way.

Appendix A

The Targeted 100 Smaller Airports
the Aviation Industry Wants to Expand

In December 2000 the National Air Transportation Association (NATA) published the following list of airports that it believes should be targeted for expansion. (Large commercial airports were not included.) "There are over 3,500 public use airports in the United States designated by the FAA to be eligible for federal funds," NATA wrote. "If America is going to have a truly national air transportation system, on par with the interstate highway system, we must identify the key airports and ensure that they are capable to meet the demands of a new century."

Inclusion on the list is based on expected demand for commercial and noncommercial aviation services, the existing or proposed "arbitrary limitations" on airport usage (such as curfews, noise restrictions, and slot controls), and "hostile political circumstances" (that is, "an organized public opposition to the airport").

AIRPORT	LOCATION
Addison	Dallas, TX
Airpark Dallas	Plano, TX
Albert Whitted	St. Petersburg, FL
Allentown Queen City Municipal	Allentown, PA
Altoona–Blair County	Altoona, PA
Anchorage Ted Stevens International	Anchorage, AK
Aspen–Pitkin County	Aspen, CO
Aurora Municipal	Aurora, Il
Bader	Atlantic City, NJ
Bismarck Municipal	Bismarck, ND
Blue Grass	Lexington, KY
Boca Raton	Boca Raton, FL
Boeing Field	Seattle, WA

179

AIRPORT	LOCATION
Boulder Municipal	Boulder, CO
Brainerd–Crow Wing County	Brainerd, MN
Brown Field	San Diego, CA
Burbank, Glendale, Pasadena	Burbank, CA
Casselton Regional	Casselton, ND
Centennial	Denver, CO
Chesapeake Regional	Chesapeake, VA
Chicago Meigs	Chicago, IL
Concord/Buchanan Field	Concord, CA
Dallas Love Field	Dallas, TX
Daugherty Field	Long Beach, CA
David Wayne Hooks	Spring, TX
Daytona Beach International	Daytona Beach, FL
Eagle County Regional	Eagle, CO
Elkhart Municipal	Elkhart, IN
Fargo Hector International	Fargo, ND
Fayetteville Regional	Fayetteville, NC
Flying Cloud	Minneapolis, MN
Fort Worth Meacham International	Fort Worth, TX
Frederick Municipal	Frederick, MD
Ft. Lauderdale Executive	Ft. Lauderdale, FL
Galveston Scholes Field	Galveston, TX
Genesee County	Batavia, NY
Georgetown Municipal	Georgetown, TX
Glenwood Springs Municipal	Glenwood Springs, CO
Grand Strand	North Myrtle Beach, SC
Greenville/Spartanburg	Greenville, SC
Greenwood Lake	West Milford, NJ
Gunnison County	Gunnison, CO
Hanscom	Boston, MA
Hawthorne	Hawthorne, CA
Hayward Executive	Hayward, CA
Hemet Ryan	Hemet, CA
Hickory Regional	Hickory, NC

AIRPORT	LOCATION
Hilton Head	Hilton Head Island, SC
Houston Southwest	Arcola, TX
Jackson	Jackson, WY
Johnson County Executive	Olathe, KS
Juneau International	Juneau, AK
Kansas City Downtown	Kansas City, MO
Lake Tahoe	South Lake Tahoe, CA
Lake Wales Municipal	Lake Wales, FL
Lantana	Lantana, FL
Leesburg Municipal	Leesburg, VA
Long Island MacArthur	Islip, NY
Mansfield Lahm	Mansfield, OH
Mid-way Regional	Midlothian, TX
Morristown Municipal	Morristown, NJ
Mount Comfort	Indianapolis, IN
Naples Municipal	Naples, FL
Oakland North	Oakland, CA
Oneida County	Utica-Rome, NY
Opa-Locka	Miami, FL
Ottumwa Industrial	Ottumwa, IA
Page Field	Fort Myers, FL
Palwaukee	Wheeling, IL
Peachtree-Dekalb	Atlanta, GA
Pearson Field	Vancouver, WA
Penn Yan–Yates County	Penn Yan, NY
Portland/Hillsboro	Hillsboro, OR
Prescott Municipal	Prescott, AZ
Reid/Hillview	San Jose, CA
Renton Municipal	Renton, WA
Republic	Farmingdale, NY
Richards-Gebaur Memorial	Kansas City, MO
Riverside Municipal	Riverside, CA
San Carlos	San Carlos, CA
Santa Barbara Municipal	Santa Barbara, CA

AIRPORT	LOCATION
Santa Monica Municipal	Santa Monica, CA
Sikorsky Memorial	Bridgeport, CT
Skypark Memorial	Woods Cross, UT
Solberg	Readington, NJ
South Jersey Regional	Lumberton, NJ
Spirit of St. Louis	St. Louis, MO
Stewart International	Newburgh, NY
Taylor County	Campbellsville, KY
Teterboro	Teterboro, NJ
Torrance Municipal	Torrance, CA
Tweed–New Haven Regional	New Haven, CT
University Park	State College, PA
Van Nuys	Van Nuys, CA
Welke	Beaver Island, MI
West Houston	Houston, TX
Westchester County	White Plains, NY
Wiley Post	Oklahoma City, OK
Witham Field	Stuart, FL
Yampa Valley Regional	Hayden, CO

Source: National Air Transportation Association, "America's 100 Most Needed Airports," December 2000. www.nata-online.org/2GovWatch/Archive/ S.20010105.100Arpts.htm.

Appendix B

RESOURCES ON AVIATION
AND THE ENVIRONMENT

Aircraft Owners and Pilots Association (AOPA)

421 Aviation Way, Frederick, MD 21701

301-695-2000; www.aopa.org

With a membership base of 360,000, AOPA serves half of all the
pilots in the United States and claims to be "the largest, most
influential aviation association in the world." AOPA's services range
from representation at federal, state, and local levels to legal services
and advice. In 1997 it founded the Airport Support Network, which
aims to have an AOPA member-volunteer at every public-use airport
in the United States to act as the association's "eyes and ears" and to
provide on-the-spot monitoring of local airport problems such as fees,
rates, and charges; curfew proposals; obstacle construction; residential
encroachment; and proposals to limit airport activity or use. AOPA
publishes *AOPA Pilot* magazine.

Air Line Pilots Association (ALPA)

535 Herndon Parkway, Herndon, VA 20170

703-689-2270; www.alpa.org

This union represents fifty-nine thousand airline pilots at forty-nine
United States and Canadian airlines. Chartered by the AFL-CIO, it
represents the collective interests of all pilots in commercial aviation
and assists in collective bargaining activities on behalf of pilots.
Safety information is published regularly on their Web site. See
also IFALPA, the International Federation of Air Line Pilots
Associations, at www.IFALPA.org.

Air Transport Association (ATA)

1301 Pennsylvania Avenue NW, Suite 1100, Washington,

DC, 20004-1707

202-626-4000; www.air-transport.org

This is the only trade organization for the principal

United States airlines.

American Association of Airport Executives

601 Madison Street, Alexandria, VA 22310

703-824-0500; www.airportnet.org

This is a professional organization for airport managers and

executives at both small and large public airports nationwide.

American Working Group for National Policy

P.O. Box 1702, Arlington Heights, IL 60006-1702

847-506-0670; e-mail info@areco.org; www.areco.org

This is a national coalition of local groups fighting airport expansion

and pollution, and seeking to ensure an accountable, equitable, and

sustainable aviation industry.

Aviation Week and Space Technology **Magazine**

1200 G Street NW, Suite 922, Washington, DC 20005

202-383-2300; fax 202-383-2346; www.aviationnow.com

This is the major trade publication of the aviation industry,

published weekly.

Centre for Sustainable Transportation

15 Borden Street, Toronto, Ontario, Canada M5S 2M8

416-923-9970; fax 416-923-6531; e-mail cstctd@web.net; www.cstctd.org

These are the publishers of *Sustainable Transportation Monitor,*

available online.

Heathrow Association for the Control of Aircraft Noise (HACAN)
Professor Walter Holland, President. P.O. Box 339, Richmond, Surrey
TW9 3RB, England
0181-876-0455; fax 0181-878-0881; www.HACAN.org.uk
> Founded in 1966, HACAN ClearSkies is the world's largest antinoise
> group. It exists to mobilize the public, and has helped to raise
> government interest in aircraft noise. In the spring of 2000 it raised
> £100,000 in two months to support its case in the European Court of
> Human Rights. It is a good source for European views.

National Air Traffic Controllers Association (NATCA)
1325 Massachusetts Avenue NW, Washington, DC 20005
202-628-5451; www.natca.org
> This is the collective bargaining unit for fourteen thousand air traffic
> controllers serving the FAA, the Department of Defense, and the
> private sector. It fights for the rights of controllers nationwide.

National Air Transportation Association (NATA)
4226 King Street, Alexandria, VA 22302
703-845-9000; www.NATA-online.org
> The national trade association representing the business interests of
> general aviation service companies at the federal level, it lobbies for
> airport expansion and sponsors a political action committee.

**National Organization to Insure a Sound-controlled Environment
(NOISE)**
Suite 900 S, 601 Pennsylvania Avenue NW, Washington, DC 20004
202-434-8163; fax 202-639-8238; www.aviationnoise.org
> A nonprofit association of local governments and others concerned
> about aircraft noise, its goals include forging partnerships with
> organizations that are committed to noise abatement, advocating noise
> abatement policies that are both responsible and acceptable to all
> parties involved, and insuring that the voice of affected communities
> is heard.

Natural Resources Defense Council (NRDC)

40 West 20th Street, New York, NY 10011

212-727-2700; fax 212-727-1773; www.nrdc.org

> This general environmental activism organization published the report
> "Flying Off Course: Environmental Impacts of America's Airports,"
> October, 1996.

Noise Pollution Clearinghouse (NPC)

Box 1137, Montpelier, VT 05601

888-200-8332; www.nonoise.org

> A national nonprofit organization with extensive online noise-related
> resources, NPC seeks to raise awareness about noise pollution and to
> strengthen laws and governmental efforts to control noise pollution.

United States Congress

www.access.GPO.gov/Congress

> Congressional publications include the Federal Register, the
> Congressional Record, and pending bills. At this Web site, online
> databases are searchable.

United States Environmental Protection Agency (EPA)

www.epa.gov/global warming/climate/index.html

www.epa.gov/globalwarming/faq/index.html

> See also www.ncdc.noaa.gov/ and
> www.publicaffairs.noaa.gov/releases2000/

United States Federal Aviation Administration (FAA)

800 Independence Avenue SW, Washington, DC 20591

202-366-4000; www.FAA.gov

Appendix C

FEDERALLY DESIGNATED HIGH-SPEED RAIL CORRIDORS

The following is excerpted from the American Railroad Revitalization, Investment, and Enhancement Act, also known as the Arrive 21 Act.

(1) California Corridor connecting the San Francisco Bay area and Sacramento to Los Angeles and San Diego.

(2) Chicago Hub Corridor Network with the following spokes:

    (A) Chicago to Detroit.

    (B) Chicago to Minneapolis/St. Paul, Minnesota, via Milwaukee, Wisconsin.

    (C) Chicago to Kansas City, Missouri, via Springfield, Illinois, and St. Louis, Missouri.

    (D) Chicago to Louisville, Kentucky, via Indianapolis, Indiana, and Cincinnati, Ohio.

    (E) Chicago to Cleveland, Ohio, via Toledo, Ohio.

    (F) Cleveland, Ohio, to Cincinnati, Ohio, via Columbus, Ohio.

(3) Empire State Corridor from New York City, New York, through Albany, New York, to Buffalo, New York.

(4) Florida High-Speed Rail Corridor from Tampa through Orlando to Miami.

(5) Gulf Coast Corridor from Houston Texas, through New Orleans, Louisiana, to Mobile, Alabama, with a branch from New Orleans, through Meridian, Mississippi, and Birmingham, Alabama, to Atlanta, Georgia.

(6) Keystone Corridor from Philadelphia, Pennsylvania, through Harrisburg, Pennsylvania, to Pittsburgh, Pennsylvania.

(7) Northeast Corridor from Washington, District of Columbia, through New York City, New York, New Haven, Connecticut,

and Providence, Rhode Island, to Boston, Massachusetts, with a
branch from New Haven, Connecticut, to Springfield, Massachusetts.

(8) New England Corridor from Boston, Massachusetts, to Portland and
Auburn, Maine, and from Boston, Massachusetts, through Concord,
New Hampshire, and Montpelier, Vermont, to Montreal, Quebec.

(9) Pacific Northwest Corridor from Eugene, Oregon, through
Portland, Oregon, and Seattle, Washington, to Vancouver,
British Columbia.

(10) South Central Corridor from San Antonio, Texas, through
Dallas/Fort Worth to Little Rock, Arkansas, with a branch
from Dallas/Fort Worth through Oklahoma City, Oklahoma,
to Tulsa, Oklahoma.

(11) Southeast Corridor from Washington, District of Columbia, through
Richmond, Virginia, Raleigh, North Carolina, Columbia, South
Carolina, Savannah, Georgia, and Jessup, Georgia, to Jacksonville,
Florida, with—

(A) a branch from Raleigh, North Carolina, through Charlotte,
North Carolina, and Greenville, South Carolina, to Atlanta,
Georgia; a branch from Richmond, to Hampton
Roads/Norfolk, Virginia;

(B) a branch from Charlotte, North Carolina, to Columbia,
South Carolina, to Charleston, South Carolina;

(C) a connecting route from Atlanta, Georgia, to Jessup, Georgia;

(D) a connecting route from Atlanta, Georgia, to Charleston,
South Carolina; and

(E) a branch from Raleigh, North Carolina, through Florence,
South Carolina, to Charleston, South Carolina, and Savannah,
Georgia, with a connecting route from Florence,
South Carolina, to Myrtle Beach, South Carolina.

(12) Southwest Corridor from Los Angeles, California, to Las Vegas,
Nevada.

Source: The American Railroad Revitalization, Investment, and Enhancement Act,
S. 1961, 108th Congress, introduced November 25, 2003, www.thomas.loc.gov.

Epigraph Sources

Page 11

Abigail Adams. Letter to Mercy Otis Warren, 1774.

Lynne Pine, president's speech at General Witham Airport Action
Alliance (WAAM) meeting, November 3, 2003. www.waam.ws.

Page 16

Henry David Thoreau, *Journal,* entry for December 5, 1856.

Jay Kaufman, personal communication.

Page 24

Edinburgh Center for Carbon Management, Edinburgh, Scotland.
Calculations reported in Harry Rijnen, "Offsetting Environmental
Damage by Planes," from the *New York Times,* February 18, 2003.

Les Blomberg, executive director, Noise Pollution Clearinghouse,
personal communication.

Page 43

Lexington, Massachusetts, town bylaws, art. 28, sec. 1, 2000.

David McCullough, quoted in Joanna Weiss, "Airport Foes Deploy
the Minute Man, Activists Contend Park Is Threatened," *Boston Globe,*
May 30, 2003.

Page 68

Declaration of Independence, in Congress, July 4, 1776. A Declaration
by the Representatives of the United States of America, in General
Congress Assembled.

Progressive Governance in the 21st Century, quoted in E. J. Dionne, Jr.,
"The Wisdom of the Progressive Tradition in a New Era," *Boston
Globe,* June 10, 2000.

Page 84

"Predict and Provoke," *Economist* (February 22, 2003): 52-53.

Noam Chomsky, *Class Warfare* (Monroe, ME: Common Courage Press, 1996), 51. Reprinted by permission of Common Courage Press.

Page 96

John Clabes, quoted in "Texas Town Fines Low-flying Plane," *Austin American-Statesman,* April 12, 1999.

Susan Fargo, interview with the author.

Page 121

William Greider, *Who Will Tell the People,* 169. Reprinted with the permission of Simon & Schuster Adult Publishing Group, from WHO WILL TELL THE PEOPLE: The Betrayal of American Democracy, by William Greider. Copyright © 1992 by William Greider. All rights reserved.

Anonymous, personal communication.

Page 133

Charles Péguy, quoted in W. H. Auden and Louis Kronenberger, eds., *The Viking Book of Aphorisms* (New York: Dorset Press, 1981), 305.

Jack Saporito, US-CAW, presentation to US-EPA Federal Facilities Conference, August 15, 2001.

Page 152

Marcus Tullius Cicero, Roman orator, first century B.C.

Jay Kaufman, personal communication.

Page 167

Peter D. Enrich, activist and law professor specializing in state and local government, personal communication.

United States–Citizens Aviation Watch, personal communication.

Page 174

Ken Burns, editorial, *Boston Globe,* October 17, 2003.

Airline passenger, personal communication.

Notes

1. The Quest for Environmentally Sustainable Aviation

1. David W. Chen, "With Major Airports Overcrowded, Regional Hubs Are Gearing Up," *New York Times,* October 24, 2000.
2. National Air Transportation Association, "America's 100 Most Needed Airports," December 2000. www.nata-online.org/ 2GovWatch/Archive/S.20010105.100Arpts.htm.
3. See John Whitelegg and Nick Williams, *The Plane Truth: Aviation and the Environment* (London: The Ashden Trust and Transport 2000 Trust, 2000). See also Paul Upham et al., *Towards Sustainable Aviation* (London: Earthscan Publications Ltd., 2003).

2. The Airport in My Garden

1. "Massachusetts Port Authority Enabling Act of 1956, chapter 465, as amended through December, 1996" (Boston: Massachusetts Port Authority, 1996): 46.
2. Massport spokesman Richard Walsh in a telephone interview November 3, 2000, said Hanscom is thirteen hundred acres, with five hundred acres devoted to the airport and the remainder to wetlands and undeveloped upland areas. He did not know how many acres are undeveloped land. According to the EPA, the adjacent Hanscom Air Force Base is 1,120 acres, including 396 acres owned by the United States Air Force and 724 acres leased by the Air Force from the Commonwealth of Massachusetts. See U.S. Environmental Protection Agency, "NPL Site Narrative for Hanscom Field/Hanscom Air Force Base," 27989–27996 *Federal Register* 59, no. 103 (May 31, 1994).
3. Davis Bushnell, "Corporate Jets on the Rise at Hanscom," *Boston Globe,* March 5, 2000.
4. Davis Bushnell, "Court Clears Airline for Hanscom," *Boston Globe,* September 28, 1999.
5. Davis Bushnell, "Massport Looking to Expand Facilities at Hanscom Field," *Boston Globe,* December 12, 1999.

3. Aviation Pollution Today

1. John Mislow and Richard Kassel, *Under the Flight Path* (New York: Natural Resources Defense Council, 1997).

2. Jack Saporito, past president of U.S.–Citizens Aviation Watch Association (US-CAW) and president of Alliance of Residents Concerning O'Hare, in testimony to the U.S. Environmental Protection Agency, "Comments to Add Standard Industrial Classification Code 45, Transportation by Air, to List of Facilities Required to Report Toxic Releases," April 2, 1998.

3. "Predict and Provoke," *Economist,* February 22, 2003: 52–53.

4. Jack Saporito, US-CAW. Presentation to the EPA Federal Facilities Conference, August 15, 2001.

5. Coralie Cooper, Dave Park, Jake Schmidt, Ingrid Ulbrich, and Steve Winkelman, *Controlling Airport-Related Air Pollution* (Boston: Northeast States for Coordinated Air Use Management [NESCAUM] and Center for Clean Air Policy [CCAP], June 2003): I-3.

6. *Code of Federal Regulations,* title 40, volume 14, and interview with Bryan Manning, mechanical engineer, Office of Transportation and Air Quality, Environmental Protection Agency, November 1, 2000.

7. Sidney A. Shapiro, "Lessons from a Public Policy Failure: EPA and Noise Abatement," *Ecology Law Quarterly* 19, no.1 (1992): 1–61.

8. Letter to the Honorable Carol Browner, administrator, U.S. Environmental Protection Agency, April 16, 1997, Re: Petition to Add Standard Industrial Classification Code 45, Transportation by Air, to the List of Facilities Required to Report Releases of Toxic Chemicals, from Peter Lehner, senior attorney, Natural Resources Defense Council, and others, [and] communication from Jack Saporito, president, US–Citizens Aviation Watch Association, June 6, 2000.

9. Jennifer Stenzel, "Flying Off Course: Environmental Impacts of America's Airports," a 1996 report of the Natural Resources Defense Council.

10. Cooper et al., *Controlling Airport-Related Air Pollution.*

11. M. Rosenlund et al., "Increased Prevalence of Hypertension in a Population Exposed to Aircraft Noise," *Occupational Environmental Medicine* 58 (Dec. 2001): 769–73.

12. E. G. Knox and E. A. Gilman, "Hazard Proximities of Childhood Cancers in Great Britain, 1953–80," *Journal of Epidemiology and Community Health* 51, no. 2 (April 1997): 151–59.

13. Seattle-King County Department of Public Health, report to the Georgetown Crime Prevention and Community Council, June 20, 1997.

14. City of Park Ridge, Illinois, "Preliminary Study and Analysis of Toxic Air Pollutant Emissions from O'Hare International Airport and the Resulting Health Risks Created by These Toxic Emissions in Surrounding Residential Communities," August 2000.

15. City of Park Ridge, Illinois, "Preliminary Study and Analysis of Toxic Air Pollutant Emissions": 14.

16. Brian Dumser, *Winthrop Community Health Survey,* Winthrop Environmental Health Facts Subcommittee of the Winthrop Airport Hazards Committee, Winthrop Board of Health, and AIR, August 18, 1999.

17. Cooper et al., *Controlling Airport-Related Air Pollution.*

18. Ibid., II-13.

19. Ibid., I-10.

20. "Health Effects of Inhalable Particles: Implications for British Columbia—Overview and Conclusions," Air Resources Branch, British Columbia Ministry of Environment, June 1995. See also R. T. Burnett et al., "The Role of Particulate Size and Chemistry in the Association between Summertime Ambient Air Pollution and Hospitalization for Cardiorespiratory Diseases," *Environmental Health Perspectives* 105 (1997): 614–20.

21. Justin Pope, "Study Links Particle Pollution with Deaths and Hospitalizations," Associated Press, June 28, 2000.

22. C. A. Pope, III, et al., "Particulate Air Pollution as a Predictor of Mortality in a Prospective Study of US Adults," *American Journal of Respiratory Critical Care Medicine* 151 (1995): 669–74, and C. A. Pope III, et al., "Lung Cancer, Cardiopulmonary Mortality, and Long-term Exposure to Fine Particulate Air Pollution," *Journal of the American Medical Association* 287, no. 9 (March 2002): 1132–41.

23. Stenzel, "Flying Off Course." See NRDC.org for a summary of findings.

24. This analysis is based on the *Illinois Annual Air Quality Report for 1998,* which reports estimated annual emissions of 134,995 tons of volatile organic compounds and 509,676 tons of nitrogen oxide. Illinois Environmental Protection Agency, Bureau of Air, September 1999.

25. Cooper, *Controlling Airport-Related Air Pollution:* II-14.

26. Ibid., II-13.

27. Ibid.,VI-1.

28. Roy R. Gould, biophysicist and environmental policy fellow at Harvard University, 1980–83, in a letter to John P. DeVillars, secretary, Boston Department of Environmental Affairs, July 25, 1990.

29. Tony Colman, *Parliamentary Debates,* Commons (March 21, 2000), col. 168WH.

30. Geoffrey Lean, "We Regret to Announce that the Flight to Malaga Is Destroying the Planet: Air Travel Is Fast Becoming One of the Biggest Causes of Global Warming," *The Independent* (August 26, 2001).

31. *Intergovernmental Panel on Climate Change Special Report: Aviation and the Global Atmosphere* (New York: World Meteorological Organization and the United Nations Environment Programme, 1999).

32. House Committee on Transportation and Infrastructure, "GAO Study Links Aircraft Emissions to Global Warming," *San Diego Earth Times,* April 2000.

33. Patrick Minnis, J. Kirk Ayers, and Steven P. Weaver, "Surface-based Observations of Contrail Occurrence Frequency over the U.S., April 1993–April 1994," NASA RP-1404, December 1997, pp. 83 ff. Also, "NASA Believes Jet Contrails Contribute to Climatic Changes," transcript from *NBC News,* July 28, 1998.

34. Rosemary Frei, "Fly the Filthy Skies," *Toronto Globe and Mail,* September 28, 2002.

35. "Atmospheric Sciences Significant Events," NASA Radiation and Aerosols Branch, June 25, 1999, www.larc.nasa.gov (accessed June 20, 2000).

36. *Natural Resources Defense Council, Inc., Airport Environmental Coalition, Humane Society of the United States, and US Citizens Aviation Watch v. the Maryland Aviation Administration.* United States District Court for the District of Maryland, 1998.

37. A. R. Bielefeldt, R. LaPlante, and T. Illangasekare, "The Impact of Biogradation of De-Icing Chemicals on the Conductivity and Dispersivity of Porous Media," in *Proceedings of the 2000 Conference of Hazardous Waste Research: Environmental Challenges and Solutions to Resource Development, Production and Use* (Manhattan, KS: Great Plains/Rocky Mountain Hazardous Substance Research Center, Kansas State University, 2000).

38. *Natural Resources Defense Council v. the Maryland Aviation Administration,* 1998.

39. Devon A. Cancilla, Jennifer Martinez, and Graham C. Van Aggelen, "Detection of Aircraft De-icing/Anti-icing Fluid Additives in a Perched Water Monitoring Well at an International Airport," *Environmental Science and Technology* 32, no. 23 (1998): 3834–35.

40. Lila Guterman, "Toxic Takeoffs: Aircraft De-icers Hold a Hidden Hazard," *New Scientist* (January 9, 1999): 7.

41. Science Applications International Corporation, SIC Code Profile 45: Transportation by Air (1994). See also U.S. Environmental Protection Agency, *Economic Analysis of the Proposed Rule to Add Certain Industries to EPCRA Section 313* (June 1996).

42. Environmental Defense Scorecard: "Threats and Contaminants at Hanscom Field," www.scorecard.org/env-releases/land/site.tcl?epa_id = MA8570024424#threats (accessed June 8, 2000).

43. For a review, see Arline L. Bronzaft, "Noise Pollution: A Hazard to Physical and Mental Well-Being," in *Handbook of Environmental Psychology,* ed. Robert B. Bechtel and Arza Churchman, 499–510 (New York: John Wiley & Sons, 2002).

44. Gary Evans and Lorraine Maxwell, "Chronic Noise Exposure and Reading Deficits: The Mediating Effects of Language Acquisition," *Environment and Behavior* 29, no. 5 (September 1997): 638–56.

45. M. M. Haines, S. A. Stansfeld, R. F. S. Job, B. Berglund, and J. Head, "Chronic Aircraft Noise Exposure, Stress Responses,

Mental Health and Cognitive Performance in School Children," *Psychological Medicine* 31 (2001): 265–77.

46. Gary Evans, Monika Bullinger, and Staffan Hygge, "Chronic Noise Exposure and Physiological Response: A Prospective Study of Children Living Under Environmental Stress," *Psychological Science* 9, no. 1 (January 1998): 75–77.

47. Richard McGowan, "Noise from Hanscom: It's Enough, Already," *Lexington Minuteman,* September 30, 1999.

48. Birgitta Berglund and Thomas Lindvall, eds., *Community Noise* (Stockholm, Sweden: Center for Sensory Research, 1995): 15. An excellent analysis of metrics can also be found in H. E. von Gierke and L. C. Johnson, "Noise Control—Where Do We Stand Today?" *Noise Control Engineering Journal* (1996). This is a report of papers presented at a special session on national environmental noise policy at the Acoustical Society of America.

49. Tom Henderson, "The Physics Classroom," www.glenbrook.k12.il.us (accessed 1998).

50. Donald F. Anthrop, "The Noise Crisis," in James L. Hildebrand, ed., *Noise Pollution and the Law* (Buffalo, NY: William S. Hein & Company, 1970): 8.

51. Alice H. Suter, "Noise and Its Effects," Administrative Conference of the United States, November 1991.

52. Birgitta Berglund, Thomas Lindvall, and Dietrich H. Schwela, eds., *Guidelines for Community Noise* (New York: World Health Organization, 1999); www.who.int (accessed June 1, 2000).

53. From the "Alarming Quick Facts" page of the Save Our Heritage Web site. www.saveourheritage.com/Alarming_Quick_Facts.html (accessed June 1, 2000).

54. Davis Bushnell, "Corporate Jets on Rise at Hanscom," *Boston Globe,* March 5, 2000.

55. Federal Aviation Administration Advisory Circular 91-36c, "Visual Flight Rules (VFR) Flight Near Noise-Sensitive Areas," October 19, 1984.

56. Russell E. Train, *Aviation Noise: Let's Go on with the Job* (Washington, DC: U.S. Environmental Protection Agency, 1976): 17.

57. Evans et al., "Chronic Noise Exposure and Reading Deficits."

58. S. Cohen and N. Weinstein, "Non-auditory Effects of Noise on Behaviour and Health," *Journal of Social Issues* (1981): 37.

59. S. Hygge, "A Comparison Between the Impact of Noise from Aircraft, Road Traffic and Trains on Long-term Recall and Recognition of a Text in Children Aged 12–14 Years," *Schriftenreihe des Vereins für Wasser-, Boden-, und Lufthygiene* 88 (1993): 416–27.

60. K. Schmeck and F. Ponstka, "Psychophysiological and Psychiatric Tests with Children and Adolescents in a Low-altitude Flight Region," *Schriftenreihe des Vereins für Wasser-, Boden-, und Lufthygiene* 88 (1992): 301–6.

61. W. W. Holland. *Noise and Health* (London: Heathrow Association for the Control of Aircraft Noise, June 1997): 5; www.hacan.org.uk.

62. Evans et al., "Chronic Noise Exposure and Physiological Response."

63. Cornell University press release, "Airport Noise Is Harmful to the Health and Well-being of Children," *Cornell News,* March 4, 1998; www.news.cornell.edu/releases/March98/noise.stress.ssl.html (accessed November 10, 1999).

64. Donald Goldman, letter to John P. DeVillars, secretary, Boston Department of Environmental Affairs, July 12, 1990.

4. Facing Up to Airport Expansion

1. General Accounting Office, "General Aviation Airports: Unauthorized Land Use Highlights Need for Improved Oversight and Enforcement," GAO/RCED-99-109, May 1999.

2. From a statement to the Hanscom Area Towns meeting on June 24, 1999, by Kathi Anderson, executive director of the Walden Woods Project and the Thoreau Institute.

3. Bernie Sanders, "Falling Behind in Boom Times," *New York Times,* January 12, 2000. Bernie Sanders is the U.S. representative from Vermont.

4. Sidney Verba, Kay Lehman Schlozman, and Henry E. Brady, *Voice and Equality: Civic Voluntarism in American Politics* (Cambridge, MA: Harvard University Press, 1995): 292–93.

5. Caroline Louise Cole, "Towns Urge Regional Approach to Planning," *Boston Sunday Globe,* March 12, 2000.

6. See the Save Our Heritage Web site: www.saveourheritage.com/Learn_about_SOH.htm (accessed March 21, 2000).

7. Neil Rasmussen, letter to the editor, "Hanscom Plan Could Weaken Our Schools," *Lexington Minuteman,* November 11, 1999.

8. I. E. Feitelson, R. E. Hurd, and R. R. Mudge, "The Impact of Airport Noise on Willingness to Pay for Residence," *Transportation Research* 1, no. 1 (1996): 1–14.

9. Rasmussen, "Hanscom Plan Could Weaken Our Schools."

10. This quote is taken from the descriptions of regional airport usage on Massport's Web site: www.massport.com (accessed December 1, 1999).

11. This process is described in the Town of Lexington's *1998 Annual Report:* 49.

12. Memorandum of Understanding, revision 11, June 9, 1998 (unpublished).

13. Mark R. Cestari, "Airline Says It's Filling Public Need," *Boston Globe,* April 23, 2000.

14. Marcella Bombardieri, "325 Protest Commercial Flights at Hanscom," *Boston Globe,* September 29, 1999.

15. Virginia Buckingham, "Thinking Regionally about Logan Airport," *Boston Globe,* January 8, 2000.

16. Matthew Brelis, "Cleared for Takeoff," *Boston Globe,* December 9, 1999.

17. Buckingham, "Thinking Regionally about Logan Airport."

18. Communities Against Runway Expansion, "Runway 14/32: An Airport-Expansion Proposal in Disguise," undated flier.

19. Mislow and Kassel, *Under the Flight Path.* I am indebted to this report for much of the information presented here on Westchester County Airport.

20. Ibid.

21. Ibid., 18.

22. Ibid., 13.

23. This is from a statement by Betty Ann Kane from the National Organization to Insure a Sound-controlled Environment before the House Committee on Transportation and Infrastructure–Subcommittee on Aviation, regarding the reauthorization of the Airport Improvement Program, March 25, 1998.

24. Ibid.

25. Mislow and Kassel, *Under the Flight Path:* 7.

26. Ibid.

27. Berglund et al., *Guidelines for Community Noise.*

28. Mislow and Kassel, *Under the Flight Path.*

29. Stephen Kiehl and Howie Paul Hartnett, "Florida Residents Complain of Increasing Noise from Witham Field Airport," *Palm Beach Post,* April 18, 1999.

30. Melissa E. Holsman and Suzanne Latshaw, "Willie Gary Is King of Local Soft Money," *Stuart News,* May 14, 2000.

31. Jerry M. Gution, "Director Reports on Witham's Ability to Handle 737," *Stuart News,* April 7, 2000.

32. Ibid.

33. Ibid.

34. Jerry M. Gution, "Gary Endorses 'Friends' Advocating Airport Upgrade," *Stuart News,* April 11, 2000.

35. Melissa E. Holsman, "Those on Both Sides of Airport Debate Oppose 737 Idea," *Stuart News,* April 12, 2000.

36. Melissa E. Holsman, "Gary Vows Fight for Landing Rights," *Stuart News,* April 13, 2000.

37. Jerry M. Gution, "Officials: Din Raised Over Wrong Issue: Noise, Not Weight, Matters in Airport Debate," *Stuart News,* April 13, 2000.

38. Dorothy Coutant, letter to the editor, *Stuart News,* April 17, 1999.

39. Stephen Kiehl, "300 Witham Field Residents Vent Frustration Over Airport Noise and Pollution at Public Meeting," *Palm Beach Post,* April 20, 1999.

40. Gabriel Margasak, "Boat, Car Horns to Protest Airport," *Stuart News,* April 21, 2000.

41. Jerry M. Gution, "Unanimous Commission OKs Airport Noise Study," *Stuart News,* May 3, 2000.

42. Jerry M. Gution, "Airport Ideas Upset Group," *Stuart News,*
    May 19, 2000.

43. Jerry M. Gution, "Melzer Will Press for Halt of Airport Study,"
    Stuart News, May 20, 2000.

44. Paul T. Rosynsky, "Emotions Unsettling in Airport Controversy,"
    Stuart News, May 25, 2000.

45. For details see www.WAAM.ws.

46. "Judge Seals Documents in O'Hare Suit," *Chicago Tribune,* June 9, 2000.

47. *Business Wire,* "ETRPA Request County Reopen Comments to
    El Toro EIR," press release, August 24, 2000.

48. "Judge Seals Documents in O'Hare Suit."

49. Gary is not alone. Larry Ellison, CEO of Oracle Corporation, has
    filed suit in the U.S. District Court for Northern California to fly his
    private jet into San Jose International Airport during the nighttime
    curfew. The city has been threatening to sue Ellison for frequently
    violating the curfew. See Carolyne Zinko, "Ellison Sues Over Airport
    Rule on Noise at Night: He Wants to Land His Jet Anytime,"
    San Francisco Chronicle, January 7, 2000.

50. Richard Goodwin, column on campaign finance reform, *Boston
    Globe,* February 5, 1997.

5. Massport: The Aviation Industry's Model Organization

1. Bombardieri, "325 Protest Commercial Flights at Hanscom."

2. Donald S. Bronstein, letter to John P. DeVillars, secretary, Boston
   Department of Environmental Affairs, July 31, 1990.

3. Bushnell, "Massport Looking to Expand Facilities at Hanscom Field."

4. Ibid.

5. "Massachusetts Port Authority Enabling Act of 1956": 6.

6. Ibid., 24.

7. Ibid.

8. James M. Coull, "Massport Hiring Is Defended," *Lexington
   Minuteman,* October 7, 1999.

9. "Massachusetts Port Authority Enabling Act of 1956."

10. Joe Battenfeld, "Cellucci Locks Pals into Massport Posts,"
    Boston Globe, May 1, 2000.

11. *Massport 1999 Annual Report.* For financial details, see www.massport.com/1999annual/financials.html (accessed January 13, 2000).

12. Former Governor William Weld issued an executive order requiring state agencies to incorporate local land-use plans into their growth plans, but Massport has declared themselves exempt from this order. See Quick Facts on the Save Our Heritage Web site, www.saveourheritage.com (accessed June 1, 2000).

13. "Massachusetts Port Authority Enabling Act of 1956": 8.

14. Coull, "Massport Hiring Is Defended."

15. See www.massport.com/about/faq.html (accessed December 1, 1999).

16. Ibid.

17. "Massachusetts Port Authority Enabling Act of 1956": 9.

18. *Lexington Education Foundation News,* spring 2000. Massport is listed as a business benefactor, the highest level, for an annual fundraiser, along with Cablevision and the Westin Hotel, and it donated between $1,000 and $2,500 to the Lexington Education Foundation as a corporation.

19. Massport, "Tobin Memorial Bridge Turns 50 Years Old," press release, February 28, 2000. www.massport.com/about/press_news_tob50.html (accessed June 12, 2000).

20. Doug Hanchett, "Audit of Massport Uncovers Wild Spending and Donations," *Boston Herald,* December 15, 2000.

21. Massachusetts Port Authority, *Hanscom Field Master Plan and Environmental Impact Statement,* June 15, 1978: 8.

22. Ibid., 9.

23. Ibid., 39.

24. Ibid., 15.

25. Ibid., 17.

26. Ibid., 8.

27. Ibid., 15.

28. Ibid., 37.

29. Ibid., 5.

30. Ibid., 40.

31. Ibid., 10.

32. Ibid., 12.

33. Ibid., 13.

34. Ibid., 14.

35. Ibid., 15. Quote from Massport *Master Plan for Logan International Airport,* April 1976: 13.

36. Massachusetts Port Authority, *General Rules and Regulations for Laurence G. Hanscom Field,* Part F, effective July 31, 1980: 3.

37. Massachusetts Port Authority, *Hanscom Field Master Plan:* 38–39.

38. Ibid., 40.

39. "Hanscom Field: A Delicate Balance," Massachusetts Port Authority, circa 1986: 12.

40. Massachusetts Port Authority, *Hanscom Field Master Plan:* 15.

41. 14 Code of Federal Regulations (CFR), Part 139—Certification and Operations: Land Airports Serving Certain Air Carriers.

42. Massachusetts Port Authority, response to the *Strategic Assessment Report* produced by Arthur D. Little for the Massachusetts Aeronautics Commission, Meeting of the Policy, Planning, and Public Affairs Committee, October 19, 1993.

43. Massachusetts Water Resources Authority, Governance and Organization; www.mwra.state.ma.us.

44. John P. DeVillars, "Privatizing the MWRA Could Spell Relief for Greater Boston," *Boston Globe,* May 18, 2000.

6. How the Air Transportation Industry Pursues Growth

1. James T. McKenna, "Despite Claims, Costs of Delays Are Unproven," *Aviation Week & Space Technology* (October 25, 1999): 70–72.

2. Michael A. Dornheim, "Jump in Delays Shows ATC Bumping into Capacity Limits," *Aviation Week & Space Technology* (October 25, 1999): 90–94.

3. Stenzel, "Flying Off Course."

4. Paul Proctor, "Global Competitive Concerns Could Boost Airport Expansion," *Aviation Week & Space Technology* (October 25, 1999): 88–90. See also "Predict and Provoke," *Economist* (February 22, 2003): 52–53.

5. David W. Chen, "With Major Airports Overcrowded, Regional Hubs Are Gearing Up," *New York Times,* October 24, 2000.

6. Jack Saporito, "Phony Flight Delays," press release, US–Citizens Aviation Watch Association, March 5, 2001. Saporito now heads the American Working Group for National Policy.

7. Jane F. Garvey, administrator, Federal Aviation Administration, "Airport Capacity: Demand Management," remarks to the Transportation Research Board, Washington, DC, February 16, 2001.

8. Paul Hudson, "Flight Delays—The Real Story," report of the Aviation Consumer Action Project, Washington, DC, November 5, 1999.

9. Rod Stewart, letter to the editor, *San Jose Mercury News,* undated.

10. "Predict and Provoke."

11. McKenna, "Despite Claims, Costs of Delays Are Unproven": 70–72.

12. Ibid.

13. David M. North, "Action Plan for Air Travel," *Aviation Week & Space Technology* (October 25, 1999).

14. Ibid.

15. Aircraft Owners and Pilots Association, "Management Reform of the Federal Aviation Administration," issue brief, February 1999. See www.aopa.org.

16. North, "Action Plan for Air Travel."

17. Mary Schiavo, *Flying Blind, Flying Safe* (New York: Avon Books, 1997): 193.

18. Robert McCoppin, "Demand for Pilots Sending Many to School," *Daily Herald,* February 12, 2001.

19. Schiavo, *Flying Blind, Flying Safe:* 48–49.

20. Ibid., 204.

21. Coalition for a Global Standard on Aviation Noise, press release on PRNewswire, July 27, 2000.

22. Aaron Bernstein, *Grounded: Frank Lorenzo and the Destruction of Eastern Airlines* (New York: Simon & Schuster, 1990): 125.

23. Peter Nulty, "America's Toughest Bosses," *Fortune* (February 27, 1989): 41.

24. Bernstein, *Grounded: Frank Lorenzo:* 220.

25. Ibid., p. 157.

26. "Union-buster Gets Grounded," fall 1996,
    www.uaw.org/strong/unity/iam-side.htm.

27. James P. Woolsey, "Say Goodby, Frank," *Air Transport World* 27
    (October 1990): 23.

28. Bridget O'Brian, "For Lorenzo, Getting a New Airline Aloft Is
    Proving Treacherous," *Wall Street Journal,* January 25, 1994.

29. Lore Croghan, "Viewpoint: A Chat with Frank Lorenzo,"
    Financial World 165 (January 2, 1996): 48–50.

30. O'Brian, "For Lorenzo."

31. "ATX fights ruling," *Aviation Week & Space Technology* 140
    (April 11, 1994): 34.

32. Carolyn Phillips and Bridget O'Brian, "Lorenzo's Plan for New
    Airline Provokes Labor," *Wall Street Journal,* June 28, 1993.

33. "Nations Air's Connection to Lorenzo Questioned," *Atlanta Journal
    and Constitution,* September 12, 1995.

34. U.S. Department of Transportation news release (DOT 149-95),
    September 7, 1995.

35. "Nations Air's Connection to Lorenzo Questioned."

36. U.S. Department of Transportation news release (DOT 149-95),
    September 7, 1995.

37. Croghan, "Viewpoint: A Chat with Frank Lorenzo": 48–50.

38. Ibid.

39. Application of Shuttle America Corporation for a Certificate of
    Public Convenience and Necessity Pursuant to 49 U.S.C.* 41102
    to Engage in Interstate Scheduled Air Transportation. U.S.
    Department of Transportation, docket OST 98-, exhibit 3: 12.

40. Ibid.

41. Ibid.

42. "Lorenzo's Ex-associates Plan Start-up Airline," *Airline Industry
    Information* (October 1, 1997).

7. How Noise Laws Fail Communities

1. See *City of Burbank et al. v. Lockheed Air Terminal, Inc., et al.,* 411 U.S.
   624, appeal from the U.S. Court of Appeals for the Ninth Circuit,
   no. 71-1637 (May 14, 1973).

2. HR Rep. 36, 88th Congress, 1st Session.

3. HR Rep. 1463, 90th Congress, 2nd Session, 4.

4. Ibid.

5. Ibid.

6. Ibid.

7. *United States v. Causby,* 328 U.S. 256 (1946).

8. *Griggs v. Allegheny County,* 369 U.S. 84, 89–90 (1962).

9. *United States v. Clarke,* 445 U.S. 253 (1980).

10. As discussed in *The Quiet Communities Act of 1997,* HR 536, 105th Cong., 1st sess. (February 4, 1997).

11. *City of Burbank. v. Lockheed Air Terminal:* 626–40.

12. Ibid.

13. Ibid.

14. Ibid.

15. Kristin L. Falzone, "Airport Noise Pollution: Is There a Solution in Sight?" *Boston College Environmental Affairs Law Review* 26 (1999): 769–807.

16. For codification of the *Noise Control Act,* see 42 U.S.C. 4901–4918 and 49 U.S.C. 44715.

17. Kenneth M. Mead, director, Transportation Issues, Resources, Community and Economic Development Division, "Issues that Need to Be Considered in Formulating Strategies to Reduce Aviation Noise," statement before the Subcommittee on Transportation, Aviation and Materials, Committee on Science, Space and Technology, U.S. House of Representatives, September 27, 1990.

18. Ibid.

19. *Airport Capacity Act,* S 3094, *Congressional Record* (September 24, 1990): S13619.

20. Ibid.

21. *1994–1995 Airport Noise Summary* (Washington DC: National Business Aircraft Association, 1995).

22. Mead, "Issues That Need to Be Considered in Formulating Strategies to Reduce Aviation Noise": 9.

23. Falzone, "Airport Noise Pollution": 775.

24. Nicholas P. Miller, "Ldn Necessary But Not Sufficient," *Internoise* (July 20–22, 1992).

25. Paul Schomer, "Assessment of Airport Noise Annoyance," report for U.S. delegation to the International Organization for Standardization Acoustics and Noise committees (Champaign, IL: Schomer and Associates, January 12, 2001).

26. U.S. Environmental Protection Agency, "Information on Levels of Environmental Noise Requisite to Protect Public Health and Welfare with an Adequate Margin of Safety," 550/9-74-004 (March 1974): 8.

27. Mead, "Issues That Need to Be Considered in Formulating Strategies to Reduce Aviation Noise": 10.

28. Ibid.

29. Miller, "Ldn Necessary But Not Sufficient": 984.

30. Falzone, "Airport Noise Pollution": 787–88.

31. Massachusetts Port Authority, *Hanscom Field Master Plan:* 37–38.

32. Ibid.

33. Ibid., 9.

34. Falzone, "Airport Noise Pollution": 775.

35. Massachusetts Port Authority, *Monthly Statistics Report—Hanscom Field,* April 2000.

36. Ibid.

37. Federal Aviation Administration, Department of Transportation, *Code of Federal Regulations* (2000), chapter 1, "Aeronautics and Space," part 36, appendix C: 822.

38. Mead, "Issues That Need to Be Considered in Formulating Strategies to Reduce Aviation Noise": 8.

39. Federal Aviation Administration, Department of Transportation, *Aviation Noise Abatement Policy,* in *Federal Register* 65, no. 136 (July 14, 2000): 43,802.

40. Frank Swoboda, "US Airways Introduces Earlier Shuttle Between Washington and New York After Acquiring Quieter Planes; Addition Expected to Attract Business Travelers," *Washington Post,* November 23, 1999.

41. "The Power in the Tower Is Out of Local Control," *Washington Post,* March 24, 2000.

42. Associated Press, "T. F. Green Airport in Warwick, Rhode Island Plans to Buy 260 Homes to Mitigate Noise," January 31, 2000.

43. Massachusetts Port Authority, *Hanscom Field Master Plan:* 31.

44. Ibid., 36.

45. Virginia Buckingham, "Massport Director Defends Growth," *Boston Globe,* April 23, 2000.

46. The Wendall H. Ford Aviation Investment and Reform Act allowed for slot exemptions for flights out of LaGuardia Airport in New York.

47. See the Airports Data Base for current regulations, www.boeing.com.

48. Paul Proctor, "Global Competitiveness Concerns Could Boost Airport Expansion," *Aviation Week & Space Technology* (October 25, 1999): 88–90.

49. Nancy Dunne, "US Claims European Union's Ban on Aircraft Noise Law Costs Billions: US Seeks Ban in EU Voting Rights," *London Financial Times,* December 10, 1999.

50. Adam Entous, "European Union and US Battle over Aircraft Noise Law," *Journal of Commerce* (December 10, 1999): 12.

51. "US Pleased with EU Hushkit Ban Changes But Suspicious of New Rules," Agence France Presse, March 26, 2002.

52. Virginia Godfrey of Kew, England, writing on the Heathrow Association for the Control of Aircraft Noise Web site, hacan.org.uk, June 1997.

53. "European Court Agrees to Hear Plea by Residents Wanting Night Flight Ban," *The Independent* (May 17, 2000).

54. Sarah Lyall, "Under Noisy Skies, Britons Assert a Right to Sleep," *New York Times,* October 14, 2001.

55. "Heathrow Neighbors Lose Appeal at European Court of Human Rights," *The Independent,* July 9, 2003.

56. *City of Burbank v. Lockheed Air Terminal.*

57. Ibid.

58. "European Court Agrees to Hear Plea," *The Independent.*

59. Reuters (Brussels), "European Union Will Fight U.S. Complaint over Europe's Refusal to Accept 'Hushkit' Aircraft," July 20, 2000.

60. BankBoston Economics Department, "MIT: The Impact of Innovation," MIT News Office (Cambridge, MA), 1995.

61. "Massachusetts Port Authority Enabling Act of 1956": 24.

62. *Communities, Inc. v. Busey,* 9 F.3d 242 (6th Cir. 1992).

63. *National Parks and Conservation Association v. Federal Aviation Administration,* 998 F.2d 1523 (10th Cir. 1993).

64. *Millard Refrigerated Services, Inc. v. Federal Aviation Administration,* no. 95-1535 (DC Cir., October 25, 1996).

65. These numbers are based on a 1994 Natural Resources Defense Council online search of all airport noise lawsuits on the WESTLAW Online Legal Database (West Publishing Company, 1994).

66. Mislow and Kassel, *Under the Flight Path.*

67. Falzone, "Airport Noise Pollution": 768–807.

68. Ibid., 803.

69. *Quiet Communities Act of 1997,* HR 536, 105th Cong., 1st sess. (February 4, 1997). See also "U.S. Congress" in appendix B.

70. Ibid.

71. *Quiet Communities Act of 1999,* HR 2702.

72. Mislow and Kassel, *Under the Flight Path:* 37–38.

73. City of Park Ridge, Illinois, "Preliminary Study and Analysis of Toxic Air Pollutant Emissions from O'Hare International Airport and the Resulting Health Risks Created by These Toxic Emissions in Surrounding Residential Communities," August 2000: 7.

74. *Griggs v. Allegheny County,* 369 U.S. 84, 89–90 (1962).

75. For a summary of the legal framework for airport proprietor liability, see Plaintiff's Reply Brief in Support of Their Motion for Summary Judgment and Response, submitted to the Circuit Court for the Eighteenth Judicial Circuit, Du Page County, Wheaton, Illinois, by James E. Ryan, DuPage County State's Attorney, et al., July 16, 1993.

8. How Will Citizen Involvement Solve These Problems?

1. Charles Rolls, "Heathrow Noise Damage Across London" (London: Heathrow Association for the Control of Aircraft Noise, June 1997): 10; www.hacan.org.uk.

2. Ibid.

3. Charles Derber, *Corporation Nation* (New York: St. Martin's Press, 1998): 315.

4. Noam Chomsky, *Class Warfare* (Monroe, ME: Common Courage Press, 1996): 117.

5. Simon Romero, "Weavers Go Dot-com, and Elders Move In," *New York Times,* March 28, 2000.

6. Interview with Kay Tiffany, September 8, 2000.

7. William Greider, *Who Will Tell the People: The Betrayal of American Democracy* (New York: Simon & Schuster, 1992): 249.

8. Stanley Milgram, *Obedience to Authority* (New York: Harper Colophon Books, 1969): 205.

9. Derber, *Corporation Nation:* 328.

10. John Ehrenberg, *Civil Society: The Critical History of an Idea* (New York and London: New York University Press, 1999): 248–49.

11. Milgram, *Obedience to Authority.*

12. Victor Klemperer, *I Will Bear Witness* (New York: Random House, 2000).

9. The People Play Defense

1. Thomas Petzinger, Jr., *Hard Landing: The Epic Contest for Power and Profits that Plunged the Airlines into Chaos* (New York: Times Books, 1995).

2. Robert B. Reich, *Tales of a New America: The Anxious Liberal's Guide to the Future* (New York: Vintage Books, 1987): 210.

3. Ibid., 219.

4. Buckingham, "Thinking Regionally about Logan Airport."

5. Matthew Brelis, "Opposition Mounting to Hanscom Expansion," *Boston Globe,* April 6, 2000.

6. Molly Hochkeppel, "Hull, Mass., Voices Grievances to Massport about Logan Air Traffic and Noise," *Patriot Ledger,* April 14, 1999.

7. Communities Against Runway Expansion, "Runway 14/32: An Airport-Expansion Proposal in Disguise," undated flier.

8. Matthew Brelis, "Runway Foes Gather New Ammunition," *Boston Globe,* May 27, 2001.

9. Alan Lupo, "Former Rivals Explore a Union to Fight Massport," *Boston Globe,* November 7, 1999.

10. Trevor Hughes, "Logan, Hanscom Neighbors Join Forces to
    Seek Regional Transit Plan," State House News Service (Boston),
    June 27, 2000.

11. From the Executive Summary of the *Boston Region MPO
    Transportation Plan 2000–2025* (Boston: Boston Metropolitan
    Planning Organization, 2002): 6.

12. Hughes, "Logan, Hanscom Neighbors Join Forces."

13. Rick Harnish, "Forty-seven Organizations Sign Agreement to Promote
    Federal Investment in Modern Nationwide Passenger Rail System,"
    Midwest High Speed Rail Coalition press release, January 16, 2003.

14. "Texas Appellate Court Says Restrictions on Airport Development in
    Bond Issue Violated Airline Deregulation Act," *Star-Telegram*
    (Fort Worth, TX), May 25, 2000.

15. "International Business Travel Guide," *New York Times,* April 25, 2000.

16. Pierre Sparaco, "Lagging ATM Imperils Europe's Air Efficiency,"
    Aviation Week & Space Technology (October 25, 1999): 97.

17. Rail Europe, "France's Latest High-speed Rail Line, TGV
    Mediterranée, Takes 60% of Market Share of Paris-Marseille Route
    Within 6 Months of Operation," press release (White Plains, NY),
    December 19, 2001.

18. Jean-Pierre Loubinoux, "Improving the Link Between Air
    and Rail," Testimony before the U.S. House of Representatives
    Committee on Transportation and Infrastructure–Subcommittee
    on Aviation and Subcommittee on Railroads, February 26, 2003.

19. John Tagliabue, "Travel Advisory: Correspondent's Report; Airlines
    Feel Pressure of Europe's Fast Trains," *New York Times on the Web,*
    August 12, 2001.

20. Kay Tiffany, letter to the editor, *Lexington Minuteman,* March 9, 2000.

21. Massachusetts Port Authority, "Support Proposed Runway 14/32:
    Change Is in the Air at Logan, but Only with Your Support,"
    www.massport.com/logan/runway.asp (accessed June 11, 2000;
    page now discontinued).

22. Heathrow Association for the Control of Aircraft Noise, "Market
    Pricing Solution to Pressure on Heathrow," news release, September
    10, 1996.

23. David Hughes, "Pilots See Shrinking Margin for Error," *Aviation Week & Space Technology* (October 25, 1999): 73.

24. Paul Proctor, "Global Competitiveness Concerns Could Boost Airport Expansion," *Aviation Week & Space Technology* (October 25, 1999): 88.

25. Edward O. Wilson, *Consilience: The Unity of Knowledge* (New York: Vintage Books, 1998): 325.

26. Ibid., 319.

27. Peter L. Berger and Richard John Neuhaus, *To Empower People: From State to Civil Society* (Washington, DC: American Enterprise Institute Press, 1996): 206.

10. Aviation with Representation

1. Marcia D. Lowe, "The Global Rail Revival," Worldwatch Institute, Worldwatch Paper 118, 1995.

2. Michael S. Dukakis, "Common Sense Can Solve Logan's Problems," *Boston Globe,* April 25, 1999.

3. This is from a statement by Betty Ann Kane from the National Organization to Insure a Sound-controlled Environment before the House Committee on Transportation and Infrastructure–Subcommittee on Aviation, regarding the reauthorization of the Airport Improvement Program, March 25, 1998.

4. Chris Mullin, Parliamentary under-secretary of state for the Environment, Transport and the Regions, *Parliamentary Debates,* Commons (March 21, 2000), cols. 168WH–174WH.

5. Reich, *Tales of a New America:* 232.

6. Bernie Sanders, "Falling Behind in Boom Times," *New York Times,* January 12, 2000.

7. Michael S. Dukakis, statement to the Save Our Heritage Advisory Board, Concord, MA, undated.

8. Brian O'Connell, *Civil Society: The Underpinnings of American Democracy* (Tufts University, Hanover, NH, and London: University Press of New England, 1999): 125.

9. Ibid., 123–24.

10. Ibid.

11. How to Work for Sustainable Aviation

1. Coralie Cooper, Dave Park, Jake Schmidt, Ingrid Ulbrich, and Steve Winkelman, "Controlling Airport-Related Air Pollution," pamphlet (Boston: Northeast States for Coordinated Air Use Management [NESCAUM] and Center for Clean Air Policy [CCAP], June 2003).

2. For discussions of using antitrust laws as a political tool to advance social goals, see Charles R. Geisst, *Monopolies in America* (New York: Oxford University Press, 2000), and Jeremy Rifkin, *The Age of Access* (New York: Penguin Putnam, 2000).

3. National Air Transportation Association, "America's 100 Most Needed Airports," December 2000; www.nataonline.org/ 2GovWatch/Archive.

4. "Unwelcome Intrusion: Congress Should Stay Out of Homestead Fray," editorial, *Miami Herald,* April 12, 2001.

5. Paul Clinton, "Cox Unveils El Toro Sell-off," *Los Angeles Times,* March 7, 2002.

6. Calculations by the Edinburgh Center for Carbon Management, Scotland, reported in Harry Rijnen, "Offsetting Environmental Damage by Planes," *New York Times,* February 18, 2003.

7. Susan Staples, personal communication.

8. Jonathan D. Salant, "Airline Lobbying Expenses Up; Industry Expects to Lose $7 Billion This Year," Associated Press, October 15, 2002.

9. Leslie Wayne and Michael Moss, "Bailout for Airlines Showed the Weight of a Mighty Lobby," *New York Times,* October 10, 2001.

10. Denise Marois, "Congress Unlikely to Grant More Aid, Regulate Industry," *Aviation Daily,* May 1, 2003.

11. Matthew Brelis, "Complaints Against Airlines Up 130%," *Boston Globe,* April 11, 2000.

12. Susan Carey, "Airlines Go to Trial over Antitrust Case," *Wall Street Journal,* November 2, 2000.

13. Frank Swoboda, "Lawmakers Seek Answers to Rise in Flight Delays," *Washington Post,* September 29, 2000.

Epilogue

1. Letter from Miguel Vasconcelos, director of airports for the Aircraft Owners and Pilots Association, to Mr. Vincent Scarano, manager, Airports Division, Federal Aviation Administration, March 29, 2000. Copy made public at the April 18, 2000, meeting of the Hanscom Field Advisory Committee. See 49 USCS 47524 (2000) for the law on which this suit is based.

2. Nancy A. Nelson, letter to friends and colleagues, February 10, 2000.

3. Barbara Foster, "Federal Agencies Involved in Hanscom Field Struggle," *Lexington Minuteman,* June 21, 2000.

4. Joe and Vicky Bartolo, letter to ShhAir, January 29, 2001.

5. Robin Washington and Ellen J. Silberman, "Runway Gets OK: Court Ruling Lifts '76 Ban on New Strip at Logan," *BostonHerald.com,* November 19, 2003.

6. Natural Resources Defense Council, Friends of the Earth, Defenders of Wildlife, Sierra Club, and Environmental Defense, "Oppose Limits on Environmental Review and Public Participation in FAA Conference Report," press release, November 7, 2003.

Bibliography

"Aircraft Noise Raises Resident Blood Pressure," *Sydney Morning Herald,* November 13, 2001.

Aircraft Owners and Pilots Association. "Management Reform of the Federal Aviation Administration." Issue brief, February 1999. www.aopa.org.

"Air Shuttle Rankles Lexington, Concord." *Hartford Courant,* September 18, 1999.

Anthrop, Donald F. "The Noise Crisis." In *Noise Pollution and the Law,* edited by James L. Hildebrand, 3–20. Buffalo, NY: William S. Hein & Company, 1970.

Atlanta Journal and Constitution. "Nations Air's Connection to Lorenzo Questioned." September 12, 1995.

"ATX Fights Ruling." *Aviation Week & Space Technology* 140 (April 11, 1994): 34.

BankBoston Economics Department. "MIT: The Impact of Innovation." Cambridge, MA: MIT News Office, 1995.

Barnard, Bruce. "Brussels' Night-Flight Ban Is Latest in European Trend of Noise Restrictions; Policies Hurt Cargo Companies the Most." *Journal of Commerce* (January 5, 2000).

Battenfeld, Joe. "Cellucci Locks Pals into Massport Posts." *Boston Globe,* May 1, 2000.

Berger, Peter L., and Richard John Neuhaus. *To Empower People: From State to Civil Society.* Washington, DC: American Enterprise Institute Press, 1996.

Berglund, Birgitta, and Thomas Lindvall, eds. *Community Noise.* Stockholm, Sweden: Center for Sensory Research, 1995.

Berglund, Birgitta, Thomas Lindvall, and Dietrich H. Schwela, eds. *Guidelines for Community Noise.* New York: World Health Organization, 1999.

Bernstein, Aaron. *Grounded: Frank Lorenzo and the Destruction of Eastern Airlines.* New York: Simon and Schuster, 1990.

Bielefeldt, A. R., R. LaPlante, and T. Illangasekare. "The Impact of
    Biogradation of De-Icing Chemicals on the Conductivity and
    Dispersivity of Porous Media." In *Proceedings of the 2000 Conference of
    Hazardous Waste Research: Environmental Challenges and Solutions to
    Resource Development, Production and Use.* Manhattan, KS: Great
    Plains/Rocky Mountain Hazardous Substance Research Center,
    Kansas State University, 2000.

Bombardieri, Marcella. "325 Protest Commercial Flights at Hanscom."
    Boston Globe, September 29, 1999.

Boston Region MPO Transportation Plan 2000–2025. Boston: Boston
    Metropolitan Planning Organization, 2002.

Brelis, Matthew. "Cleared for Takeoff." *Boston Globe,* December 9, 1999.

———. "Complaints Against Airlines Up 130%." *Boston Globe,* April 11,
    2000.

———. "Opposition Mounting to Hanscom Expansion." *Boston Globe,*
    April 6, 2000.

———. "Runway Foes Gather New Ammunition." *Boston Globe,* May
    27, 2001.

Bronzaft, Arline L. "Noise Pollution: A Hazard to Physical and Mental
    Well-Being." In *Handbook of Environmental Psychology,* edited by
    Robert B. Bechtel and Arza Churchman, 499–510. New York: John
    Wiley & Sons, 2002.

"Brussels, Belgium Will Ban Night Flights after 2003." *AFX European
    Focus* (January 3, 2000).

Buckingham, Virginia. "Massport Director Defends Growth." *Boston
    Globe,* April 23, 2000.

———. "Thinking Regionally about Logan Airport." *Boston Globe,*
    January 8, 2000.

Burnett, R. T., S. Cakmak, J. R. Brook, and D. Krewski. "The Role of
    Particulate Size and Chemistry in the Association between
    Summertime Ambient Air Pollution and Hospitalization for
    Cardiorespiratory Diseases." *Environmental Health Perspectives* 105
    (1997), 614–20.

Bushnell, Davis. "Corporate Jets on the Rise at Hanscom." *Boston Globe,*
    March 5, 2000.

———. "Court Clears Airline for Hanscom." *Boston Globe,* September 28, 1999.

———. "Massport Looking to Expand Facilities at Hanscom Field." *Boston Globe,* December 12, 1999.

Business Wire. "ETRPA Request County Reopen Comments to El Toro EIR." Press release, August 24, 2000.

Button, Kenneth. *Aviation and the Environment—A General Perspective. Findings Workshop Report, Environmental Research Beyond 2000.* (Washington, DC: Office of Environment and Energy, Federal Aviation Administration, 1998).

Cancilla, Devon A., Jennifer Martinez, and Graham C. Van Aggelen. "Detection of Aircraft De-icing/Anti-icing Fluid Additives in a Perched Water Monitoring Well at an International Airport." *Environmental Science and Technology* 32, no. 23 (1998): 3834–35.

Carey, Susan. "Airlines Go to Trial over Antitrust Case." *Wall Street Journal,* November 2, 2000.

Cestari, Mark R. "Airline Says It's Filling Public Need." *Boston Globe,* April 23, 2000.

Chen, David W. "With Major Airports Overcrowded, Regional Hubs Are Gearing Up." *New York Times,* October 24, 2000.

Chicago Tribune. "Judge Seals Documents in O'Hare Suit." June 9, 2000.

Chomsky, Noam. *Class Warfare.* Monroe, ME: Common Courage Press, 1996.

City of Burbank et al. v. Lockheed Air Terminal, Inc., et al. 411 U.S. 624. Appeal from the United States Court of Appeals for the Ninth Circuit, no. 71-1637 (May 14, 1973).

Clinton, Paul. "Cox Unveils El Toro Sell-off." *Los Angeles Times,* March 7, 2002.

Cohen, S., and N. Weinstein. "Non-auditory Effects of Noise on Behaviour and Health." *Journal of Social Issues* (1981): 36–70.

Cole, Caroline Louise. "Towns Urge Regional Approach to Planning." *Boston Sunday Globe,* March 12, 2000.

Colman, Tony. Parliamentary Debates Commons (March 21, 2000), col. 168WH.

Communities Against Runway Expansion. "Runway 14/32:
  An Airport-Expansion Proposal in Disguise." Undated flier.
Communities, Inc. v. Busey. 9 F.3d 242 (6th Cir. 1992).
Cooper, Coralie, Dave Park, Jake Schmidt, Ingrid Ulbrich, and Steve
  Winkelman. *Controlling Airport-Related Air Pollution.* Boston: Northeast
  States for Coordinated Air Use Management (NESCAUM) and
  Center for Clean Air Policy (CCAP), June 2003.
Cornell University press release. "Aircraft Noise Is Harmful to the
  Health and Well-being of Children." *Cornell News,* March 4, 1998.
  www.news.cornell.edu/releases/March98/noise.stress.ssl.html.
Coull, James M. "Massport Hiring Is Defended." *Lexington Minuteman,*
  October 7, 1999.
Coutant, Dorothy. Letter to the editor. *Stuart News,* April 17, 1999.
Croghan, Lore. "Viewpoint: A Chat with Frank Lorenzo." *Financial World*
  165 (January 2, 1996): 48–50.
Derber, Charles. *Corporation Nation.* New York: St. Martin's Press, 1998.
DeVillars, John P. "Privatizing the MWRA Could Spell Relief for
  Greater Boston." *Boston Globe,* May 18, 2000.
Dornheim, Michael A. "Jump in Delays Shows ATC Bumping into Capacity
  Limits." *Aviation Week & Space Technology* (October 25, 1999): 90–94.
Dukakis, Michael S. "Common Sense Can Solve Logan's Problems."
  Boston Globe, April 25, 1999.
Dumser, Brian. *Winthrop Community Health Survey.* Winthrop, MA:
  Winthrop Environmental Health Facts Subcommittee of the
  Winthrop Airport Hazards Committee, Winthrop Board of Health,
  and AIR, August 18, 1999.
Dunne, Nancy. "US Claims European Union's Ban on Aircraft Noise
  Law Costs Billions: US Seeks Ban in EU Voting Rights." *London
  Financial Times,* December 10, 1999.
Ehrenberg, John. *Civil Society: The Critical History of an Idea.* New York
  and London: New York University Press, 1999.
Entous, Adam. "European Union and US Battle over Aircraft Noise Law."
  Journal of Commerce (December 10, 1999): 12.
"European Court Agrees to Hear Plea by Residents Wanting Night
  Flight Ban." *The Independent* (May 17, 2000).

Evans, Gary, Monika Bullinger, and Staffan Hygge. "Chronic Noise Exposure and Physiological Response: A Prospective Study of Children Living Under Environmental Stress." *Psychological Science* 9, no. 1 (January 1998): 75–77.

Evans, Gary, and Lorraine Maxwell. "Chronic Noise Exposure and Reading Deficits: The Mediating Effects of Language Acquisition." *Environment and Behavior* 29, no. 5 (September 1997): 638–56.

Falzone, Kristin L. "Airport Noise Pollution: Is There a Solution in Sight?" *Boston College Environmental Affairs Law Review* 26 (1999): 769–807.

Federal Aviation Administration, Department of Transportation. *Aviation Noise Abatement Policy. Federal Register* 65, no. 136 (July 14, 2000): 43,802.

―――. *Code of Federal Regulations* (2000). Chapter 1, "Aeronautics and Space," part 36, appendix C.

―――. Federal Aviation Administration Advisory Circular 91-36c. "Visual Flight Rules (VFR) Flight Near Noise-Sensitive Areas." October 19, 1984.

Feitelson, I. E., R. E. Hurd, and R. R. Mudge. "The Impact of Airport Noise on Willingness to Pay for Residence." *Transportation Research* 1, no. 1 (1996): 1–14.

Foster, Barbara. "Federal Agencies Involved in Hanscom Field Struggle." *Lexington Minuteman,* June 21, 2000.

Frei, Rosemary. "Fly the Filthy Skies." *Toronto Globe and Mail,* September 28, 2002.

Geisst, Charles R. *Monopolies in America.* New York: Oxford University Press, 2000.

General Accounting Office. "General Aviation Airports: Unauthorized Land Use Highlights Need for Improved Oversight and Enforcement." GAO/RCED-99-109. May 1999.

Greider, William. *Who Will Tell the People: The Betrayal of American Democracy.* New York: Simon & Schuster, 1992.

Griggs v. Allegheny County, 369 U.S. 84, 89–90 (1962).

Guterman, Lila. "Toxic Takeoffs: Aircraft De-icers Hold a Hidden Hazard." *New Scientist* (January 9, 1999).

Gution, Jerry M. "Airport Ideas Upset Group." *Stuart News,* May 19, 2000.

———. "Director Reports on Witham's Ability to Handle 737." *Stuart News,* April 7, 2000.

———. "Gary Endorses 'Friends' Advocating Airport Upgrade." *Stuart News,* April 11, 2000.

———. "Melzer Will Press for Halt of Airport Study." *Stuart News,* May 20, 2000.

———. "Officials: Din Raised over Wrong Issue: Noise, Not Weight, Matters in Airport Debate." *Stuart News,* April 13, 2000.

———. "Unanimous Commission OKs Airport Noise Study." *Stuart News,* May 3, 2000.

Haines, M. M., S. A. Stansfeld, R. F. S. Job, B. Berglund, and J. Head. "Chronic Aircraft Noise Exposure, Stress Responses, Mental Health and Cognitive Performance in School Children." *Psychological Medicine* 31 (2001): 265–77.

Halstead, Ted. "A Politics for Generation X." *Atlantic Monthly* (August 1999).

Hanchett, Doug. "Audit of Massport Uncovers Wild Spending and Donations." *Boston Herald,* December 15, 2000.

Harnish, Rick. "Forty-seven Organizations Sign Agreement to Promote Federal Investment in Modern Nationwide Passenger Rail System." Midwest High Speed Rail Coalition press release, January 16, 2003.

Heathrow Association for the Control of Aircraft Noise. "Market Pricing Solution to Pressure on Heathrow." News release, September 10, 1996.

Hochkeppel, Molly. "Hull, Mass., Voices Grievances to Massport about Logan Air Traffic and Noise." *Patriot Ledger,* April 14, 1999.

Holland, W. W. "Noise and Health." London: Heathrow Association for the Control of Aircraft Noise, June 1997.

Holsman, Melissa E. "Gary Vows Fight for Landing Rights." *Stuart News,* April 13, 2000.

———. "Those on Both Sides of Airport Debate Oppose 737 Idea." *Stuart News,* April 12, 2000.

Holsman, Melissa E., and Suzanne Latshaw. "Willie Gary Is King of Local Soft Money." *Stuart News,* May 14, 2000.

House Committee on Transportation and Infrastructure. "GAO Study Links Aircraft Emissions to Global Warming." *San Diego Earth Times* (April 2000).

Hudson, Paul. "Flight Delays—The Real Story." Report of the Aviation Consumer Action Project, Washington, DC, November 5, 1999.

Hughes, David. "Pilots See Shrinking Margin for Error." *Aviation Week & Space Technology* (October 25, 1999).

Hughes, Trevor. "Logan, Hanscom Neighbors Join Forces to Seek Regional Transit Plan." State House News Service (Boston), June 27, 2000.

Hygge, S. "A Comparison Between the Impact of Noise from Aircraft, Road Traffic and Trains on Long-term Recall and Recognition of a Text in Children Aged 12–14 years." *Schriftenreihe des Vereins für Wasser-, Boden-, und Lufthygiene* 88 (1993): 416–27.

Illinois Environmental Protection Agency, Bureau of Air. *Illinois Annual Air Quality Report for 1998.* September 1999.

Intergovernmental Panel on Climate Change Special Report: Aviation and the Global Atmosphere. New York: World Meteorological Organization and the United Nations Environment Programme, 1999.

"International Business Travel Guide." *New York Times,* April 25, 2000.

Kiehl, Stephen, and Howie Paul Hartnett. "Florida Residents Complain of Increasing Noise from Witham Field Airport." *Palm Beach Post,* April 18, 1999.

Klemperer, Victor. *I Will Bear Witness.* New York: Random House, 2000.

Knox, E. G., and E. A. Gilman. "Hazard Proximities of Childhood Cancers in Great Britain from 1953–80." *Journal of Epidemiology and Community Health* 51, no. 2 (April 1997): 151–59.

Lean, Geoffrey. "We Regret to Announce that the Flight to Malaga Is Destroying the Planet: Air Travel Is Fast Becoming One of the Biggest Causes of Global Warming." *The Independent* (August 26, 2001).

"Logic 101." *Noise Regulation Report* 28, no. 7 (July 2001).

"Lorenzo's Ex-associates Plan Start-up Airline." *Airline Industry Information* (October 1, 1997).

Lowe, Marcia D. "The Global Rail Revival." Worldwatch Paper 118, Worldwatch Institute, 1995.

Lupo, Alan. "Former Rivals Explore a Union to Fight Massport." *Boston Globe,* November 7, 1999.

Lyall, Sarah. "Under Noisy Skies, Britons Assert a Right to Sleep." *New York Times,* October 14, 2001.

Margasak, Gabriel. "Boat, Car Horns to Protest Airport." *Stuart News,* April 21, 2000.

Massachusetts Port Authority. *General Rules and Regulations for Laurence G. Hanscom Field.* Effective July 31, 1980.

———. "Hanscom Field: A Delicate Balance." Circa 1986.

———. *Hanscom Field Master Plan and Environmental Impact Statement.* June 15, 1978.

———. "Massachusetts Port Authority Enabling Act of 1956." Chapter 465, as amended through December, 1996.

———. *Monthly Statistics Report—Hanscom Field.* April 2000.

———. Response to the *Strategic Assessment Report* produced by Arthur D. Little for the Massachusetts Aeronautics Commission, Meeting of the Policy, Planning, and Public Affairs Committee, October 19, 1993.

Massachusetts Water Resources Authority. Governance and Organization. www.mwra.state.ma.us.

McCoppin, Robert. "Demand for Pilots Sending Many to School." *Daily Herald,* February 12, 2001.

McGowan, Richard. "Noise from Hanscom: It's Enough, Already." *Lexington Minuteman,* September 30, 1999.

McKenna, James T. "Despite Claims, Costs of Delays Are Unproven." *Aviation Week & Space Technology* (October 25, 1999): 70–72.

Milgram, Stanley. *Obedience to Authority.* New York: Harper Colophon Books, 1969.

Millard Refrigerated Services, Inc. v. Federal Aviation Administration. No. 95-1535 (DC Cir., October 25, 1996).

Miller, Nicholas P. "Ldn Necessary But Not Sufficient." *Internoise* (July 20–22, 1992).

Minnis, Patrick, J. Kirk Ayers, and Steven P. Weaver. "Surface-based

Observations of Contrail Occurrence Frequency over the U.S., April 1993–April 1994." NASA RP-1404, December 1997: 83 ff.

Mislow, John, and Richard Kassel. *Under the Flight Path.* New York: Natural Resources Defense Council, March 1997.

Moore, James. *The Death of Competition.* New York: HarperBusiness, 1996.

Mullin, Chris. *Parliamentary Debates,* Commons (March 21, 2000), cols. 168WH–174WH.

"NASA Believes Jet Contrails Contribute to Climatic Changes." *NBC News* transcript of broadcast, July 28, 1998.

National Air Transportation Association, "America's 100 Most Needed Airports," December 2000. www.nata-online.org.

National Parks and Conservation Association v. Federal Aviation Administration, 998 F.2d 1523 (10th Cir. 1993).

Natural Resources Defense Council, Friends of the Earth, Defenders of Wildlife, Sierra Club, and Environmental Defense. "Oppose Limits on Environmental Review and Public Participation in FAA Conference Report." Press release, November 7, 2003.

1994–1995 Airport Noise Summary. Washington, DC: National Business Aircraft Association, 1995.

North, David M. "Action Plan for Air Travel." *Aviation Week & Space Technology* (October 25, 1999).

Nulty, Peter. "America's Toughest Bosses." *Fortune* (February 27, 1989): 41.

O'Brian, Bridget. "For Lorenzo, Getting a New Airline Aloft Is Proving Treacherous." *Wall Street Journal,* January 25, 1994.

O'Connell, Brian. *Civil Society: The Underpinnings of American Democracy.* Tufts University, Hanover, NH, and London: University Press of New England, 1999.

Park Ridge, Illinois, City of. "Preliminary Study and Analysis of Toxic Air Pollutant Emissions from O'Hare International Airport and the Resulting Health Risks Created by These Toxic Emissions in Surrounding Residential Communities." August 2000.

Petzinger, Thomas, Jr. *Hard Landing: The Epic Contest for Power and Profits that Plunged the Airlines into Chaos.* New York: Times Books, 1995.

Phillips, Carolyn, and Bridget O'Brian. "Lorenzo's Plan for New Airline Provokes Labor." *Wall Street Journal,* June 28, 1993.

Pope, C. A., III, et al. "Lung Cancer, Cardiopulmonary Mortality, and Long-term Exposure to Fine Particulate Air Pollution." *Journal of the American Medical Association* 287, no. 9 (March 2002): 1132–41.

———. "Particulate Air Pollution as a Predictor of Mortality in a Prospective Study of US Adults." *American Journal of Respiratory Critical Care Medicine* 151 (1995): 669–74.

"The Power in the Tower Is Out of Local Control." *Washington Post,* March 24, 2000.

"Predict and Provoke." *Economist* (February 22, 2003): 52–53.

Proctor, Paul. "Global Competitiveness Concerns Could Boost Airport Expansion." *Aviation Week & Space Technology* (October 25, 1999): 88–90.

Rail Europe. "France's Latest High-speed Rail Line, TGV Mediterranée, Takes 60% of Market Share of Paris-Marseille Route Within 6 months of Operation." Press release (White Plains, NY), December 19, 2001.

Rasmussen, Neil. "Hanscom Plan Could Weaken Our Schools." Letter to the editor. *Lexington Minuteman,* November 11, 1999.

Reich, Robert B. *Tales of a New America: The Anxious Liberal's Guide to the Future.* New York: Vintage Books, 1987.

Rifkin, Jeremy. *The Age of Access.* New York: Penguin Putnam, 2000.

Rolls, Charles. "Heathrow Noise Damage Across London." London: Heathrow Association for the Control of Aircraft Noise, June 1997.

Romero, Simon. "Weavers Go Dot-com, and Elders Move In." *New York Times,* March 28, 2000.

Ryan, James E., et al. Plaintiff's Reply Brief in Support of Their Motion for Summary Judgment and Response, submitted to the Circuit Court for the Eighteenth Judicial Circuit, Du Page County, Wheaton, Illinois, July 16, 1993.

Sanders, Bernie. "Falling Behind in Boom Times." *New York Times,* January 12, 2000.

Saporito, Jack. "Phony Flight Delays." Press release, US–Citizens Aviation Watch Association, March 5, 2001.

Schiavo, Mary. *Flying Blind, Flying Safe.* New York: Avon Books, 1997.

Schmeck, K., and F. Ponstka. "Psychophysiological and Psychiatric Tests with Children and Adolescents in a Low-altitude Flight Region." *Schriftenreihe des Vereins für Wasser-, Boden-, und Lufthygiene* 88 (1992): 301–6.

Schomer, Paul. "Assessment of Airport Noise Annoyance." Report for U.S. delegation to the International Organization for Standardization Acoustics and Noise committees (Champaign, Illinois: Schomer and Associates, January 12, 2001).

Shapiro, Sidney A. "Lessons from a Public Policy Failure: EPA and Noise Abatement." *Ecology Law Quarterly* 19, no. 1 (1992): 1–61.

Sparaco, Pierre. "Lagging ATM Imperils Europe's Air Efficiency." *Aviation Week & Space Technology* (October 25, 1999): 97.

Stenzel, Jennifer. "Flying Off Course: Environmental Impacts of America's Airports." A 1996 report of the Natural Resources Defense Council. The report's major findings, along with detailed recommendations for regulation, are available at NRDC.org.

Suter, Alice H. "Noise and Its Effects." Administrative Conference of the United States, November, 1991.

Swoboda, Frank. "Lawmakers Seek Answers to Rise in Flight Delays." *Washington Post,* September 29, 2000.

———. "US Airways Introduces Earlier Shuttle Between Washington and New York After Acquiring Quieter Planes; Addition Expected to Attract Business Travelers." *Washington Post,* November 23, 1999.

Tagliabue, John. "Travel Advisory: Correspondent's Report; Airlines Feel Pressure of Europe's Fast Trains." *New York Times on the Web,* August 12, 2001.

"Texas Appellate Court Says Restrictions on Airport Development in Bond Issue Violated Airline Deregulation Act." *Star-Telegram* (Fort Worth, TX), May 25, 2000.

United States v. Causby. 328 U.S. 256 (1946).

United States v. Clarke. 445 U.S. 253 (1980).

"Unwelcome Intrusion: Congress Should Stay Out of Homestead Fray." Editorial, *Miami Herald,* April 12, 2001.

Upham, Paul, Janet Maughan, David Raper, and Callum Thomas, eds. *Towards Sustainable Aviation* (London: Earthscan Publications Ltd., 2003).

U.S. Department of Transportation. Application of Shuttle America Corporation for a Certificate of Public Convenience and Necessity Pursuant to 49 U.S.C.* 41102 to Engage in Interstate Scheduled Air Transportation. Docket OST 98-, exhibit 3: 12.

U.S. Environmental Protection Agency. "Information on Levels of Environmental Noise Requisite to Protect Public Health and Welfare with an Adequate Margin of Safety," 550/9-74-004 (March 1974).

————. "NPL Site Narrative for Hanscom Field/Hanscom Air Force Base." 27989–27996 *Federal Register* 59, no. 103 (May 31, 1994).

Vedal, Sverre. "Health Effects of Inhalable Particles: Implications for British Columbia—Overview and Conclusions." British Columbia Ministry of Environment, Water, Air, and Climate Change Branch, Victoria, BC, June 1995.

Verba, Sidney, Kay Lehman Schlozman, and Henry E. Brady. *Voice and Equality: Civic Voluntarism in American Politics.* Cambridge, MA: Harvard University Press, 1995.

Von Gierke, H. E., and L. C. Johnson. "Noise Control—Where Do We Stand Today?" *Noise Control Engineering Journal* (1996).

Washington, Robin, and Ellen J. Silberman. "Runway Gets OK: Court Ruling Lifts '76 Ban on New Strip at Logan." *BostonHerald.com,* November 19, 2003.

Wayne, Leslie, and Michael Moss. "Bailout for Airlines Showed the Weight of a Mighty Lobby." *New York Times,* October 10, 2001.

Whitelegg, John, and Nick Williams. *The Plane Truth: Aviation and the Environment.* London: The Ashton Trust and Transport 2000 Trust, 2000. Available at us-caw.org.

Wilson, Edward O. *Consilience: The Unity of Knowledge.* New York: Vintage Books, 1998.

Woolsey, James P. "Say Goodby, Frank." *Air Transport World* 27 (October 1990): 23.

Index

abatement, noise: and bans on Stage
Two aircraft, 101–2; defined, 108;
DNL contours and, 58–59; in
Federal Aviation Act, 97; Massport
and, 77; and quieter aircraft, 58–59,
108–10
accountability: aviation with
representation and, 158–59; of
government, 68–69; as prerequisite
for citizen involvement, 130–32; as
prerequisite for democracy, 126
acetone, 36
acid rain, 29
activism. *See* citizen involvement;
empowerment
ADAFs. *See* aircraft de-icing/anti-icing
fluids
Adams, Abigail, 11
additives, de-icing, 35
Advisory Council on Historic
Preservation, 170
Aeromexico, 90
Aeroports de Paris, 90
Agriculture, U.S. Department of, 41
Airbus Industrie, 90
air cargo operations, 58
aircraft de-icing/anti-icing fluids
(ADAFs), 34–36; additives in, 35; at
Hanscom Field, 75, 77; health
effects of, 34–35; main ingredients
of, 34
aircraft disturbance reports, 21, 57
Aircraft Owners and Pilots Association
(AOPA), 87, 175, 183
Air France, 90, 142
Airline Deregulation Act (1978), 141
Air Line Pilots Association, 90, 93, 183

air pollution, 29–32, 111, 171. *See also*
emissions
Airport and Airway Trust Fund, 88
airport expansion: airports targeted for,
13, 43, 179–82; citizen opposition
to, 11–12; citizens' master plan for,
65–67; community reactions to,
121–24; complexity of issue, 12,
168; control of, and infrastructure
reduction, 64; incrementalist tactics
used for, 43–44; and loss of local
autonomy, 14–15; no caps on, 54;
secrecy and, 64–65; and traffic
congestion, 31–32; and urban
sprawl, 162–63; as urban/suburban
phenomenon, 13. *See also* Hanscom
Airfield/Field expansion; *specific
airports*
Airport Noise and Capacity Act of
1990 (ANCA): aviation industry
pressure to liberalize, 116; and
DNL measurements, 103–8; and
FAA, 102–3; failure of, 57, 103–8;
implementation of, 103; and noise
abatement, 108–10; and noise
mitigation, 110–11; passage of,
101–2; undebated in Congress,
102, 113
Airport Operating Certificate, 80
Airports Council International, 112
air quality, at Hanscom Field, 75
air traffic controllers strike (1981), 76,
91–92
Air Transport Association (ATA), 86,
184
Air Transport World, 92
allergies, 28

All Nippon Airways, 90
ambient sound, 104
American Airlines, 19, 90
American Association of Airport
    Executives, 146–47, 184
American Cancer Society, 30
American Railroad Revitalization,
    Investment, and Enhancement Act,
    141, 187
American Working Group for National
    Policy, 184
Amsterdam Airport Schiphol, 111
Amtrak, 141, 154
ANCA. *See* Airport Noise and
    Capacity Act of 1990
annoyance, 38, 105–6
anti-icing. *See* aircraft de-icing/anti-
    icing fluids
antitrust laws, 67, 143, 172
AOPA. *See* Aircraft Owners and Pilots
    Association
apathy: and institutional
    unaccountability, 131–32; and
    special interest influence, 22–23,
    164–65
aquatic life, 35
Aretakis, Gregory, 91, 94–95
Army Corps of Engineers, 177
Arrive 21 Act, 141, 187
Ashley, Thomas, 126
asthma, 26, 28, 29
ATA. *See* Air Transport Association
ATX, Inc., 93, 94
aviation, general: airports restricted to,
    66; emissions from unmonitored,
    25; FAA control of, 157–58; at
    Hanscom Field, 19, 51, 54, 76; lead-
    based fuel used for, 31; lobbying
    efforts of, 175
aviation, international: Kyoto Protocol
    and emissions from, 33; and noise

regulation, 89–90, 111–13; and
    sustainable transportation, 172–73
aviation industry: and accountability,
    132; airport expansion promoted
    by, 14, 84–85; and citizen
    opposition, 12, 144–46; community
    competitiveness against, 148–51;
    and delays, 85–87; and FAA, 12–13,
    169, 172; Frank Lorenzo and,
    91–95; lobbying efforts of, 89–90,
    171–72; 9/11 attacks and, 171–72,
    177; and noise regulation, 89–90,
    119–20; political influence of,
    12–13, 23, 84, 169, 171–72;
    reregulation of, 172; and
    restructuring of FAA, 71, 87–88, 89;
    and safety standards, 88–89;
    strategies of, 13–14, 135–36;
    subsidization of, 13, 120, 168; and
    sustainable transportation, lack of,
    167–68
Aviation Safety and Noise Abatement
    Act (1979), 102–3, 107
Aviation Week & Space Technology, 86,
    87–88, 184
aviation with representation, 20; and
    accountability, 158–59; citizens'
    master transportation plan, 65–66;
    and demand management strategy,
    157; and multimodal transportation
    policy, 154–55; and NIMBY label,
    159–61; and noise regulation,
    155–56; and pollution, 155, 156;
    and security, 157–58; and
    sustainable transportation, 152–54
Avidyne Corporation, 19

BAA, plc, 90
BankBoston, 116
Bartolo, Joe and Vicky, 176
Battle Road Trail, 46–47

Bedford (Mass.), 14, 19, 46
benzene, 26
Berlin (Germany), 112
Bernstein, Aaron, 91–92
Big Dig, 72
Blackmun, Henry A., 101
Blomberg, Les, 24, 105
blood pressure, impact of noise on, 41–42
Blute, Peter, 51–53
Boeing Company, 90
Boeing 747, emissions from, 171
Boston, 13–15. *See also* Logan Airport; *specific suburbs*
Boston Globe, 53–54, 137–38
Bradley Airport. *See* Hartford Bradley Airport
Brennan, William J., 101
British Airways, 90
bronchitis, 29
Buckingham, Virginia, 54, 137–38
Burbank et al. v. Lockheed Air Terminal, Inc., 99–101, 113–15
Bureau of Labor Statistics, 86
Burger, Warren E., 101
Burns, Ken, 49, 174
Bush, George H. W., 92
Bush, George W., 92, 177
butadiene, 26

campaign finance reform, need for, 67, 143, 165
cancer: Clean Air Act and, 119; impact of aviation pollution on, 26, 27, 30
capitalism, 84; citizen involvement and, 127–28; and commercial vs. community interests, 113; and common good, 81, 145–46
carbon dioxide, 24, 33, 171
CARE (Communities Against Runway Expansion), 54–55, 139
CCAP. *See* Center for Clean Air Policy

Cellucci, Paul, 53, 72, 82, 92
Center for Clean Air Policy (CCAP), 29, 30–31, 168
Centre for Sustainable Transportation, 184
certification standard, engine, 89–90
certified passenger air carrier operations: at Hanscom Field, 75, 76–77, 80; passenger commuter operations vs., 78–79
Charles de Gaulle Airport (Paris), 142
Chek Lap Kok Airport (Hong Kong), 142
Chicago, City of, 27, 169. *See also* O'Hare International Airport
children: cancers in, 26; impact of noise on, 22, 36, 39, 40–42
chloroform, 36
Chomsky, Noam, 84, 124
Cicero, 152
citizen involvement: accountability and, 130–32; effectiveness of, 124; effect of special interests on, 65, 66–67; lack of, in Massport, 80–83; in Lexington (Mass.), 45–46, 47; master transportation plan as result of, 65–66; in MWRA, 82; need for, 15, 80–83; prerequisites for, 124–30; reconceptualization of, 132; social-psychological skills for, 128–30. *See also* aviation with representation
City of Burbank et al. v. Lockheed Air Terminal, Inc., 99–101, 113–15
Civil Aeronautics Board, 78
civil organizations: and aviation with representation, 165; goals for competitiveness, 149–51; limitations of, 143–46, 149, 165; opposition to Hanscom Field expansion, 81–82, 125, 146; practical importance of, 164. *See also specific organizations*

civil society: citizen involvement and,
127; deterioration of, and
democracy, 163–65
Clabes, John, 96
Clean Air Act, 119
Clean Elections Law, 143
climate change, 32–34
Clinton, William Jefferson, 60, 174
CNEL (community noise equivalent
level), 118–19
Coalition for a Global Standard on
Aviation Noise, 89–90, 120
Coalition of Airline Pilots Association,
90
Cohasset (Mass.), 138
commercial interests: community
interests vs., 113–17; strategies of,
135–36. *See also* aviation industry;
special interests
Common Cause, 159
common good: community strategies
and, 136; community vs.
commercial definitions of, 142–46;
and industrial subsidization, 168
communities, local: accountability to,
68–69; aviation with representation
and, 161–63; citizens' master
transportation plan for, 65–66;
emotional reactions to airport
expansion, 121–24; empowerment
of, 15, 163–66; goals for
competitiveness, 148–51;
government/industry strategies
against, 13–14, 43–44, 64–65;
impact of air pollution on, 29–32;
impact of aviation pollution on,
26–28; impact of ground pollution
on, 34–36; impact of noise
pollution on, 36–42; local victories
of, 169–70; loss of autonomy in,
12–15, 22–23, 96, 148; and

multimodal transportation policy,
140; and NIMBY label, 159–61;
and noise regulation, 119; strategies
of, 136–37, 170; survival of, in
organizational ecosystem, 146–48;
and sustainable transportation,
168–71. *See also* aviation with
representation; citizen involvement;
noise regulation; *specific communities*
Communities Against Runway
Expansion. *See* CARE
community noise equivalent level
(CNEL), 118–19
Concord (Mass.), 14, 17, 46, 177
Concorde, 112
congestion. *See* delays/congestion;
ground traffic
Congress, U.S., 186; ANCA undebated
in, 102, 113; aviation industry
influence on, 112, 168–69; and
FAA noise reviews, 118; subsidies
awarded by, 168. *See also specific
legislation*
Conservation Law Foundation, 159
Constitution, U.S.: Article 5, 99;
Article 10, 96, 101; Supremacy
Clause, 100
Continental Airlines: antitrust action
against, 172; Frank Lorenzo and
bankruptcy of, 76, 91, 93, 94–95;
and Hanscom Field expansion, 42;
and Westchester County Airport
expansion, 19
Continental Express, 69–70, 94, 170
contrails, 33–34
Controlling Airport-Related Air Pollution
(CCAP/NESCAUM), 168
Cornell University, 40–41
Corporate Air Service, Inc., 69
corporate jet traffic, 39–40
Corporation Nation (Derber), 123

Corsi, Steve, 35
County of San Bernadino Airports, 90
Cox, Rebecca, 172
CTC Communications, 19
curfews: aviation with representation
    and, 155; *Burbank v. Lockheed* and,
    99–101, 113–14; community
    strategies for enforcement of, 170;
    in EU, 111; Hanscom Field Master
    Plan and, 79; penalties for violating,
    21, 118; violations of, 200n49; at
    Westchester County Airport, 59,
    170; at Witham Field, 63

Dallas-Fort Worth Airport, 141–42
D'Amato, Alfonse M., 118
Danforth, John C., 102
Daschle, Linda Hall, 172
Day-Night Average Sound Level
    (DNL). *See* DNL
decibels (dB): ANCA noise limits,
    108–9; dBA vs. dBC measurement
    of, 37–38, 155–56; and Ldn
    measurement, 103–4
Declaration of Independence, 68
Defenders of Wildlife, 25–26
de-icing. *See* aircraft de-icing/anti-icing
    fluids
delays/congestion, 85–87, 102
Delta Air Lines, 90
democracy: accountability as
    prerequisite for, 126, 130–32;
    capitalism and, 127; and
    centralization of power, 173; citizen
    involvement and, 80–83, 130–32;
    and civil society, deterioration of,
    163–65; effect of special interests
    on, 13, 50–51, 66–67, 173
Denver International Airport, 104,
    141
Derber, Charles, 123, 127

DNL, 103–8
DNL contour, 58–59, 118, 156
DOT. *See* Transportation, U.S.
    Department of
Douglas, William O., 101
Dukakis, Michael J., 140–41, 154,
    162–63
Dulles Airport, 108
Dutch Aviation Act (1978), 111

Eastern Airlines, 76, 91, 93, 95
Economist, The, 84, 86, 150
ecosystem of organizations, 146–48
Ehrenberg, John, 127
Ellison, Larry, 200n49
Elm Brook, 74
El Toro Airport (Orange County,
    Calif.), 64, 170
EMC Corporation, 19
eminent domain, 19
emissions: aviation with representation
    and, 155; from Boeing 747, 171;
    environmental effects of, 32–34;
    health effects of, 27, 30–31;
    insufficient monitoring of, 25; local
    concentration of, 30; at O'Hare, 30,
    194n24
emphysema, 29
empowerment: accountability and,
    130–32; community need for, 15,
    163–66; community strategies for,
    148–51; in Lexington (Mass.), 130;
    prerequisites for, 124–30; social-
    psychological skills for, 128–30. *See
    also* aviation with representation;
    citizen involvement
Enrich, Peter D., 167
environmental organizations, 141,
    146–47
Environmental Protection Act
    (Canada), 35

Environmental Protection Agency
(EPA), 186; aviation with
representation and, 155, 156; and
enforcement of Noise Control Act,
118; and ground pollution, 35–36;
insufficient monitoring by, 25–26;
and Ldn guidelines, 104, 105–6;
monitoring role curtailed, 177; and
noise pollution, 40; and support for
sustainable transportation, 178. *See
also* Office of Noise Abatement and
Control
Environmental Science & Technology, 35
European Court of Human Rights,
112–13, 115
European Union (EU): CNEL used in,
118; and demand management
strategy, 157; and FAA certification
standards, 90; high-speed rail in,
142; noise regulations as "trade
barriers" in, 115; noise regulations
of, 59, 90, 111–13. *See also specific
countries*
Evans, Gary, 40–42
eye irritation, 34–35

Falzone, Kristin L., 117, 119
Fargo, Susan, 53, 92, 96
Federal Aviation Act (1958), 96–98
Federal Aviation Administration (FAA),
186; and airport noise compatibility
programs, 102–3; aviation industry
influence on, 12–13, 87–88, 89,
117–18, 169, 172; aviation with
representation and, 156, 157; and
cost of delays, 86–87; DOT and, 87;
and Hanscom Field expansion, 80;
and New England regional
planning, 139; noise guidelines of,
105–6; noise impact estimates of,
116; on noise pollution and

property values, 50; noise pollution
regulated by, 14, 40, 99; and safety
standards, 88–89; and Stage
Two/Stage Three engine
conversions, 58; and support for
sustainable transportation, 178; and
Witham Field expansion, 63
Federal Aviation Administration
Reauthorization Act (1996), 155,
174
FedEx, 90
Financial World, 94
fines, for nighttime flying, 21, 118
Fish and Wildlife Service, 177
fish kills, 35
flight consolidation, 66, 157
Flight 100–Century of Aviation
Reauthorization Act, 177
Flying Blind, Flying Safe (Schiavo), 89
Foote, Shelby, 49
Ford, Wendell H., 102, 109
formaldehyde, 26
France, 90, 142
Freedom of Information Act, 53
Friends of the Earth, 177
Friends of Witham Field, 63

Garvey, Jane, 85
Gary, Willie, 60–64
general aviation. *See* aviation, general
General Electric, 90
Generic Environmental Impact
Report, 175
Geological Survey, 35
Germany, 112, 142
globalization, 67, 76, 145
global warming, 32–34, 146
glycol ethers, 36
glycols, 25–26, 34–35
Goldman, Donald, 42
Goodwin, Richard, 66–67

Great Britain, 24, 26, 86, 145
Great Meadows National Wildlife
    Refuge, 17, 46
greenhouse gases, 32–33
Greider, William, 15, 121
Griggs v. Allegheny County, 119
Grounded (Bernstein), 91–92
ground pollution, 34–36, 74–75, 77,
    155
ground traffic, 31–32, 46–47, 111
Gulf Oil Corporation, 56

HACAN. *See* Heathrow Association for
    the Control of Aircraft Noise
Hackett, David, 91, 94–95
Haiti, civil society in, 124–25
Hale and Dorr (law firm), 50
Hanscom Airfield/Field: aircraft
    disturbance reports filed against, 21;
    citizens' master plan for, 65–66;
    curfews at, 79; current size of, 19,
    191n2 (ch.2); DNL measurements
    at, 103–4, 108; flight path of, 16–17;
    as general aviation reliever airport,
    19, 51, 54, 76; ground pollution at,
    74–75, 77; ground traffic congestion
    near, 32, 46–47; historic sites near,
    46–47; impact of noise on schools
    near, 37; noise abatement at, 108;
    noise mitigation at, 110–11; noise
    pollution near, 47, 75; operations at,
    22, 39–40, 111; ownership of, 19;
    passenger commuter operations at,
    78–80; penalty for nighttime flights
    at, 21; SuperFund pollution site at,
    36; urban sprawl near, 162–63
Hanscom Airfield/Field expansion,
    174–77; aviation industry strategies
    for, 13–14; and corporate jet traffic,
    39; FAA certification and, 80;
    Hanscom Field Master Plan and,

74–80; impact on communities
    near, 14–15; Massport long-term
    plan for, 110–11; Massport strategies
    for, 17–18, 51–55; 9/11 attacks and,
    176–77; no caps on, 54; opposition
    to, 20–22, 81–82, 125, 146
Hanscom Air Force Base, 19, 76, 191n2
    (ch.2)
Hanscom Area Towns Committee
    (HATS), 48, 52
"Hanscom Field: A Delicate Balance"
    (Massport), 79
Hanscom Field Advisory Committee
    (HFAC): citizen involvement and,
    83; establishment of, 48; and
    Hanscom Field Master Plan, 75; and
    Hanscom Field user fees, 175;
    Massport and, 18, 20, 52, 77, 81–82;
    powerlessness of, 68–69, 81–82,
    122, 149
Hanscom Field Master Plan and
    Environmental Impact Statement,
    74–80; adopted by Massport, 76;
    and certified passenger air carrier
    operations, 75, 76–77; and
    commercial operations, 40;
    difficulty of obtaining, 68–69, 122;
    and ground pollution, 74–75, 77;
    and ground traffic levels, 111;
    Hanscom Task Force and, 75–76;
    hidden agenda of, 77–80; and noise
    pollution, 75, 107
Hanscom Task Force, 75–76
Hard Landing (Petzinger), 135
Hartford Bradley Airport (Conn.), 30,
    138, 139–40
HATS. *See* Hanscom Area Towns
    Committee
Havern, Robert, 139
haze, 29
headaches, 35

Health Effects Institute, 29–30
Heathrow Airport (London), 36,
    112–13, 115, 123
Heathrow Association for the Control
    of Aircraft Noise (HACAN),
    112–13, 185
HFAC. *See* Hanscom Field Advisory
    Committee
highways, subsidization of, 168
Hingham (Mass.), 138
Hollywood-Burbank Airport, 99–101
Homestead Air Force Base, 169–70
Hong Kong, 142
House Committee on Interstate and
    Foreign Commerce, 96–98, 114
Howe, Jonathan, 112
hub-and-spoke system, 85, 173
Huizenga, Wayne, 61
Hull (Mass.), 138–39, 177
Humane Society of the United States,
    25–26
hushkits, 57, 59, 111–12
hydrocarbons, 24, 29

Iberia, 90
Illinois, State of, 169
influenza, 26
infrastructure: investment in, and
    airport expansion, 43–44; need for
    challenged, 86; reduction of, and
    control of airport expansion, 64. *See
    also* runway construction
Interior, U.S. Department of the,
    175–76
International Association of Machinists
    and Aerospace Workers, 94–95
international aviation. *See* aviation,
    international
International Civil Aviation
    Organization, 112
International Organization for

Standardization Acoustics and
    Noise, 105
Internet, 159, 168
involvement, political. *See* citizen
    involvement
Ireland, 73
isopropyl alcohol, 36

Jet Fuel A, 28
John F. Kennedy International Airport,
    57
Johnson Controls World Services, 56

Kaufman, Jay, 16, 20, 152
King County International Airport
    (Seattle), 26
Klemperer, Victor, 129
Kyoto Protocol, 33

LaGuardia Airport (New York City):
    Hanscom compared to, 19; and
    Hanscom Field expansion, 138,
    175; landing slots at, 87, 111,
    174–75; management of, 73; size of,
    19; Westchester County Airport
    compared to, 57
LanChile, 90
landing fees, 111
landing slots, 145
Lautenberg, Frank R., 118
Ldn, 103–8, 155
lead-based fuel, 31
leukemia, 26
Lexington (Mass.), 17; civil
    organizations in, 125, 146;
    description of, 44–46, 47–48;
    empowerment in, 130; as
    endangered historic site, 177;
    environmental impact study not
    performed at, 36; impact of aviation
    pollution on, 110–11; loss of local

autonomy in, 14, 121–23; noise ordinances in, 43; political involvement in, 45–46, 47. *See also* Hanscom Airfield/Field

Lexington Education Foundation News, 201n18

Liberty Mutual Insurance, 19

Lincoln (Mass.), 14, 46

local communities. *See* communities, local

Logan Airport (Boston): and aviation industry strategies, 14; expansion of, and health risks, 27–28; Hanscom Field as general aviation reliever airport for, 19, 51, 76; nitrogen oxide emissions at, 30–31; noise mitigation near, 110; operations at, 55; opposition to expansion of, 54–55; passenger activity at, 140; runway construction at, 14, 54–55, 138–39, 177; security at, 177

London (England): impact of noise pollution in, 36, 123; landing slot dispute in, 145; opposition to night flights in, 112–13, 115

London City Airport, 112

Lorenzo, Frank, 76, 91–95

Louisville (Ky.), 116

Love Field (Dallas), 141

Lufthansa, 90, 142

Manchester Airport (N.H.): FAA investment in, 138; Hanscom compared to, 19; Massport regional strategy and, 138, 139–40; and multimodal transportation policy, 154, 162–63; nitrogen oxide emissions at, 30

Marshall, Thurgood, 100

Maslow, Abraham, 124–25

Massachusetts, Commonwealth of:

citizen involvement in state agencies, 82; Clean Elections Law in, 143; Generic Environmental Impact Report, 175; Joint Committee on Transportation, 53

Massachusetts Environmental Protection Agency, 20

Massachusetts Institute of Technology (MIT), 116

Massachusetts Port Authority Enabling Act, 71

Massachusetts Water Resources Authority (MWRA), 82

Massport (Massachusetts Port Authority), 90; and accountability, 158; aircraft disturbance reports filed against, 21; charitable contributions of, 73; communities unrepresented in, 80–83; divide-and-conquer strategies of, 13–14, 54; establishment of, 71; General Rules and Regulations for Hanscom, 78–79; "Hanscom Field: A Delicate Balance," 79; and Hanscom Field expansion, 17–18, 39, 74–80, 110–11; Hanscom Field owned/operated by, 19; incrementalist development strategies used by, 51–55; as independent authority, 71–74, 201nn12,18; inefficiency of, 74; and Logan Airport security, 177; and noise abatement, 108; and noise mitigation, 110–11; public relations campaigns of, 144–45, 176; and regionalization, 137–38; and regional planning, 138–40; secrecy of, 68–71, 81–82

Maxwell, Lorraine, 40–41

McCain, John, 102, 109, 172

McCullough, David, 43, 49

Meigs Field Airport (Chicago), 169
methylene chloride, 36
methyl ethyl ketone, 36
Metropolitan Washington Airports
    Authority, 90
Miami-Dade Airport Authority, 74
Midway Airport (Chicago), 26
Milgram, Stanley, 128–30
Milwaukee (Wis.), 35
Minneapolis/St. Paul International
    Airport, 90
Minneskwa State Park and Reserve, 171
Minute Man National Historical Park:
    community strategies for protection
    of, 170; as endangered historic site,
    177; impact of aviation pollution
    on, 46–47, 175–76; lawsuit over,
    175–76; Massport and, 52
mitigation, noise, 110–11
Mohawk Air, 69
monopolies, 143, 169
Montgomery Consulting Group, 139
Moynihan, Daniel Patrick, 118
Mullin, Chris, 84
multimodal transportation policy:
    aviation with representation and,
    154–55; need for, 12, 14, 15, 140–42
Munich (Germany), 36–37, 41
Mystic River Bridge Authority, 71

National Aeronautics and Space
    Administration (NASA), 34
National Air Traffic Controllers
    Association, 185
National Air Transportation Association
    (NATA), 13, 169, 179, 185
National Audobon Society, 25–26
National Business Aircraft Association,
    103
National Environmental Policy Act,
    118

National Heart, Lung and Blood
    Institute, 40–41
National Historic Preservation Act,
    175–76
National Institutes of Health, 41
National Noise Policy, 102. *See also*
    Airport Noise and Capacity Act of
    1990
National Organization to Insure a
    Sound-Controlled Environment
    (NOISE), 57–58, 159, 185
National Park Service, 170
National Trust for Historic
    Preservation, 177
Nations Air, 93
Natural Resources Defense Council
    (NRDC), 186; and FAA noise
    reviews, 118; on Flight 100 Act,
    177; and glycols, 25–26; as
    information resource, 159; and
    ONAC reauthorization, 117; and
    Westchester County Airport
    expansion, 56–57, 59
NESCAUM. *See* Northeast States for
    Coordinated Air Use Management
Netherlands, the, 111
Newark International Airport, 171
New England: multimodal
    transportation policy for, 154;
    nitrogen oxide emissions in, 30–31;
    regionalization in, 137–38; regional
    planning in, 138–42
New England Regional Transportation
    Summit, 137–38
Newman, Paul, 49
New York Times, 172
NIMBY, 121, 159–61
nitrogen oxides, 24, 29, 30–31
NOISE. *See* National Organization to
    Insure a Sound-Controlled
    Environment

noise complaints. *See* aircraft
disturbance reports
noise contour. *See* DNL contour
Noise Control Act (1972), 99, 101,
118–19
noise/noise pollution: ambient, 104;
anxiety disorders and, 38–39,
124–25; aviation industry and
worldwide standards for, 89–90;
cardiovascular effects, 36; children's
reading and, 36, 40–42; citizen
involvement and, 171; court cases
fought over, 116–17; FAA
regulation of, 14; high blood
pressure and, 41–42; impact on
property values, 50; insufficient
monitoring of, 25; liability for, 107,
119; measurement of, 37–38,
155–56; numbers affected by, 11;
schools and, 37, 40–42; and Stage
Two/Stage Three engine
conversions, 57–59; stress and,
124–25
Noise Pollution Clearinghouse, 159, 186
noise regulation: aviation with
representation and, 155–56; *Burbank
v. Lockheed* and, 99–101; community
vs. commercial interests and,
113–17, 119–20; in EU, 111–13;
legal resolution of, 117–20; state vs.
federal power of, 96–101;
technology-based controls, 119. *See
also* Airport Noise and Capacity Act
of 1990
nongovernmental organizations, quasi-
autonomous (quangos), 73
Norman, Greg, 61
Northeast States for Coordinated Air
Use Management (NESCAUM),
29, 30–31, 168
Northwest Airlines, 19, 90, 172

Occupational Safety and Health
Administration (OHSA), 34
O'Connell, Brian, 163–64
Office of Noise Abatement and
Control (ONAC): defunding of, 14,
25, 101; establishment of, 99;
reactivation of, 117–18
O'Hare International Airport (Chicago):
expansion of, 169; health risks to
communities near, 27, 30; operations
at, 30; secrecy and expansion plans
at, 64; as world's largest stationary
pollution source, 24
OHSA (Occupational Safety and
Health Administration), 34
Omnibus Budget Reconciliation Act
(1990), 102
ONAC. *See* Office of Noise Abatement
and Control
operations: certified passenger air
carrier vs. passenger commuter,
78–79; in U.S., 84–85. *See also under
specific airports*
ozone, 29
ozone layer, 32–34

Pacific Southwest Airlines, 99
Paris (France), 90, 142
Park Ridge (Ill.), 27
particulates, 26, 27, 29–30
Part 150 Program, 103
Part 150 study, 62, 175
passenger commuter operations, 78–79
passenger time, 86
Peck, Gregory, 49
Péguy, Charles, 133
penalties, for nighttime flying, 21, 118
People Against Hanscom Expansion,
49, 69. *See also* Safeguarding the
Historic Hanscom Area's
Irreplaceable Resources

Petzinger, Tom, Jr., 135
pilots, student, 157
pilot training, 89
Pine, Lynne, 11
Plane Truth, The (Whitelegg and
    Williams), 173
pneumonia, 26
pollution, aviation, 22–23; and climate
    change, 32–34; health effects of, 26;
    insufficient monitoring of, 25–26;
    sources of, 24–26; strategies for
    fighting, 178. *See also* air pollution;
    ground pollution; noise/noise
    pollution
Port Authority (New York City), 73
Port of Boston Commission, 71
Powell, Lewis F., 101
power: centralization of, 173; Massport
    and, 71–74; resistance to, 128–30.
    See also empowerment
Pratt and Whitney, 112
pregnancy complications, 26
Progressive Governance in the 21st
    Century, 68
property values, 50
Providence (R.I.), 154. *See also* T. F.
    Green Airport
public interest. *See* common good

Qantas Airways, 90
quangos (quasi-autonomous
    nongovernmental organizations), 73
Quiet Communities Act, 109, 117–18

rail: and multimodal transportation
    policy, lack of, 14, 15; and regional
    planning, 138, 141; supposed
    subsidization of, 168; underfunding
    of, 13
rail, high-speed: aviation with
    representation and, 152–53, 154–55,

162–63; in EU, 15, 142; need for,
    15; in U.S., 187–88
Raytheon, 19
Reagan, Ronald/Reagan
    administration, 76, 92, 101
Reagan National Airport (Washington,
    D.C.), 108, 109
Reeve, Christopher, 49
regionalization, 137–38
regional planning, 138–42
Rehnquist, William H., 100
Reich, Robert, 135–36, 159
representation, aviation with. *See*
    aviation with representation
reregulation, of airlines, 156, 172
respiratory disease, 26, 28, 34–35
Rijnen, Harry, 24
Robb, Charles S., 118
Rolls-Royce, plc, 90
runway construction: delays unaffected
    by, 85; expansion of, 14, 138–39,
    177; government/industry strategies
    for, 43, 64; Massport and, 138–39;
    opposition to, 54–55, 139. *See also*
    airport expansion

Safeguarding the Historic Hanscom
    Area's Irreplaceable Resources
    (ShhAir), 48–49, 52, 69, 83,
    175–76
safety standards, 88–89
San Bernadino County Airports
    (Calif.), 90
San Jose International Airport (Calif.),
    200n49
San Jose Mercury News, 85–86
Saporito, Jack, 133
Save Our Heritage, 49–50, 83, 175
Savoy Capital, 93–94
Schiavo, Mary, 88–89
Schriber, William, 94–95

Seattle-King County Department of
Public Health, 26
security, 157–58
Senate Commerce Committee, 98
SENLs. *See* single event noise levels
September 11 terrorist attacks (2001):
aviation industry exploitation of,
171–72; corporate jet traffic
increases and, 39; economic effects
of, 177; and rail transportation, 12–13
Shawsheen River, 74
ShhAir. *See* Safeguarding the Historic
Hanscom Area's Irreplaceable
Resources
Shuttle America, 91, 94–95, 174, 176–77
Sierra Club, 159
single event noise levels (SENLs), 105,
155
sinusitis, 28
Sixth Circuit Court of Appeals, 116
Skyway Airlines, 89
sleep disruption, 22, 38–39, 109,
124–25
SNCF International, 142
Snecma Moteurs, 90
snow removal. *See* aircraft de-
icing/anti-icing fluids
Society for the Psychological Study of
Social Issues, 41
South African Airways, 90
special interests: community values and,
127; and loss of local autonomy,
66–67; and Massport, 82; political
influence of, 12–13, 22–23, 65–67.
See also aviation industry;
commercial interests
spills, 74–75
Stage Three aircraft: ANCA and, 57,
108–9, 116; and international
engine certification standard,
89–90; noise problems of, 57–59

Stage Two aircraft: ANCA and, 108–9;
international restrictions on, 111;
local bans on, 101–2; noise
problems of, 57–59
Staples, Susan, 171
State Airport Management Board, 71
Stewart, Potter, 100
Stuart (Fla.), 60–64
Stuart News, 61
student pilots, 157
subsidies, 13, 120, 168, 173
suburban communities: aviation industry
strategies against, 13–14; impact of
noise pollution on, 50, 105
sulfur oxides, 24
SuperFund pollution, at Hanscom
Field, 36
supersonic jets, 33, 156
Supreme Court: *Burbank v. Lockheed*,
99–101, 113–15; *Griggs v. Allegheny
County*, 119
sustainable transportation: aviation with
representation and, 152–53, 161–62;
community work for, 168–71;
individual choices and, 171; lack of,
aviation industry and, 167–68; local
autonomy and, 15
Swedish Environmental Protection
Agency, 41

TACA International, 90
taxes, 72, 80, 86, 157, 168
Tempelhof Airport (Berlin), 112
Tenth Circuit Court of Appeals, 116
Texas Air Corporation, 91–92, 94
T. F. Green Airport (Providence, R.I.):
Hanscom compared to, 19;
Massport regional strategy and, 138,
139–40; and multimodal
transportation policy, 154, 162–63;
noise mitigation at, 110

TGV (high-speed rail), 142
Thoreau, Henry David, 16
ticket prices, 157, 161–62
Tiffany, Kay, 124
To Empower People (Berger), 149
toluene, 36
tolyltriazoles, 35
Torricelli, Robert G., 118
Train, Russell E., 40
Transportation, Secretary of, 155, 177
Transportation, U.S. Department of
    (DOT), 54, 87, 93, 170, 174. *See also*
    Federal Aviation Administration
trichloroethylene, 36

UAL Corporation, 172
union busting, 91–92
United Airlines, 90
United Parcel Service, 90
United Technologies, 90
University of Wisconsin–Whitewater, 34
urban communities: airport expansion
    and, 13; aviation industry strategies
    against, 13–14; noise impact in, 105;
    sprawl in, 162–63
US Airways, 19, 176
US Airways Express, 177
US Airways Group, 172
US–Citizens Aviation Watch (US-CAW),
    159, 167
user fees, 157, 175

Valujet, 88

WAAM. *See* Witham Airport Action
    Majority
Walden Pond, 46, 47
Wall Street Journal, 150

Walsh, Richard, 191n2 (ch.2)
Walters, Barbara, 91
Washington Post, 109–10
weight, aircraft, 21, 62, 175
Weld, William F., 69, 73, 201n12
Wellstone, Paul, 118
Wendell H. Ford Aviation Investment
    and Reform Act for the 21st
    Century, 174
Westchester County Airport (N.Y.):
    community micromanagement
    strategies at, 170; expansion of,
    18–19, 55–60; Hanscom compared
    to, 39; operations at, 56–57
wetlands, and ground pollution, 74–75
White, Byron R., 100
Whitelegg, John, 173
White Plains (N.Y.), 55. *See also*
    Westchester County Airport
Who Will Tell the People (Greider), 15
Williams, Nick, 173
Wilson, Edward O., 147
Winthrop (Mass.), 27–28
Wisconsin–Whitewater, University of,
    34
Witham Airport Action Majority
    (WAAM), 61–62, 63–64
Witham Field (Stuart, Fla.), 60–64
Woodward, Joanne, 49
Worcester Airport (Mass.): as alternative
    to Hanscom, 133–34; Massport
    operating agreement with, 52;
    Massport regional strategy and, 138,
    140; and multimodal transportation
    policy, 154, 162–63
World Health Organization, 38, 58–59

xylene, 36